Seventeenth-Century Water Gardens and the Birth of Modern Scientific Thought in Oxford

The Case of Hanwell Castle

Stephen Wass

WINDgather PRESS

Windgather Press is an imprint of Oxbow Books

Published in the United Kingdom in 2022 by
OXBOW BOOKS
The Old Music Hall, 106–108 Cowley Road, Oxford, OX4 1JE

and in the United States by
OXBOW BOOKS
1950 Lawrence Road, Havertown, PA 19083

© Windgather Press and Stephen Wass 2022

Paperback Edition: ISBN 978-1-914427-16-9
Digital Edition: ISBN 978-1-914427-17-6

A CIP record for this book is available from the British Library

Printed in the United Kingdom by Short Run Press

For a complete list of Windgather titles, please contact:

United Kingdom
OXBOW BOOKS
Telephone (01865) 241249
Email: oxbow@oxbowbooks.com
www.oxbowbooks.com

United States of America
OXBOW BOOKS
Telephone (610) 853-9131, Fax (610) 853-9146
Email: queries@casemateacademic.com
www.casemateacademic.com/oxbow

Oxbow Books is part of the Casemate group

Front and back cover: Author's own images

Contents

Acknowledgements

Work on this thesis is entirely down to the encouragement and hospitality of Rowena E. Archer and Christopher Taylor, for whom no statement of acknowledgement or gratitude would go far enough. The huge level of support both domestically and professionally from my wife, Verna, demands the highest level of thanks. The other members of my supervisory team, Jon Healey and Julian Munby, also deserve great thanks for going above and beyond what might normally be expected of supervisors, especially in terms of making journeys into the wilds of north Oxfordshire to discuss the work in hand. Fellow researcher and member of the Cope family Bill Cope was enormously helpful over aspects of the family's early history. Architect Bryan Martin was kind enough to make a number of visits to discuss technical aspects of construction.

The entire project would not have been possible without the input of a large number of volunteers. Foremost amongst these is Sarah Beaujean, who first came to us from Belgium, as a 16-year-old schoolgirl, and who returned repeatedly as she went on to complete her first degree in archaeology at Durham before going on to do a master's in museum and artefact studies and then returning to help with cataloguing and displaying our extraordinary repository of finds. Also deserving special mention is Peter Spackman, who in the early years of the project assisted tirelessly with the digging and, after having health problems, returned to undertake the first tentative restorations of some of the garden urns. Special thanks also to Chris Mitchell, for photography. Long-term local supporters include Ian Harris, Chris Walker, Helen Wickenden and Andries Bosland (who also supplied translation from Dutch), as well as Peter Palmer, who drove up regularly from Enfield to assist us. More recently John and Olwen Akhurst and Alan Berck-May have joined the team. Other occasional mature volunteers have included Karen Bullen, Rosie Burchell, Philip Bushell-Mills, Peter Christopher, Brenda and Stephen Day, Elaine Dorset, Pinelopi Flaouna, Oliver Garbett, Elizabeth Gardner, Georgina Hall, Georgia Hawkins, Mike Leonard, Viv Mead, Pat and Albert Meadows, William and Philip Molesworth, Maurice O'Brien, Rupert Willday and Jim Williams.

We have enjoyed the company of students at all stages in their post-16 education. Here are their names: Sebastian Anstis, Severine Bernard, Kate Bickerton, Emilia Bjornsdottir, Josef Bloomfield, Edyta Cehak, Paolo Coruzzi, Adam Douthwaite, Christian East, Nina Elphick, George Ferguson, Federica Fionda, Amber Furnage, Lucy Gallard, Luke Gibbs, Sam Govan, Nathan Hanson, Noelia Hernandez, Jack Hudson, Matthew and Katt Jones, Saskia Judd, Andrew MacKenzie, Sabrina Marchant, Jasmine Maton, Toby McLusky, Shereen Mee, Mika Alvarez Nishio, Yefren Nye, Emma Parker, Chelsea Peer, Samuel Phipps, Kendra Sarah, Maria Slatterbod, Isobel and Naomi Smith, Chris Sopp, Hamish

Southworth, Hannah Street, Kathryn Stone, Oliver Westmoreland-Caunter, Maddy Walsh, Kirsten Wilkes and Kate Willday. We also have a number of volunteers whose surnames have not been recorded: Ray, Tony, Hebe, Eve, Hannah, Christine, Sophie, Annie, Charlie, Jerome, Abigail, Meg and James. Thank you all.

And finally and most importantly, endless thanks to my wife, Verna, who has been a tireless supporter of the project and who has contributed endlessly to the supervision of excavations, the management of volunteers and the processing and cataloguing of finds.

Abbreviations and Conventions

A/TC   Collection relating to Hanwell Castle and the Cope family in the possession of Rowena E. Archer and Christopher Taylor, The Coach House, Hanwell Castle

Hants. CRO   Hampshire County Record Office

ODNB   *Oxford Dictionary of National Biography*

Oxon. HER   Oxfordshire Historic Environment Record

RCHME   Royal Commission on Historic Monuments (England)

HOP   *History of Parliament*

OED   *Oxford English Dictionary*

TNA   The National Archives

VCH   Victoria County History

Archaeological Labelling Conventions

In the example HANK21/009/3, HAN = the abbreviation of the site name, Hanwell; K = the 'K' site; 21 = the year; 009 = numbering of individual archaeological feature or context; and 3 = numbering of individual find or artefact.

NOTE: At the outset of this study, ample use was made of printed sources and manuscripts thanks to the good offices of the Bodleian Library. Unfortunately during the Covid-19 pandemic, access was severely restricted and sources that were examined in hard copy were increasingly referred to online. In cases where they were originally consulted in a library or archive, the references are given in standard form. Sources that were only accessed online are also referenced appropriately. In cases where work began in the library before shifting to an online version, the bibliographic details and page numbering, for example, may have changed. In these instances, I have generally stuck with the original referencing to hard copies. Some key documents were purchased as high-resolution scans, and these are treated as if the original paper were to hand.

All photographs and drawings are by the author unless otherwise stated. Every effort has been made to contact the relevant organisations for permission to reproduce other images.

A full plan of the site showing the layout and location of all significant archaeological features is presented as Plate 31.

CHAPTER ONE

Introduction

....

Voyages to the House of Diversion: Investigating Hanwell

The idea of a 'lost garden' has become something of a cliché, but that, to all intents and purposes, was the situation we found ourselves dealing with in the case of the park at Hanwell. Security considerations have meant that little publicity has been sought or given to the Hanwell project until now, an appropriate time to give an account of more than a decade's worth of research and discovery. In 2010–11 the author was engaged in an M.A. at Leicester University in Historical Archaeology, a part of which involved researching and writing a dissertation based on studies of the gardens and park of a National Trust property, Farnborough Hall, in Warwickshire. This involved many weeks of work primarily on site, but in the course of reading around the subject of other historic gardens in the area, references to Plot's *Oxfordshire* and the well-known waterworks at Enstone leapt off the page. Having read about the Enstone Marvels, I was intrigued by an account of similar waterworks at Hanwell, in the north of Oxfordshire. Here was a description of a 'House of Diversion' on an island in a pool. A moment with the relevant Ordnance Survey map showed that there was indeed a large pool with an island in the grounds of Hanwell Castle that was crying out for exploration (Plate 1). The wonders of Enstone were reputed to be long gone, but could something significant survive of a seventeenth-century garden with attendant wonders just down the road? A number of queries led me to get in touch with the owners, Rowena E. Archer and Christopher Taylor, who greeted me with the remark, 'We've been waiting for thirty years for someone to turn up and show an interest in our garden.' After further discussions and a subsequent lengthy site visit that established the extent of the gardens and the potential for significant archaeological remains to survive, it was agreed that a detailed plan to explore the site should be drawn up, with a view to launching a programme of research in the new year, 2013 (Plate 2). As the potential of the site and its associated history became clearer, it was also decided that the investigation could form an appropriate topic for a programme of D. Phil. research at the University of Oxford, under the banner of architectural history and with the title 'Voyages to the House of Diversion, Seventeenth-Century Water Gardens and the Birth of Modern Science'.

Over the next 10 years, a series of closely targeted excavations were carried out, alongside survey work and documentary research into the family and the period. A team of local volunteer diggers had already cut their teeth on a number of small-scale excavations carried out for the National Trust at Farnborough and elsewhere, and these diggers were augmented by increasing numbers of students during the summer vacations. These students came to us from secondary and tertiary education and included A-level students thinking of reading archaeology at university and, very sensibly, wanting to try it out, as well as undergraduates seeking additional training and work experience and post-graduates wishing to build up their CVs in the search for jobs. As the work progressed, funds raised locally were used not only to cover the day-to-day running costs of excavation but also to build capacity for the processing and storage of the resulting finds.

Talks about the work were given to local historical societies, for whom visits were also occasionally organised; digging opportunities were advertised in *Current Archaeology;* and a comprehensive project web-site was set up and regularly updated [http://www.polyolbion.org.uk/Hanwell/Project.html]. In addition, once a year an open weekend, under the title of 'Stars and Snowdrops', was held to showcase the work on the Hanwell Community Observatory that occupied part of the site. This also enable visitors to admire the huge drifts of wild snowdrops that had colonised the terraces below the castle. As time went by, the archaeology began to figure increasingly largely in these events, and in September of 2021, a large-scale event was held, featuring a pop-up museum and living history displays. Behind all this – and the main inspiration for the project – is the extraordinary account by Robert Plot, whose detailed reports on Sir Anthony and his wonders provided the starting point for our investigations.

Robert Plot and Sir Anthony Cope

> … that great *Virtuoso*, the Right Worshipful *Sir Anthony Cope* of *Hanwell*… whose House I thought seemed to be the real *New Atlantis* which my Lord Viscount *Verulam* had only in Fancy. (Plot 1705, 74)

So wrote Robert Plot (1640–96) in his *The Natural History of Oxfordshire,* first published in 1677 (Plate 3). This reference to the status of Sir Anthony Cope (1636–75) as a 'great virtuoso', and the identification of his house at Hanwell as the 'real *New Atlantis*', is a remarkable one. As we shall see, it suggests that the Cope household in the years after the English Civil War resembled the early proto-scientific university as outlined in Sir Francis Bacon's visionary book of 1626, *The New Atlantis*. In this work Bacon made the argument that if progress were to be made in the realm of natural philosophy, two essential components were a community of like-minded people with an interest in experimental method and a supportive environment within which to carry out any investigations. Was Plot was describing something of real significance or simply flattering Sir Anthony with his words of praise? Whatever the case, it is useful to begin by outlining what Plot has to tell us about Sir Anthony and his interests.

Early in 1675 Robert Plot was riding by the village of Shutford when he found a large fossil bivalve.

... which being much too heavy for my Horse-portage, was afterward upon my Direction, fetch'd away by the Ingenious Sir *Anthony Cope*, since whose Decease it is come I suppose into the hands of his equally Ingenious Brother Sir *John Cope*, the Heir of his Virtues as well as Estate. (Ibid., 128)

This incident hints at a fairly close relationship with Sir Anthony that is confirmed in ten additional entries referring to the Cope family and their park at Hanwell. Plot knew the location well enough to comment on freshwater mussels in a pond (Ibid., 190). He also gave an account of a distinctive variety of small-leaved elm planted in the park (Ibid., 161). The inside of the castle was evidently also familiar to him, as he describes in some detail a water clock (Ibid., 240). Plot goes on to mention a collection of anamorphic paintings he must have examined (Ibid., 279). Presumably he had been invited to dine at the castle, as he comments on the polished stone handles of some of Sir Anthony's cutlery (Ibid., 74). Beyond that he had clearly been treated to a display of the waterworks in the garden, noting,

There are some other *Water-works* at the same Sir *Anthony Cope's, in* a House of *Diversion* built in a small *Island* on one of the *Fish-ponds*, Eastward of his House, where a *Ball* is tost by a *Column* of *Water* and artificial *Showers* descend at pleasure; within which they can yet so place a *Candle*, that though one would think it must needs be overwhelmed with *Water*, it shall not be extinguish'd. (Ibid., 240)

He had also become acquainted with a mill

[…] of wonderful contrivance, where-with that great *Virtuoso* did not only grind the *Corn* for his House, but with the same motion turned a very large *Engine* for cutting the hardest Stone […] and another for boaring of *Guns*. (Ibid., 269)

However, the most remarkable comment is that in Chapter 4, '*Of Stones*', where Plot eulogises Sir Anthony in these terms,

[…] that great *Virtuoso*, the Right Worshipful Sir *Anthony Cope* of *Hanwell*, the most eminent *Artist* and *Naturalist* while he lived, if not of *England*, most certainly of this *County*, whose House I thought seemed to be the real *New Atlantis*, which my Lord Viscount *Verulam* had only in Fancy. (Ibid., 74)

Plot mentions in his *History* a number of eminent natural philosophers, including Christopher Wren and Robert Boyle, and other members of the gentry, such as Sir Thomas Pennyston of Cornwell Park. However, no one else is treated to such a torrent of praise, all of which raises questions about Sir Anthony's potential role in the development of early scientific thinking associated with Oxford (Ibid., 99). Equally astonishing is Plot's reference, elsewhere in his *Natural History,* to 'a Learned Society of *Virtuosi*, that, During the late Usurpation lived obscurely at *Tangley*', another Cope family property, which appears to have been a venue for clandestine meetings of early experimentalists during that period of parliamentary supremacy known as the Commonwealth (Ibid., 92). Our account of Sir Anthony's life examines someone who, in the 1650s and 1660s, may have been promoting informal communities dedicated to learning and research, an enterprise akin to the later formation of the Royal Society, in 1662.

Beyond the history lies the physical fact of the garden at Hanwell that has remained largely hidden for more than three centuries. Such survivals of seventeenth-century gardens are vanishingly rare, and the garden merits study in its own right as an unusual instance of a garden of the period that was not levelled in the eighteenth century as part of the English parkland movement. This study interleaves historical analysis with archaeological fieldwork carried out at Hanwell and elsewhere over the past decade. As Roy Strong queried (1998, 6), 'What was the relationship between gardening and the advent of impulses like Baconian experimentalism which led to the Newtonian mechanistic universe? There is indeed still much to be done before one can fully comprehend the Renaissance garden in England.' This volume sets out to try and further understand that relationship and document what I believe to be a significant episode in the history of gardens.

Hanwell: Geology, Geography, Archaeology and History

The layout, usage and ultimate fate of the important seventeenth-century garden at Hanwell are all functions of the geology, topography and early history of the site (Fig. 1). The village of Hanwell lies close to the centre of a plateau of a ferruginous limestone known locally as ironstone. Indeed St Peter's Church, Hanwell, is one of the eight churches of what is called 'the Ironstone Benefice'. It is also within the region sometimes known as Banburyshire, denoting a distinctive part of northern Oxfordshire centred on the former market town of Banbury but taking in a much larger area than the historical hundred. Raymond Wood-Jones (1961, 1), in his important and pioneering account of the vernacular architecture of the area, notes that it is a 'small but quite populous agrarian area [which has] evolved a distinctive regional style of domestic building of remarkable homogeneity in material and character'. Flora Thompson (2008, 17), in her well-known memoir of village life *Larkrise to Candleford,* describes it as 'the flat, wheat-growing corner of Oxfordshire [where] all around from every quarter, the stiff clayey soil of the arable fields crept up; bare browned windswept for eight months out of twelve'. The rusty brown ironstone has been widely used locally for building, and in times of necessity it has been quarried as a low-grade iron ore (Powell 2005, 22). Geologically the area is a northern outlier of the Cotswolds: a south-tilting mass made up of Early Jurassic marine shales, limestones and sands of the lias group. The most prominent part of these deposits is a marlstone bed, which is a calcareous, sandy ironstone and which, due to its relative hardness, forms an elevated ridge. Because of this, the scarp slope, known as Edge Hill, is quite steep, with an overall height of around 50 m. The dip slope, running north-east to south-west, is dissected by streams that come together in a shallow valley around 40 m deep and 800 m wide, running north to south around 1.5 km to the east of Hanwell. The lower slopes of this valley consist of hill-wash and eroded material derived from the underlying marlstone, while the valley bottom is composed of alluvial deposits

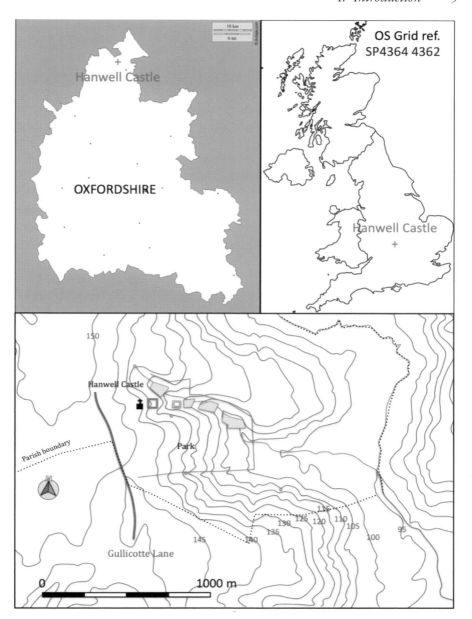

FIGURE 1. Hanwell, location and topography. © Crown Copyright and Landmark Information Group Limited (2021). All rights reserved.

of silt, clay and gravel. The castle lies at the head of a small, eastward-flowing tributary that is fed by a series of springs around the 130 m contour. As Timothy Mowl (2007, 23) puts it, 'Hanwell stands above a narrow valley that oozes with springs.' The resulting stream has carved out quite a steep-sided little valley, around 10 m deep and 120 m wide at its midpoint. This formed the basis for the water gardens of the seventeenth century. The early park also took in an eastward-facing slope to the south. The village today lies beyond the church and castle, to the north and west.

Early, albeit transient, settlement of the area is attested to by the discovery of Mesolithic microliths, whereas a well-made Neolithic leaf-shaped arrowhead with its tip broken off suggests hunting within the valley. There is limited evidence for Neolithic and Bronze Age occupation in the upper Cherwell valley (for example, Hardy 2000; Stevens 2002). Developer-led excavations on the land between Banbury and Hanwell have uncovered traces of late Iron Age agriculture (Chinock 2014). Crop-marks suggested possible occupation from a similar period immediately to the north-west of the village (Oxon HER no. 28019). The proposal, following excavations on the site of the castle prior to redevelopment in 2014, that a deep ditch on the site of the castle was of Iron Age date, was not really supported by any finds (Yeates 2014). The best known site from the Roman period, lying around 700 m north-west of the church, was listed in Alfred Beesley's (1841, 41) *History of Banbury* thus: 'near the gate of the southern field some tessellated pavement was discovered some years ago'. In addition he noted rock-cut chambers, stairs, an oven and 'a profusion of burned stones, bones and pieces of Roman pottery'. Beesley also illustrated part of a hoard of more than 70 Roman coins found in a pot in 1828, some 1.2 km west of the church. The 2014 excavations produced one piece of Roman pottery, a paucity mirrored by finds farther down the valley where again only a single sherd has been discovered (Yeates 2014, 20).

Settlement of these 'redlands' in the post-Roman period is poorly documented. John Blair (1994, 16) described a situation in the seventh century whereby 'hybrid communities' were developing in the northern Cotswolds, drawing on cultural influences from 'the Avon valley Angles and the Thames valley Saxons inter-breeding with what was doubtless a British majority'. He concluded that both the nearby town of Banbury and the village of Cropredy had early minster churches and that a settlement at Prescote, just north of Cropredy, could have been one of the earliest religious foundations in the area (Ibid. 75). The settlement at Prescote lay on a route across the valley of the River Cherwell, and the *VCH* suggested that the presence of a spring adjacent to this early east–west highway, known as Hana's Weg, was the focus for the original nucleus of the village of Hanwell and that the existence of a 'never-failing spring' was sufficient later on to cause *welle* to be substituted for *weg*. Excavations in 1995 in advance of building work at Spring Farm, north of Main Street, uncovered a series of ditches with late Saxon pottery, chiefly St Neott's ware (Oxford Archaeological Unit 1995). A single sherd of Ipswich ware was not sufficient to establish whether there was a Saxon presence on the castle site (Yeates 2014, 54).

Both before the conquest and at the time of Domesday, Hanwell was held by the Saxon lord Leofwine, after which it passed into the hands of the Vernons. In 1415 the manor was conveyed to Thomas Chaucer, son of Geoffrey Chaucer the poet, and then to Thomas's daughter Alice, at that point the wife of Sir John Phelip. She carried the property to her third husband, William de la Pole, Earl of Suffolk, in 1430 (*ODNB*). The manor remained part of the holdings of the De la Poles until it was conveyed to William Cope, in 1498. The *VCH* paints a picture of a rather undistinguished, middling-sized village, a situation perhaps reinforced by the suggestion that 'it is doubtful whether there were any resident lords of the manor before the Copes and the early manor-house was presumably leased or occupied by bailiffs.' The problems of an absentee lord are illustrated by the bill of complaint taken out by John Chambre against Richard Grevil of nearby Drayton for 'forcible entry and dispossession of the manor of Hanwell' in 1455 (Hants. CRO, 43M48/93). It was alleged, and this may be a legal fiction, that the raiders, armed with 'many other forbidden weaponry', entered into the manor and drove the tenants 'from their homes for fear of their lives' before helping themselves to the livestock.

The layout of the village is interesting (Fig. 2). The church, first mentioned in 1154 and almost completely rebuilt early in the fourteenth century, occupies the high ground on the south side of the village. The surviving portion of Hanwell Castle lies around 50 m to the north-east. What is striking is the area of open ground to the north of the castle and church, which the main road through the village skirts round. It is possible that this area simply reflects the boundary of the manorial enclosure broken into by Grevil and his thugs in 1455. One notable feature of this open ground is a large area of raised ground immediately

FIGURE 2. Hanwell village, possible medieval features. © Crown Copyright and Landmark Information Group Limited (2021). All rights reserved.

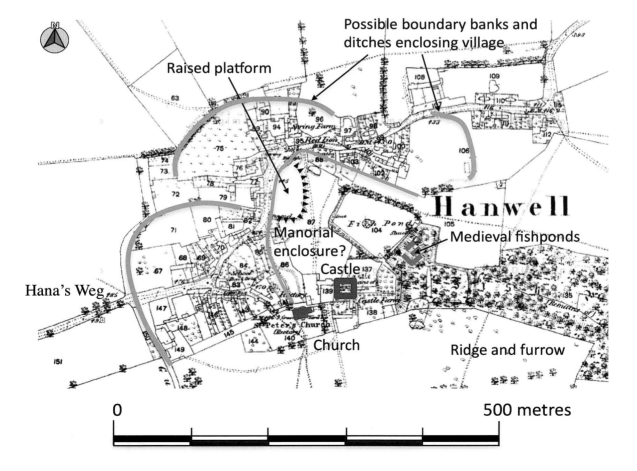

adjacent to the current boundary wall on the west side of the plot. Whether this is evidence for significant building activity on this part of the site or possibly even the remains of an early earthwork fortification remains unknown; however, data from the 2014 excavation do indicate early medieval occupation on the castle site, possibly associated with a defensive ditch (Yeates 2014, 24). The *VCH* suggests that the village was subject to an early form of ribbon development along the line of the through road because of the presence of open fields to the north and south. There is certainly evidence of ridge and furrow to the south-east, later truncated by enclosure into the castle park. Excavations in 1974 demonstrated that late-medieval occupation extended to the east of the centre of the village (Chambers 1974). Furthermore, it was noted that this area was bounded by a bank and ditch that may have extended around the village to the north, and there is evidence of a number of other possible earthwork features surrounding the village. This was the setting that one William Cope acquired in 1498, with plans to build his new house.

Bibliography

Bacon, F., *The New Atlantis* (originally published London, 1626), in Bruce, S. (ed.) *Three Early Modern Utopias: Utopia, New Atlantis and The Island of Pines* (Oxford, 2008)

Beesley, A., *The History of Banbury* (London, 1841)

Blair, J., *Anglo-Saxon Oxfordshire* (Stroud, 1994)

Chambers, R., 'Excavations at Hanwell nr. Banbury, Oxon. 1974', *Oxoniensia* 40 (1975)

Chinock, C., *Trial Trench Evaluation at Hanwell Fields, Banbury, Oxfordshire, September 2014* (Museum of London Archaeology, unpublished report, 2014)

Hants. CRO, 43M48/93 (transcript of petition or bill of complaint of John Chambre of Northampton against Ralph Grevill for forcible entry and dispossession of the manor of Hanwell on 7 January 1455)

Hardy, A., 'The Excavation of a Medieval Cottage and Associated Agricultural Features at Manor Farm, Old Grimsbury, Banbury', *Oxoniensia* 65 (2000)

Mowl, T., *The Historic Gardens of England: Oxfordshire* (Stroud, 2007)

ODNB, Archer, R.E., 'Alice Chaucer (c. 1404–75)'

Oxford Archaeological Unit, *Spring Farm, Main Street, Hanwell Archaeological Evaluation,* Ref. CHN. 391/93 (Oxford, 1995)

Plot, R., *The Natural History of Oxfordshire* (London, second edition 1705; facsimile edition Paul Minnet, Scolar Press, Menston, Yorkshire, 1972)

Powell, P., *The Geology of Oxfordshire* (Wimborne, 2005)

Stevens, C., *Iron Age and Saxon Settlement at Jugglers Close, Banbury, Oxfordshire,* John Moore Heritage Services, unpublished report (2002)

Strong, R., *The Renaissance Garden in England* (London, 1998)

Thompson, F., *Larkrise to Candleford* (London, 2008)

Wass, S., 'A Way with Water – Water Resources and the Life of an Eighteenth-Century Park', *Industrial Archaeology Review* 38(1) (2016)

Wood-Jones, R., *Traditional Domestic Architecture in the Banbury Region* (Manchester, 1963)

Yeates, S., *Archaeological Excavation and Watching Brief at Hanwell Castle, Main Street, Hanwell, Oxfordshire,* John Moore Heritage Services, unpublished report (2014)

CHAPTER TWO

The Sixteenth Century

William Cope and the Building of Hanwell House

Although the main focus of this story will be on the 4th baronet, it is inevitable that his interests in and opportunities to develop the gardens at Hanwell drew on the deep well of his family's fortunes. William Cope (d.1513) was born into a lesser branch of the Cope family of Deanshanger, in Northamptonshire, and took service with Lady Margaret Beaufort and subsequently her husbands, Henry, Lord Stafford and Thomas, Lord Stanley. William Cope was among the most intimate of Lady Margaret's circle and served her in the management of her estates (Jones and Underwood 1992, 79). American researcher and descendant Bill Cope (2017, 240) proposed that it was here that he was schooled in the intricacies of accounting and property management and that it was here also that he acquired an appetite for the acquisition of large holdings of land. After the Battle of Bosworth, in 1485, William was drawn into the service of Margaret Beaufort's son, Henry VII, although there is no evidence he actually fought. After sitting in the parliament of 1491, William became the Sergeant of the Catery, with the task of supplying provisions to the king's household (*HOP* 1938, 710). On 30 September 1494 he was promoted to the role of cofferer, or accountant, for the royal household. Bill Cope drew attention to an agreement executed between the king and the royal household officials that, he suggested, established a system where responsibilities and accountabilities were clearly spelt out, a measure which not only improved the financial security of the Crown but also set the pattern for William's future business dealings. While in possession of a house in Banbury in 1496, William took a lease on the manor of Hardwick, a small, moated manor, still partially surviving as an earthwork, some 2.3 km south-east of Hanwell. In 1498 William was granted the nearby manors of Fenny Compton and Wormleighton, both in Warwickshire, the latter village being depopulated and enclosed for sheep grazing. Harty Thorpe (1965, 51) gave the following account of what happened. 'He promptly set about purchasing all the lands and tenements of minor lords in Wormleighton […] Having gained control of the entire parish he proceeded in 1499 to destroy 12 messuages and 3 cottages, converting 240 acres of arable land to enclosed pasture for animals and driving 60 persons from the land.' William secured the Hanwell property in February 1498, from Edmund de la Pole, 3rd Duke of Suffolk. The duke was attainted in Parliament in January of 1503/4 for treason, meaning that William had to rely on Henry VII to guarantee the transfer of the manor into his ownership (Hants. CRO, 43M48/94 17). William does not seem to have taken the same wholesale approach to clearances and enclosure here as was taken at many of his other holdings. This may be linked to his intention to develop Hanwell into his family seat by ordering the construction of a new residence.

This grand house would have formed the centre piece for activities in the seventeenth century that led to Plot's identification of the space as the real New *Atlantis,* and so it is important to consider how its original layout, rather reminiscent of an Oxford college, came about. We do not have a precise date for the start of building work, but it must have followed fairly closely on the family taking control, in 1498. Although the term architect is not necessarily anachronistic, as a structure firmly anchored in the medieval tradition, it would probably be better to consider the role of a master mason in the design of this building. It is clear that architectural drawings were in use, as there is a reference in William's will charging his executors to 'finish and make my house in like manner and proportions as it is begun and according to a plat [plan] hereof made' (Hants. CRO, 43M48/96). While we have no idea about the dialogues between William as client and his master mason as contractor, it must have been a costly undertaking. No building accounts survive, but it is perhaps significant that in 1506 the property at Wormleighton was sold to his wife's cousin, John Spencer, for the large sum of £2,000 (Thorpe 1965, 57). Bill Cope (2017, 148) made the entirely plausible suggestion that much of this cash would have been siphoned off to help cover the costs of the possibly halting progress with the building work at Hanwell. Work began on the Spencers' brick manor house at Wormleighton in 1516. It being a local project to construct a major brick build-ing, it is possible that the same gang of brick makers, bricklayers and masons moved from one property to work on the other.

The surviving remnant of Hanwell Castle, as it is commonly called today, is clearly a shadow of its former self, and some effort needs to be made to appre-ciate its form during its heyday in the mid-seventeenth century. Fortunately a number of engravings of the castle have survived, although it is possible that they all post-date the castle's partial destruction in the eighteenth century. The building today is surrounded by later accretions, the most recent of which were constructed between 2012 and 2017. It is now quite difficult to imagine its strict-ly symmetrical facade (Fig. 3). This, according to John Goodall (2011, 362), was a typical composition of tower, turret, gatehouse, turret and tower. Some doubt the building's castle credentials: 'not a castle in the true sense', say Sherwood and Pevsner (1974, 632). Even so, it is likely that such a prestigious building, with its martial trappings, would have been viewed within the long tradition of castle building by those who put it up and those who came under its sway, even if it was constructed in what would have been an overtly modern material: brick. It is possible to read this as an example of how, as Matthew Johnson (1992, 45) saw it, 'aristocracy and upper gentry in 16th-century England manipulated symbolic structures relating to the feudal past to lend ideological support to the Tudor social order'. The early images indicate that the castle was built as a series of two-storey ranges, set around a square courtyard with three-storey

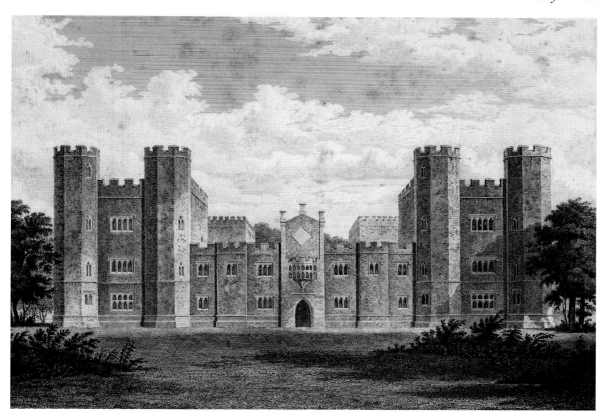

FIGURE 3. *Hanwell Castle in Its Former State*, by John Fittler, 1827. Author's collection.

towers at each corner. Using the dimensions of the existing south range and the engravings of the north and west fronts, with the additional information that the length of that frontage was 109 feet (Beesley 1841, 191), it has been possible to reconstruct the ground plan. A further assumption was made based on the degree of symmetry found at new properties, such as Herstmonceux, of 1441; Kirby Muxloe, of 1480; and, showing the persistence of the form, Toddington, of 1560. This results, as we have noted, in a layout strikingly reminiscent of a contemporary Oxford college (Fig. 4). Goodall (2011, 363) made much of the 'distinctive rhythm of elements [...] that was to recur in major English buildings into the late sixteenth century', which, he suggested, was a characteristic of buildings with royal connections or pretensions. At Hanwell the strongly symmetrical west front is typical of this pattern, appearing to comprise two large, square flanking towers with octagonal turrets on the western elevation; two smaller, square turrets in intermediate positions; and a comparatively restrained central gatehouse. This has an oriel window below a sculptured plaque, which in turn is below a gabled pediment finished off with three square finials.

An exact parallel for this arrangement is surprisingly hard to find. The corner towers in particular appear unique in their specific setting. They resemble on a smaller scale Ralph, Lord Cromwell's, great brick tower of 1446 at Tattershall. Ralph also figured in the nation's financial affairs as treasurer to Henry VI

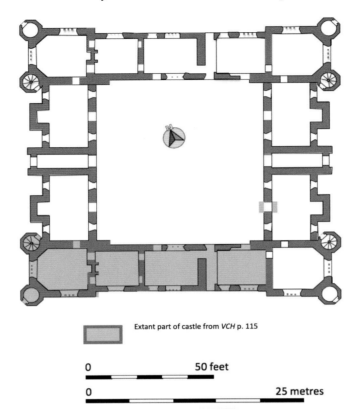

Extant part of castle from *VCH* p. 115

0   50 feet

0   25 metres

FIGURE 4. Hanwell Castle, reconstructed plan.

(ODNB). Perhaps Cope hoped to reflect some of the glory of his illustrious predecessor. A closer parallel in terms of date is the tower begun in the 1470s at Buckden, in Huntingdonshire, by Thomas Rotherham, Bishop of Lincoln, but in both cases we are dealing with single towers. Hanwell has four, albeit slightly smaller in scale. The most common parallels for a tower with octagonal turrets are of course the many late-medieval brick gatehouses, starting with Herstmonceux and running through Hertford, from 1463, Kirby Muxloe, from 1480, and Esher, from 1484, to the extravagances of Oxburgh, from 1482. At Hanwell the gatehouse is under-emphasised and the corner towers, with their octagonal turrets, remain an unusual and distinctive element in the design.

In practice the work on completing the castle was delayed. Whether this was because of technical difficulties with construction, supply of materials, disputes with contractors or, as seems most likely, simply a shortage of ready cash, remains uncertain. What is documented is the court of chancery case that followed William Cope's death, in 1513. In 1518 his oldest son and heir, Anthony Cope, sued the executors, his older half-brother Stephen and one William Bustard, for failing to finish the castle in accordance with William's will (TNA, C 1/399/39). The case presumably was resolved, at which point the building must have been completed to a satisfactory standard to create what John Leland (1908, 40) described in the 1540s as 'a very pleasaunt and gallaunt house'.

While the building of the house was consuming the site of the earlier manor house, work was probably under way to improve the adjacent gardens within the setting of the surrounding manorial enclosure and also to extend, or even introduce, a large park. However, given the difficulties that were encountered in finishing the castle, it may be that work on the surrounding park plus gardens was postponed until into the sixteenth century. When Anthony's mother, Jane Spencer Saunders Cope, died in 1525, her will listed 'Item, I give to my said sonne, Anthony, to the making of his poole £20 in forme followinge, viz., at the beginning of the making of the said poole £10, and when it is full made and finished other ten pounds' (TNA, Prerogative Court of Canterbury, PROB 11/11/125). This considerable amount would have made a substantial contribution to work on the garden, perhaps reflecting his mother's frustration that more progress had not been made. This pool may be the precursor of a water parterre that later became home to Sir Anthony Cope's House of Diversion. The dam to the east is rather modest in size compared with the other dams engineered up and down the valley and would have created a square pool with a sense of formality absent from the other bodies of water. It is notable how very little early brick is encountered within the wider park and garden, a material one might expect to come across if improvements had been underway during the building of the castle. Where walls are seen, especially on the eastern terraces and surrounding the deer park to the south, they are well made, with ashlar blocks, and may, as will be suggested later, date to the opening decades of the seventeenth century. Whatever the case, developments in the park and garden early in the sixteenth century would have taken place within a tradition of garden making continuing from the Middle Ages and subject to a number of native and some continental influences.

The Origins of Early Modern Water Gardens

To appreciate the features described by Plot at Hanwell in the seventeenth century, it is helpful to keep in mind an outline account of the factors that supported the development of the garden within what appears to be a local tradition of working with water. In 1991 archaeologist Paul Everson remarked that

> The idea of medieval water management features as having an ornamental, garden-related aspect seems, then, to have considerable interest [...] Not the least importance is that it might afford an insular/non-continental background through continuity of skills and interest in water features to the almost ubiquitous employment of water features found in 16th and 17th century gardens. (Everson 1991, 11)

In looking at the origins of the gardens at Hanwell, we need to consider this proposed chain of causality in order to challenge the widespread view amongst many garden historians that all good things in gardens ultimately had Italian and therefore classical origins. The idea that John Hale (1993, 520) expressed, namely that 'it was not until the mid-fifteenth century that actual gardens began to be developed as amenities that deliberately expressed social and aesthetic ideas', is clearly not an accurate one. Louise Wickham (2012, 62) maintained, writing of the early Renaissance enclosed medieval gardens, that these *hortus conclusus* were 'opened up by new ideas inspired by classical models' and that 'this was the first time that gardens had used borrowed scenery since Roman times'. Overreliance on images has perhaps warped our views of medieval gardens. As Christopher Currie (2005, 9) pointed out, 'The compressed perspectives of medieval illustration affected perceptions that medieval gardens uniformly consisted of small closely bounded spaces'. Work over the past thirty years has opened up a whole new perspective on designed landscapes from the Middle Ages.

At the core of any study of medieval parks, gardens and managed landscapes lie the two great institutions of medieval England: the castle and the monastery. Although they are possibly more technologically advanced, monastic landscapes are limited in terms of evidence for conscious design to promote images of power and celebrate an aesthetic of beauty. In the case of secular landscapes, there has been a significant move away from regarding castles and their surroundings as solely military mechanisms, to a more subtle appreciation of their role as administrative, social and cultural hubs that formed a backdrop for economic, political and technological display. This is what Robert Liddiard (2005, 51) called 'courtly choreography'. Although a comprehensive history of medieval gardens and parks in Britain, that is, one incorporating archaeological data, has yet to be written, ample work has been done on individual sites, and so there is much evidence for extensive and sophisticated developed landscapes in England from at least the twelfth century onward. Indeed the Norman conquest is an appropriate place to begin; evidence for early Norman settlement is plentiful, and the Normans bought a degree of novelty and sophistication across western Europe from Ireland to Sicily. There are many instances of early Norman estates where the layout of castle, gardens and park clearly demonstrates the ability to use locations to establish dominance and subjugation while at the same time creating a landscape that was both productive and attractive.

At Restormel, in Cornwall, the castle was established around 1100 by the Cardinham family. Its location has many points of interest (Fig. 5). It is not the most defensible spot in the area, which lies to the south-west and is occupied by the site of a Roman fort, nor is it close enough to offer immediate protection to the town and bridge at Lostwithiel. However, it is inter-visible with the town and the surrounding countryside, which, by the mid-thirteenth century, had become an elaborate park under the control of the earls of Cornwall. In his analysis of the landscape, Oliver Creighton (2009, 17) describes how 'the building was "keyed into" a local setting that was manipulated, at least in part, with an eye for aesthetic value, thus amounting to a designed landscape'. Features included a mill and hermitage on the banks of the Fowey below the castle and the careful alignment of the park boundary so that it was invisible from the castle, creating the illusion of a much larger estate. Particularly noteworthy is the circular wall walk on the castle, which seems designed for appreciating the view but makes poor sense defensively. It may be argued that aspects of this are simply an overinterpretation of fortuitous juxtapositions within an

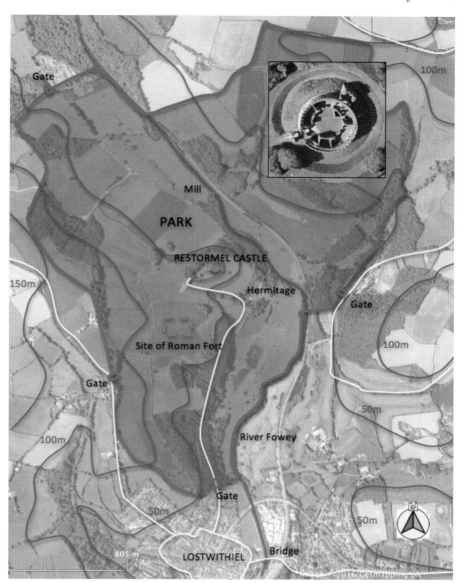

FIGURE 5. Restormel, the park (after Creighton). Inset aerial view of castle. © Google Earth.

entirely functional landscape, but these ideas can be seen further developed at Kenilworth Castle, in Warwickshire, where the physical efforts to transform the landscape were enormous. Kenilworth was also begun in the twelfth century. From a study of contemporary charters, Liddiard (2005, 120) contends that its founder, Geoffrey de Clinton, laid out a designed landscape of multiple components, which formed the setting for four centuries of refinement. Examination of the castle's plan as it stood prior to the famous siege of 1266 is instructive. A huge dam lay to the south of the main castle enclosure, and further dams lay to the east, which created an extensive mere surrounding the castle on the south and west sides (Plate 4). According to most accounts, this defensive work was further protected by a massive, crescent-shaped earthwork known as the *brayz*, and together these formed one of the most sophisticated examples of military engineering seen in the country. In practice this huge investment makes little sense militarily, as these combined defensive works could be simply ignored by mounting an attack on the weakly defended northern side of the castle. Further developments in the thirteenth century underlined the true nature of this complex as a grand ceremonial entrance to the castle, with a staged unfolding of what was a landscape of pleasure and beauty. To a person approaching from the south, the view is blocked by the brayz and only starts to appear once one has passed through the first gate. In 1374 instructions were given to create an enclosed garden, which may have been on the same site as the Elizabethan garden created in the early 1570s (Demidowicz 2013, 33). This investment continued, as in 1414 Henry V ordered the construction of a pleasaunce north-east of the castle, being a large, rectangular, moated site enclosing gardens and pavilions, all approached by boat across the mere.

This idea of a separate enclosed garden, or *pleasaunce*, finds earlier expression in the feature known as Rosamund's Bower, at the royal palace of Woodstock, in Oxfordshire. This garden, based on a water source known as Everswell, lay around 300 m to the west of the medieval palace. The surviving remains are fragmentary, but John Aubrey produced a measured sketch of the ruins in the seventeenth century that enables a tentative reconstruction to be made (Bond and Tiller 1997, 46). The site consisted of a walled garden with an entrance tower. Inside were a series of interconnected, rectangular pools and walkways with seats and niches (Fig. 6). The particular significance of this site is its early date, the 1170s, and the possible design links with the Sicilio-Norman tradition of palace and garden building. The fact that there were dynastic and cultural links at the time with both Sicily and Iberia is well established (James 1990, 54). Howard Colvin (1963, 1015), in his exhaustive *History of the King's Works*, refers specifically to the palace of La Zisa, in Palermo. The Islamic garden works surviving in Spain are well known, but the remains of a series of elite buildings, originating with the Norman kings of Sicily, are less familiar largely because they have been absorbed into the ramshackle suburbs of the Sicilian capital. The sophisticated water gardens at La Zisa were part of a tradition in Islamic architecture that developed between the ninth and twelfth centuries and included, as well as fountains and canals, a scheme for cooling the interior of the building (Colajanni 2019, 19).

Although the evidence for designed landscapes in monastic settings is less clear, it is evident that they shared with the secular community technologies of water management and in many instances managed that technology more adeptly. A case in point is the Cistercian house at Bordesley Abbey, Redditch, where investigations over nearly a quarter of a century established the diversity of applications for water, the lengthy timeframe during which water was continually managed, and the fact that management adapted as circumstances, including the climate, changed (Wass 1993, 98). Whether it is in the provision of fishponds to support the monastic diet, flowing water to carry away waste,

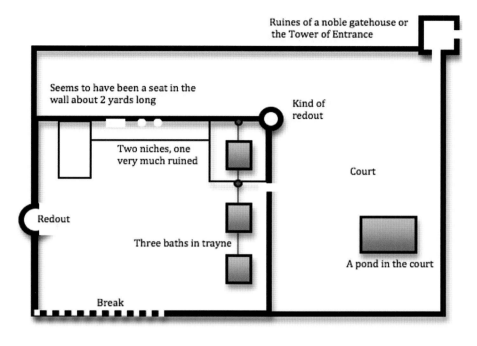

Ruines of a noble gatehouse or the Tower of Entrance

Seems to have been a seat in the wall about 2 yards long

Kind of redout

Two niches, one very much ruined

Court

Redout

Three baths in trayne

A pond in the court

Break

FIGURE 6. Everswell, 12th-century enclosed garden based on measured sketch by John Aubrey.

0   100 metres

or even as a source of power for semi-industrial applications, a huge body of expertise and a widespread legacy of managed landscapes survived into the middle of the sixteenth century and the Dissolution, as we shall see in the case of Bindon Abbey.

Throughout the Middle Ages there are examples of large- and small-scale undertakings where ground was cleared, terraced and planted for effect; enclosed gardens were built, and extensive systems of waterworks were incorporated into grand schemes of improvement and enhancement of the landscape. This is far removed from the earlier view of medieval gardens and demonstrates that there was a well-established and sophisticated tradition of garden and park construction well before the advent of the Tudors. By the early 1500s the English landscape could be characterised as one that was intensively managed and was both productive and, in places, ornamental. In terms of capacity, the gentry and the aristocracy were able to command large-scale operations that enabled the transformation of landscapes by engineering ponds, lakes and leats and by constructing banks, mounds and terraces. This proficiency in managing projects of this type typically belonged to those regions of north-western Europe where water was plentiful and the soils pliable. Frank Woodward (1982, 13) wrote, 'By the seventeenth century still-water features were being employed primarily for decorative reasons, though the influence of medieval defensive features and fishponds remains apparent.' It is this tradition of working with water that underpins the later proliferation of water gardens. As Paula Henderson (2005, 129) states, 'The inspiration for water gardens was largely indigenous.'

Water Gardens in the Sixteenth Century

Following the completion of the house at Hanwell, it is likely that work would have been undertaken to improve the park and lay out a formal garden, in line with the status and ambitions of the Cope family. The archaeological record for such early developments at Hanwell is limited, but it is worth considering contemporary instances of garden making to give some context to the works. A significant example is Henry VIII's developments at the newly acquired Hampton Court, from 1529 onwards. In competing with the formal gardens associated with the courts of France and Burgundy, his additions included the Privy Garden, the Mount Garden and the Pond Garden. The latter, sometimes termed the Pondyard, was not especially innovative in design terms, consisting of three rectangular pools surrounded by low stone walls. However, information that survives about construction is interesting in the account it present of methods and materials. In March 1535 work on 'dyggyng the fondacyons of the ponds' began. David Jacques sums up the progress of the work.

> The supply and retention of water were being worked on from April. Installation of pumps and lead pipes was commenced that month to fill the ponds from the river. The natural ground is extremely pervious sandy gravel and, so, in May the bottoms of the ponds were clayed. There were also sluices made of elmwood to enable the ponds to be drained. Various trials were made of filling and emptying the ponds from May to July. The arrangements seem to have worked, because in July a lead pipe was laid from the 'fountayne in the inner courtt to the pondds' to supplement the pumps; in September the construction of a well was being undertaken; and in December two further pumps were supplied to draw water from it. (Jacques 2005, 89)

Excavations in 1993–94 in the adjoining privy garden uncovered brick-lined drains of the period and recovered valuable information about a central fountain, albeit one probably dating from 1701 (Dix and Parry 1995, 79). Gardens at the palaces of Whitehall, in London, and Nonsuch, in Surrey, followed, but apart from the occasional fountain, neither was a water garden as such.

The degree of continuity between medieval landscapes and Tudor water gardens can be illustrated by examining the works at Raglan Castle, in Gwent. Elizabeth Whittle (1989, 83) suggested that the extensive gardens still visible as earthworks were a phenomenon of the Renaissance 'made around the existing castle between 1550 and 1646 by the 3rd., 4th. and 5th. earls of Worcester'. However, a building programme initiated in 1465 led to the creation of two courts enclosed with towers and a curtain wall lined with accommodation blocks and the truly colossal Yellow Tower of Gwent, a free-standing structure of some magnificence. Works on a comparable scale would have taken place within the associated park. Whittle reports,

FIGURE 7. Raglan Castle plan of earthworks adapted from 1970 OS 6 inch map. © Crown Copyright and Landmark Information Group Limited (2021). All rights reserved.

There is some evidence that there were gardens of a utilitarian nature at Raglan in the fifteenth century. A 'Fysshe Pole' is mentioned in an inquest in 1465 and an early fifteenth-century manuscript states of Raglan '[…] about the palace there were orchards full of apple trees and plums, and figs and cherries and grapes, and French plums, and pears and nuts, and every fruit that is sweet and delicious'. (Ibid., 83)

Although there is no hard and fast dating evidence, it seems likely that the great pool to the north of castle was a late-medieval construction, as was the terracing to the west, an ideal location for the orchards described (Fig. 7). The long pool

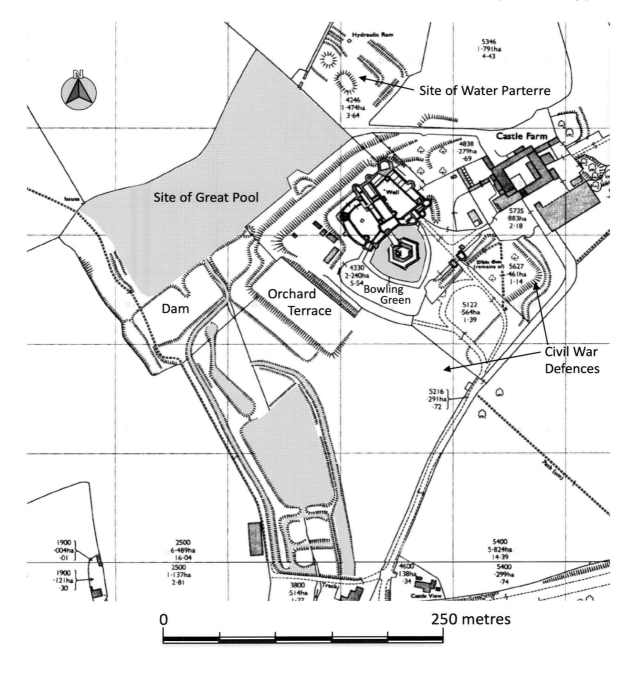

to the south-west with two rectangular islands at its southern end also seems to owe more to medieval styles of construction than those of the seventeenth century. Much is made of the terracing between the castle and the valley below as being a typically Renaissance feature, yet examination on the ground reveals that the earlier fabric of the building, hanging, as it does, above a narrow gorge to the east, needed the support of that terracing.

It is possible that additional features, such as stone steps, a balustrade and summer house, were added post-1550, but the earth moving had already been accomplished. The Renaissance influences largely occurred under the direction of Edward Somerset, the 4th earl, who, after his succession in 1589, is believed to have commissioned a series of shell-lined niches around the perimeter of the moat surrounding the great tower. These niches formerly held statues of Roman emperors, but, like other features, a water parterre for example, they were elaborations upon a landscape already fixed in the fifteenth century. General surveys of late-medieval castles with significant continuation through the sixteenth century continually demonstrate the 'bolt-on' nature of many Renaissance additions.

At Quarrendon, in Buckinghamshire, a series of water features associated with a medieval manor and settlement and the site of St Peter's Church were converted into an elaborate water garden, possibly started by Sir Robert Lee prior to 1540. The gardens reached their fully developed form later in the century, probably under the control of Sir Henry Lee (1513–1611), the Queen's champion, in anticipation of a visit by Elizabeth in 1592. Everson (2001, 24) notes that 'The earthwork remains of a grand country house and its accompanying formal gardens dating from the 16th and 17th centuries occupy the whole central section of the surveyed site. This elaborate complex is an outstanding survival of its date and type in England.' Distinctive features include huge, raised terraces flanked by water-filled ditches and a water garden based on three linked square islands (Fig. 8).

The transition post-Dissolution (1540 onwards) to Renaissance garden of the medieval monastic landscape was rather more abrupt than that of solely secular properties. As well as instances of monastic structures being adapted for residential use – Titchfield Abbey in Hampshire, Wroxton Abbey in Oxfordshire and Combe Abbey in Warwickshire, for example – we also have the wholesale takeover of associated gardens and parks and their water features. At Bindon Abbey, in Wool, Dorset, a Cistercian monastery founded in 1172, the buildings were converted into a house in 1539 by Sir Thomas Poyning, and although the house itself was destroyed during the Civil War, a fine series of earthworks illustrates the transition from monastic landscape to pleasure garden (Fig. 9). Thomas Howard purchased the property in 1544, and as, Mowl (2003, 16) suggests, 'only five years after the Dissolution there would still have been some of the nine monks who had been pensioned off, or skilled *conversi* in Wool village, who understood the system of sluices that kept the waters flowing.' Amongst a series of sluices and canals were added a lozenge-shaped pool with central

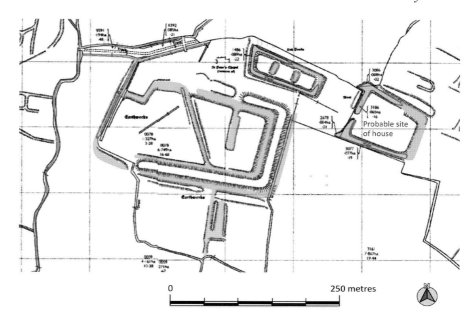

FIGURE 8. Quarrendon, plan of earthworks from 1970 OS 6 inch map. © Crown Copyright and Landmark Information Group Limited (2021).

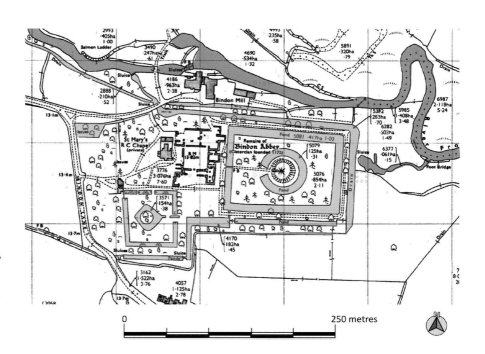

FIGURE 9. Bindon Abbey, plan of earthworks from 1970 OS 6 inch map. © Crown Copyright and Landmark Information Group Limited (2021).

island within a square, moated enclosure considered by Mowl to be the earliest instance of this form in England, a form developed and echoed at Raglan; Chipping Campden, Gloucestershire; and, to a certain extent, Hanwell as a 'water parterre', a geometric arrangement of water channels and raised ground for planting. No contemporary examples survive with planting, but an idea can be gained of their appearance by considering continental examples (Plate 5). Farther to the east was a larger, rectangular moated area within which was situated a mount surrounded by a water-filled ditch. The entire composition, according to Mowl (Ibid., 17), 'make[s] up a Tudor water garden on a grand scale, one befitting a house of a cousin of the Queen. [...] Here better than anywhere else it is possible to evoke the spirit of that great garden which William Cecil, Lord Burghley created [...] at Theobalds in Hertfordshire.' The importance of Theobalds as a model for garden design moving into the next century is hard to exaggerate. Strong (1998, 154) says, 'Planted in the decade 1575 to 1585 Theobalds was the most influential Elizabethan garden, although its actual appearance and detailed layout can only be a matter for speculation.' Situated close to the capital, the manor was purchased by William Cecil in 1564. Work on the great courtyard house was completed in 1585, the interior echoing in many ways some of the extravagances of Italian gardens of the period (Andrews 1993, 130).

The gardens were built, as had become the practice at the time, around a series of walled courts with walks, hedges and arbours and, in discrete beds, plantings of what are often termed 'knot gardens'. One of the more distinctive features of the formal garden layout was the use of 'knots': geometric plantings bordered by low hedges and sand or gravel. The origins of this motif in garden design remain obscure, but it is generally recognised that the earliest depiction is in Colonna's notoriously obscure *Hypnerotomachia Poliphili*, first printed in 1499. Tom Turner (2005, 221), amongst others, conjectures that these decorative schemes are derived from Islamic carpets. One of the first English references to knot gardens is in the contemporary account of the wedding of Catherine of Aragon to Arthur, Prince of Wales, at Richmond, in 1501.

> [...] most faire and pleasant gardeyns, with ryall knots aleyed and herbid; many a marvellous beast, as lyons, dragons, and such other of dyvers kynde, properly fachyoned and carved in the grounde, right well sandid and compassed in with lede. (Thacker 1994, 41)

Stephen Hawes's romance, Passetyme of Pleasure, or the History of Grande Amour and la Bel Pucel, published in 1509, describes the design like this:

> With Flora paynted and wrought curiously,
> In dyvers knottes of mervaylous gretenes.
> Rampande lyions stode up wondersly,
> Made all of herbes with dulcet swetenes. (Hawes 1509, lines 2010–12)

The water features at Theobalds, though extensive, were from a design perspective fairly straightforward. They consisted of a series of moats and canals defining the garden plots and enabling a visitor of 1598 to 'go into the garden, encompassed with a ditch full of water, large enough for one to have the pleasure of going in a boat and rowing between the shrubs' (Hentzner 1797) (Fig. 10). Strong (1998, 53) is of the opinion that 'This arrangement could come from only one source, France, where the evolution of the moat into the decorative canal was one of the most striking features of garden design under the Valois.' Margaret Willes (2011, 19), on the other hand, suggests that the water gardens at Wacquem, in Flanders, possibly visited by William Cecil in the 1550s, were a more likely influence. Continental input there may have been, but, as we have seen, there are ample examples of similar features laid out prior to work on the garden at Theobalds. Improvements continued to be made into the early years of the next century, at which point a certain Sir Walter Cope becomes involved.

Perhaps the finest surviving garden of the late sixteenth century, albeit only in the form of earthworks, is at Holdenby, in Northamptonshire (Fig. 11). Its significance is also enhanced by the consideration that it may be one of the earliest garden designs in the country to consciously echo some principles of Italianate design, specifically a strong sense of symmetry, terracing and the whole looking down onto a series of water features all anchored by the central positioning of the house. Constructed on the orders of Sir Christopher Hatton (1540–91) late in the 1570s, the gardens may have been subject to some alteration while held by the Crown between 1607 and 1651 (*RCHME* 1975, 106). Hatton's motivation for the vast expense involved is expressed by Wallace MacCaffrey (*ODND*) as

FIGURE 10. Theobalds, plan of gardens, reconstruction after Andrews (1993).

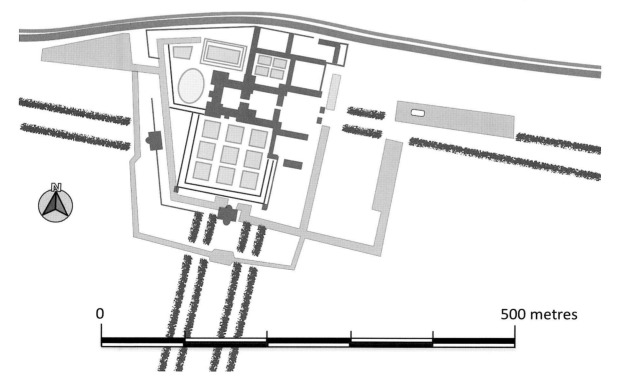

0   500 metres

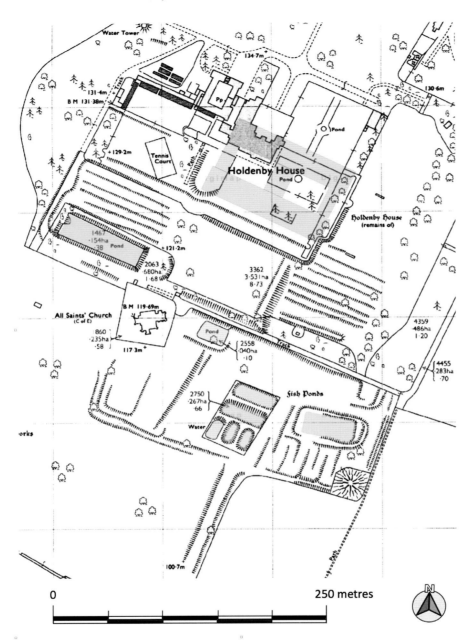

a determination, 'to surpass his colleagues' seats, such as Burghley's Theobalds, in grandeur'. He goes on to assert that 'Hatton set out to erect on his ancestral Northamptonshire manor of Holdenby a palace that would fulfil his ambition.' Despite suggestions of Catholic leanings there is no evidence that he ever travelled abroad, although his protégé, Sir Henry Unton, undertook a grand tour, including a visit to Italy, in 1575 and may have returned with material relating to garden designs (*ODNB*). Alternatively, Paula Henderson (2005, 115) suggests that a Catholic priest named Hugh Hall may have had a hand in the design, going on later to work for the notable recusant Thomas Tresham. In addition, according to Andrew Eburne (2008, 118), Pieter Morris, a well-known Dutch engineer, was advising on the hydraulic engineering. The grounds lay on a south-facing slope to the south of his huge courtyard house and consisted of a central parterre flanked by several gently descending terraces, all overlooking a complex of pools and other water features. Strong (1998, 5) considers it to be 'perhaps a distant response to gardens such as the Vatican's Villa Belvedere, the Villa D'Este and the Villa Lante, Bagnaia.' More developed and arguably more sophisticated instances of this layout can be seen at Chipping Campden and Enstone. In these cases, while some Italian influence may be discerned in the strong impetus towards symmetry and extensive use of terracing, the earth-working remains part of the native tradition. Also underway at broadly the same time was the garden of Sir Francis Carew (1530–1611) at Beddington, in Surrey. This may have been influenced by the work of the French engineer and ceramicist Bernard Palissy (c. 1510–89). Some idea of the decorative elements associated with the waterworks comes from the German traveller Baron Waldstein, who visited in 1600 and reported on

> … a most lovely garden belonging to a nobleman called Francis Carew. A little river runs through the middle of this garden, so crystal clear that you see the water-plants beneath the surface. A thing of interest is the oval fish-pond enclosed by trim hedges. The garden contains a beautiful square-shaped rock, sheltered on all sides and very cleverly contrived: the stream flows right through it and washes all around. In the stream one can see a number of different representations: the best of these is Polyphome playing on his pipe, surrounded by all kinds of animals. There is also a Hydra out of whose many heads the water gushes. (Groos 1981, 163)

A 'little house' that may have covered the water-spouting hydra was repaired in 1650, when accounts list the necessary materials as being 'Laths, lath-nails, hair and tile pins', a strong indication of a timber-framed structure with walls of lath and plaster and a tiled roof (Phillips and Burnett 2005, 166). When we come later to consider Hanwell's House of Diversion, a description from 1611 is of special interest in conveying an impression of the decorative elements.

> Not far away is an exceedingly fine pleasure house built all of mineralibus or various kinds of brass in cheerful fashion, the ceilings made like the sky from which rain pours down. Coelum pluens etc. On top is a fine and pleasant cabinet on whose ceiling Flanders Holland and Zealand etc. are beautifully painted. There is a mirror in the pleasure house which is laid in with all sorts of marble. Lapide Lydio. (quoted in Strong 1990, 235)

Excavations in 1995–96 uncovered the possible remains of a grotto and, significantly, also unearthed several fragments of Palissy-style ceramics and a small copper fish, probably designed to be animated by the flow of water (Phillips and Burnett 2005, 172).

The unfinished gardens of Lyveden New Bield, Northamptonshire, from 1597 are a further example of an elaborate water garden of the period. Anthony Brown and Christopher Taylor explained the background to the work.

> The estate at Lyveden passed to the Treshams in the mid-fifteenth century and it was this family who in 1540 obtained a licence to empark 420 acres of land around the manor house there, now known as the Old Bield. In the late 1590s Sir Thomas Tresham started work on the New Bield which was intended as a symbol of the Passion of Christ. By I 597 the building, designed by Robert Stickells, was well advanced but the work was still not complete by 1605 when Sir Thomas died and the building was abandoned. (Brown and Taylor 1972, 154)

The garden had its physical origins in an earlier moated site that lies immediately to the west. A smaller moated area that may have been an enclosed garden, incorporated into the west side, testifies to the incomplete nature of the project. The principal element of the garden was to be a large, square, moated enclosure framed by banks and with two spiral mounds projecting into the moat at the southern corners (Fig. 12). The central area was planted as an orchard, with the trees arranged in circular rings, what Eburne (2008, 71) refers to as 'a *coup de théâtre*, a dramatic revelation to the visitor as he ascended the terrace and mounts to the north. Like the lower orchard, it represented order and fecundity, beauty and productivity.' Square mounds mark the ends of terracing to the north side of the moat, and beyond that further terracing takes the garden down a slope towards the main house. Correspondence survives indicating the close interest Tresham took in the project, specifying measurements and materials for features, such as arbours, paths, a sunken alley and a bowling green, and requiring that the moat should be stocked with 'breeding congers' (Brown and Taylor 1972, 159). All this mingling of old and new ended up generating rather haphazard garden plans in an era which was striving for regularity. In terms of the overall conception of the design for the associated lodge, Eburne (2008, 119) makes a number of points relating particularly to Tycho Brahe's observatory at Uraniborg, Denmark, commenting on the geometric layout and the sophistication in its use of water and noting that it was 'an influential model for the idea of the garden lodge as place of study and meditation'. These are all points that could apply to Sir Anthony Cope's later House of Diversion at Hanwell.

No fountains have survived above ground in any of the gardens noted above, and fountains were not particularly spectacular features in English gardens at the time. Fountains in the sense of streams of water discharging into a basin under gravity had been part of the European scene since Roman times and featured in a number of monastic sites, for example in the twelfth-century plan of the plumbing at Canterbury (Trinity College MS R.17.1). An example of this type of fountain is illustrated in the 1499 edition of Colonna's *Hypnerotomachia Poliphili*, but working with high pressure pipelines, which would throw plumes of water high into the air, taxed the abilities of early engineers. Christopher Thacker (1994, 40) suggests that the 'spouting dragon headed fountain described in Stephen Hawes's *Passetyme of Pleasure* is the first reference in English to a

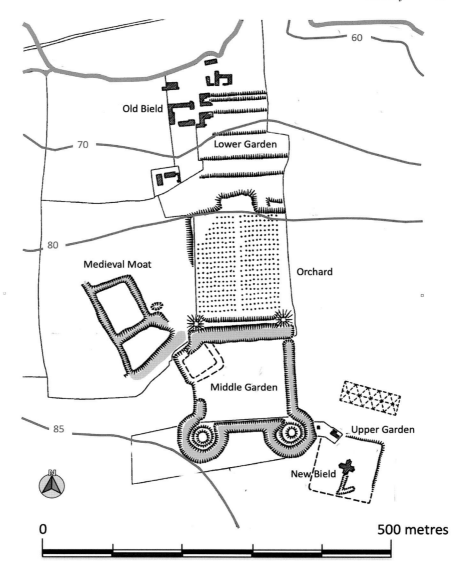

source of water operating under pressure, an achievement of Renaissance technology, unknown to the Middle Ages.' However, recent work (Peters 2011, 156) on the fountain in the marketplace at Huy, in Belgium, demonstrated water being brought and raised under pressure via lead pipes from over 1 km away in 1406. An important example of what is sometimes termed a 'candelabrum' fountain was that at the Château de Gaillon, Normandy, commissioned in 1506 from the Genoese sculptors Agostino Solari, Antonio della Porta and Pace Gazini, and which, according to Esther Godfrey (2013, 110), was 'one of the earliest and most important fountains of the sixteenth century, observed by generations of English noblemen' (Fig. 13). Similar examples were introduced into England from the latter part of the century, notably at Lumley's gardens

GAILLON

FONS MARMOREVS
SITVS IN AREA

LA FONTAINE DE
MARBRE DANS LA COVRT

FIGURE 13. Gaillon, the fountain, engraving from Du Cerceau, *Les plus excellents bastiments de France* (1576).

at Nonsuch from the 1570s, the recently re-imagined example of around 1575 at Kenilworth and the great fountain at Hampton Court from the late 1580s. However, to see instances of elaborate fountains fully integrated into garden designs, along with a host of other related engineering and architectural features, one must turn to Italy.

The sequence of great Italian water gardens, which may have provided some inspiration for and even trained technicians for later works, including those at Hanwell, is rather difficult to reconstruct in detail. There were many gardens designed around water in the 1540s and 1550s, with further developments through the remainder of the century. The conventional view is that this flowering in garden design was inspired by classical readings, notably of Pliny the Younger, and the study of ancient Roman gardens, especially Hadrian's Villa at Tivoli, which was plundered from the fifteenth century onwards. Strong (1998, 14) suggests that 'The most potent influence that reshaped the medieval into the Renaissance garden in fifteenth-century Italy was the re-creation of the villa ideal'. There are few references to the contributions from the Islamic world, especially the engineering of water features. A notable exception is the work of Lisa Golombek (2008, 243), who 'identified those elements of the Renaissance garden that could not have derived from indigenous traditions in Italy' and went on to attribute the design of such features as the water chains at Caprarola and Bagnaia to Islamic precedents. The links have been further explored in a recent volume edited by Mohammad Gharipour (2017), where such themes as 'the use of water in both Italian and Ottoman gardens of the Renaissance in the context of symbolic appropriation of land and sensual perception' are examined.

Work on the key Medici garden, Giardino di Castelli, in Tuscany, was begun in 1537 under Cosimo I (1519–74), who commissioned Niccolò di Raffaello (1500–50), known as Tribolo, to undertake the design. Luke Morgan (2013, 22) considers that this garden marked, in terms of garden design, the 'establishment of the Renaissance repertoire'. The enormous fountain based on a statue of Hercules strangling Antaeus, by the sculptor Bartolomeo Ammannati (1511–92), dominates the garden (Plate 6). Water was supplied initially via an aqueduct, which, Vasari (1963, 169) records, had to be completed prior to work on the garden starting. Water was then gathered in a pool on a raised terrace to the north, which contains a later bronze figure of a giant from 1563. Water was also conducted through a system of terracotta pipes to flow into Tribolo's famous, emblematic 'Grotto of the Animals', before feeding the fountain (Plate 7).

Perhaps the most influential, although now ruinous, of the Tuscan gardens was Pratolino. It was begun under the auspices of Francesco I de'Medici (1541–87), and much of the detailed design work was done by Bernado Buontalenti (1531–1608). Again the park occupied a huge area but contained an entire series of well-engineered water features, including pools, fountains, grottoes and automata. Work began here in 1568 to create what Maria Pozzana (2001, 90) describes as 'a thick network of galleries and chambers for various mechanisms and for decanting water forming the arteries and veins of the garden representing the peak of technical hydraulic knowledge of the times'.

However, the three greatest water gardens of the period are to be found closer to Rome: the Villa Farnese, at Caprarola (1559); the Villa Lante, at Bagnaia (1566); and the Villa d'Este, at Tivoli (1568). The first two, while having larger parks attached, have very specific areas built around a strongly linear flow of water, which is manipulated though a series of channels, cascades, fountains and pools in extraordinarily imaginative and sophisticated ways. For example, at the Villa Farnese, commissioned by Alessandro Farnese (1520–89) from the designer Jacapo Borazzi da Vignola (1507–73), a long water chain refreshes and soothes visitors during the lengthy climb up a ramp towards the Casino di Piacere (House of Pleasure). A water-cooled dining table marks the centre point of the sequence of water features within the garden of the Villa Lante, a design again attributed to Vignola and carried out at the behest of Cardinal Gianfrancesco Gambara (1533–87).

Georgina Masson (1989, 180) describes the gardens of the Villa d'Este as 'the most Roman but also most typically Renaissance garden of all Italy.' Built on a series of terraces rising up a steep slope towards the villa at the crest of the hill, each upward step is accompanied by the sound and sight of water, and each terrace has some new marvel to entertain and inspire, including a water organ and the famed walk of a hundred fountains. Kirsty McLeod (2011, 199) sums up the garden's impact and *raison d'être* in these terms: 'Water, used extravagantly and scientifically, was the medium of the garden, the means by which its complex mix of iconography, allegory, family history, learning and personal glorification could be expressed.' Standing apart from the mainstream of Italian gardens is the Parco di Monstri, at Bomarzo, formerly known as the Sacro Bosco, created by Vicino Orsini (1523–83) from 1552 onwards. While defying explanation, the park is of technical interest because of the way in which it is laid out along a valley, with water being managed through a series of conduits paralleling the valley's sides, a situation not dissimilar to the later works at Hanwell (Wass 2017, 3). The key feature demonstrated by these Italian gardens is the sophisticated ways in which comparatively limited quantities of water were gathered, husbanded and exploited through channels, conduits and pipework, a tradition born out of technical expertise as well as limited water supply, a lack that was not part of the English experience.

A further feature of Italian gardens of the period were the *giochi d'acqua*, or water jokes, aspects of which fed into some elements of English garden design. A typical account of the experience is given by Montaigne, from a visit in 1581 to Castelli.

> As they were walking about the gardening looking at its curiosities, the gardener left their company for this purpose; and as they were in a certain spot contemplating certain marble statues, there spurted upon their feet and between their legs, through an infinite number of tiny holes, jets of water so minute that they were almost invisible, imitating supremely well the trickle of fine rain, with which they were completely sprinkled by the operation of some underground spring which the gardener was working more than two hundred paces from there, with such artifice that from there on the outside he made these spurts of water rise and fall as he pleased, turning and moving them just as he wanted. This game is found here in several places. (Montaigne 2003, 43)

The full, rich panoply, and indeed consequences, of such 'amusing experiences' were detailed by French historian Charles de Brosses in the middle of the eighteenth century, when the *giochi d'acqua* were still well maintained. An excursion made by him and his companions began at the Villa Mondargone.

> [...] around a polypriapic pool, where the edge of the basin is fitted all round with hosepipes, made from leather and with copper nozzles at the end. These pipes were belying there idle and innocent, when – after the tap had been turned on – these fine creatures began to stand up in the oddest way, and, as Rabelais says, began to piss fresh water non-stop, Migieu grabbed one of these weapons and squirted it straight in Lacurne's face; he shot back and we all joined in this excellent sport, and went on half an hour until we were drenched to the skin. You'd think winter was not the best season for this little game, but the day was so cold and fine that we couldn't resist the temptation. (De Brosses 1740, quoted in Atlee 2006, 147)

After changing their clothes at the inn, he and his companions made a further excursion to the Villa Aldobrandini, the location of a garden begun in 1598 by Pietro Aldobrandini (1571–1621), under the direction of the aptly named Dominican friar and architect Giovanni Fontana (1540–1614).

> [...] we were sitting behaving ourselves, by the belvedere [...] and didn't notice a hundred treacherous little pipes distributed between the joints of the stones, when suddenly they went off in jets all over us. Well, we had no dry clothes left and so we plunged boldly into the wettest corners of then place, where we spent the rest of the evening playing the same sort of tricks. There is an especially good little curving stairway where, as soon as you are part way up, the water jets shoot out, criss-crossing in every direction, from above from below, and the sides. At the top of these steps we got our revenge on Legouz who had been responsible for our wetting by the Belvedere. He had intended to turn on a tap to squirt water at us, but the tap was designed to trick the tricker. It shot out a torrent of water, thick as your arm, and with ferocious force, straight into Legouz's stomach. Legouz bolted off, his trousers full of water, guttering down into his shoes. We all fell over with laughing and that was enough. But the end isn't as funny as it had been in the morning. We had to stay in with nothing to wear but our dressing gowns, eating a vile supper, while they dried our clothes. (De Brosses 1740, quoted in Atlee 2006, 147)

While such experiences may have made perfect sense in the context of the Italian climate, instances of similar aquatic games in England are understandably rather sparse, the Enstone Marvels being a notable exception.

The grand set piece gardens of France in the sixteenth century, such as Gaillon, Blois and Fontainebleau, owed much to links established with Italy through dynastic marriage, political manoeuvrings and military campaigns. William Adams identifies in particular the invasion of Italy by the King Charles VIII of France in 1494 as a seminal moment.

> The king was deeply impressed by the luxurious palaces, gardens and villas of Naples. The gardens with their elaborate hydraulic systems, fountains and sculptures were 'an early paradise' Charles wrote to his brother-in-law after he had inspected the elegant villas of La Duchesa and Poggio Reale. (Adams 1974, 10)

Work had ceased at Amboise upon Charles's death in 1498, but work was picked up by his successor, Louis XII, at Blois and particularly at Gaillon. Georges d'Amboise, who was made cardinal in 1498, began work on his fortress palace in 1502. While incorporating much of the feel of a medieval fortress, the detached garden featured, as well as numerous elaborate fountains, a separate pleasure house known as the Maison Blanche. A letter by Jacopo Probo d'Atri, probably written around 1510, praises the 'superb pavilions, the well-made doors, fountains in castles and the beautiful and artificial labyrinth' (Probo c. 1510, quoted in Weiss 1953, 6). The complexity of the water features associated with the garden is illustrated by Du Cerceau in his Les Plus *Excellants Bastiments de France*, published in the 1570s, where a two-storey pavilion set on an island is joined by a canal to a similarly water-girt rock termed the Parnassus de Gaillon. Water figures largely in the later work at Chantilly and Fontainebleau, where the tradition of northern French medieval moated enclosures was extended on a huge scale. However, the site that most embraced the Italian tradition of terraced gardens with attendant elaborate water works was at St Germain-en-Laye (Fig. 14). Started in 1599 by Henri IV, the gardens consisted of six huge terraces stepping down the valley side to the banks of the Seine. The terraces were home to a variety of grottoes, with automata and a water organ, canals, water parterres and, of course, fountains. These were engineered by the Italian Thomas Francini and constitute, according to Adams (1974, 46), the 'most complex water engineering to be seen in France'.

In England, those constructing fountains continued to work with medieval forms, such as seen in the courtyard fountain of 1601 at Trinity College, Cambridge (Plate 8). It seems that innovative designs had to wait on the new century and the arrival of expert engineers from the continent. The latter half of the sixteenth century saw many instances of garden making incorporating ambitious water features but drawing on an established tradition of design and a pre-existing body of engineering expertise. Significant continental influences may be discerned in the architecture of the assorted structures that were brought in late in the sixteenth century to grace the gardens of the elite. These influences also applied to the design and decor of the great houses that were associated with these gardens, although this in itself remains debatable. In analysing structural elements of the Cecils' work at Burghley in the late sixteenth century, Mark Girouard (1963, 30) suggests that 'the native Perpendicular Gothic tradition was too strong to succumb to the new style; that for thirty years or so in the middle of the century the two joined battle and classical architecture, having influential backers, nearly won the day; but that in the end the victory went to the native style.' However, it is in the nature of garden buildings that, as comparatively low-cost, sometimes ephemeral structures, they are ready arenas within which to experiment and boast of one's acquaintance with the very latest fashionable styles. Even in these architectural instances, however, as Strong (1998, 6) argues, 'the floodgates never opened until after Inigo Jones's second visit in 1613–14.' Personnel and ideas, from France in particular, were to be

FIGURE 14. Gardens at St. Germain-en-Laye, from Du Cerceau, *Les plus excellents bastiments de France* (1576).

brought in to contribute to the structural elements of gardens associated with some of the highest in the land, and water features became a major component in this continentally inspired adventure.

Evidence for early garden making, in association with the construction of the house, at Hanwell is thin on the ground. We have already looked at the 1525 bequest of £20 for the making of a pool. Excavators in 2014 recorded the terracing that was required to create a level area for the building the castle, some of which extended to the north and east, and reported on a series of shallow pits to the east of the house (Yeates 2014, 42). These may well have been planting pits for elements of a formal garden. Excavations in 2014 in an area known as the Sunken Garden indicated that this feature had originated as

FIGURE 15. Hanwell, park boundary. Field names taken from A/TC, Welch Farm Estate map, 1799. © Crown Copyright and Landmark Information Group Limited (2021). All rights reserved.

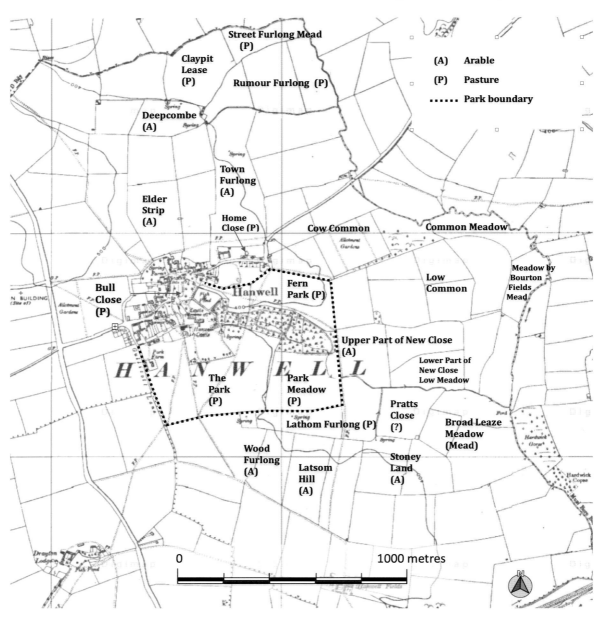

a quarry. The lack of brick fragments amongst the debris and back-fill shows that this feature arguably pre-dated the building of the castle. However, given its proximity to the castle, it seems likely that landscaping of the area would have closely followed the completion of the residence. Evidence from elsewhere in the park for the sixteenth-century layout is limited. The LiDAR image of the paddock on the south side of the valley shows clearly the way in which the ridge and furrow of the medieval open fields was cut across by a double bank and ditch (see Fig. 29). As it is probable that the process of enclosure went hand in hand with the acquisition of the manor by the Copes, this earthwork may be an indication of the boundary to the park in the early sixteenth century, prior to later expansion. The existence of a deer park in 1563 is suggested by the provision made of venison to Banbury Corporation (Beesley 1841, 230). Further evidence of the original extent of the deer park comes from the field names used late in the eighteenth century (Fig. 15). It seems likely that the next major phase in the expansion of the park and garden was at the behest of the 1st baronet, Sir Anthony, and his brother Walter Cope in the opening decades of the seventeenth century, a project undertaken with full and expert knowledge of some of gardens described above.

Bibliography

Adams, W., *The French Garden 1500–1800* (London, 1974)

Andrews, M., 'Theobalds Palace: The Gardens and Park', *Garden History* 21(2) (1993)

Atlee, H., *Italian Gardens, a Cultural History* (London, 2006)

Bond, J. and Tiller, K., *Blenheim Landscape for a Palace* (Stroud, 1997)

Brown, A.E. and Taylor, C., 'The Gardens at Lyveden, Northamptonshire', *Archaeological Journal* 129(1) (1972)

Colajanni, S., 'The Effect of Water on Passive Cooling Systems in the Arab-Norman Architecture of the Zisa Palace in Palermo', in Campbell, J.W.P. *et al.* (eds) *Water, Doors and Buildings: Studies in the History of Construction* (Cambridge, 2019)

Colvin, H., The History of the King's Works (London, 1963)

Cope, B., 'William Cope of Hanwell (c. 1450–1513)', *Cake and Cockhorse* 20(5) (2017)

Creighton, O., Designs upon the Land: Elite Landscapes of the Middle Ages (Woodbridge, 2009)

Currie, C.K., *Garden Archaeology*, Practical Handbooks in Archaeology 17 (York, 2005)

Demidowicz, G., 'The North Court Prior to Leicester's Works', in Keay, A. and Watkins, J. (eds) *The Elizabethan Garden at Kenilworth Castle* (Swindon, 2013)

Dix, B. and Parry, S., 'The Excavation of the Privy Garden', in Thurley, S. (ed.) *The Privy Garden, Hampton Court Palace* (London, 1995)

Eadwine Psalter, Trinity College, Cambridge, MS R.17.1

Eburne, A., 'The Passion of Sir Thomas Tresham: New Light on the Gardens and Lodge at Lyveden', *Garden History* 36(1) (2008)

Everson, P., 'Field Survey and Garden Earthworks', in Currie, C. (ed.) *Garden Archaeology*, Council for British Archaeology Research Report 78 (York, 1991)

Everson, P., 'Peasants, Peers and Graziers: The Landscape of Quarrendon, Buckinghamshire, Interpreted', *Records of Buckinghamshire* 41 (2001)

Gharipour, M. (ed.), *Gardens of Renaissance Europe and the Islamic Empires* (University Park, Pennsylvania, 2017)

Girouard, M., 'Elizabethan Architecture and the Gothic Tradition', *Architectural History* 6 (1963)

Godfrey, E., 'Sources for the New Fountain', in Keay, A. and Watkins, J. (eds) *The Elizabethan Garden at Kenilworth Castle* (Swindon, 2013)

Golombek, L., 'From Timur to Tivoli: Reflections on Il Giardino All'Italiana', *Muqarnas* 25 (2008)

Goodall, J., *The English Castle* (New Haven, 2011)

Groos, G.W. (translator), *Diary of Baron Waldstein: A Traveller in Elizabethan England* (London, 1981)

Hale, J., *The Civilization of Europe in the Renaissance* (London, 1993)

Hants. CRO, 43M48/94 17 (release of rights in the manor of Hanwell, Oxon. 17 October 1498)

Hants. CRO, 43M48/96 (office copy of will and probate of William Cope Esq. 1513)

Hawes, S., *Passetyme of Pleasure, or the History of Grande Amour and la Bel Pucel*, ed. Mead, W.E., Early English Text Society 19 (London, 1928), lines 2010–12

Henderson, P., *The Tudor House and Garden* (New Haven, 2005)

Henderson, P., 'Clinging to the Past: Medievalism in the English "Renaissance" Garden', in Samson, A. (ed.) *Locus Amoenus, Gardens and Horticulture in the Renaissance* (Chichester, 2012)

Hentzner, P., *Travels in England During the Reign of Queen Elizabeth* (London, 1797)

Jacques, D., 'The "Pond Garden" at Hampton Court Palace: One of the Best-Known Examples of a Sunk Garden', *Garden History* 33(1) (2005)

James, T., *The Palaces of Medieval England c.1050–1550: Royalty, Nobility, the Episcopate and Their Residences from Edward the Confessor to Henry VIII* (London, 1990)

Johnson, M., 'Meanings of Polite Architecture in Sixteenth Century England', *Historical Archaeology* 26(3) (1992)

Jones, M. and Underwood, M., *The King's Mother: Lady Margaret Beaufort, Countess of Richmond and Derby* (Cambridge, 1992)

Leland, J., *The Itinerary of John Leland in or About the Years 1535–1543*, ed. Smith, L.T. (London 1908)

Liddiard, R., *Castles in Context* (Macclesfield, 2005)

Masson, G., *Italian Gardens* (London, 1989)

McLeod, K., *The Best Gardens in Italy, a Traveller's Companion* (London, 2011)

Montaigne, M. de, *The Complete Works: Essays, Travel Journal, Letters*, ed. Frame, D. (London, 2003)

Morgan, L., *A Cultural History of Gardens in the Renaissance* (London, 2013)

Mowl, T., *The Historic Gardens of Dorset* (Stroud, 2003)

ODNB, Reeves, A.C., 'Cromwell, Ralph, Third Baron Cromwell (1393?–1456)'

ODNB, MacCaffrey, W., 'Hatton, Sir Christopher (c. 1540–1591)'

ODNB, Greengrass, M., 'Unton [Umpton], Sir Henry (c. 1558–1596)'

Peters, C., 'Huy: Archaeological Study Prior to the Restoration of the Market Fountain Called li bassini', *Chronicle of Walloon Archeology* 18 (2011)

Phillips, J. and Burnett, N., 'The Chronology and Layout of Francis Carew's Garden at Beddington, Surrey', *Garden History* 33(2) (2005)

Pozzana, M., *Gardens of Florence and Tuscany* (Florence, 2001)

Royal Commission on Historic Monuments (England), *An Inventory of the Historical Monuments in Dorset, Volume 2, South East* (London, 1970)

Royal Commission on Historical Monuments (England), *An Inventory of the Historical Monuments in the County of Northamptonshire, Volume 3, Archaeological Sites in North-West Northamptonshire* (London, 1975)

Sherwood, J. and Pevsner, N., *The Buildings of England: Oxfordshire* (London, 1974)

Strong, R., 'Sir Francis Carew's Garden at Beddington', in Chancey, E. and Mack, P. (eds) *England and the Continental Renaissance: Essays in Honour of J.B. Trapp* (Woodbridge, 1990)

Thacker, C., *The Genius of Gardening: The History of Gardens in Britain and Ireland* (London, 1994)

Thorpe, H., 'The Lord and the Landscape, Illustrated through the Changing Fortunes of a Warwickshire Parish, Wormleighton', *Birmingham Archaeological Society, Transactions and Proceedings* 80 (1965)

TNA, C 1/399/39 (Cope v. Cope, 1515–1518)

TNA, Prerogative Court of Canterbury, PROB 11/11/125 (will of Jane Spencer Saunders Cope, 1525)

Turner, T., *Garden History, Philosophy and Design* (London, 2005)

Vasari, G., *The Lives of the Painters, Sculptors and Architects, vol. 3* (London, 1963)

Wass, S., 'Subsidiary Excavations Through the Tailrace', in Astill, G. (ed.), *A Medieval Industrial Complex and Its Landscape: The Metalworking Watermills and Workshops of Bordesley Abbey*, Council for British Archaeology Research Report 92 (York, 1993)

Wass, S., 'Parco di Monstri, Bomarzo: Some Preliminary Observations on the Use of Water', *Garden History* 45(1) (2017)

Wedgwood, J. and Holt, A., *History of Parliament, 1439–1509*, vol. 2 (London, 1938)

Weiss, R., 'The Castle of Gaillon in 1509–10', *Journal of the Warburg and Courtauld Institutes* 16 (1953)

Whittle, E., 'The Renaissance Gardens of Raglan Castle', *Garden History* 17(1) (1989)

Wickham, L., *Gardens in History: A Political Perspective* (Macclesfield, 2012)

Willes, M., *The Making of the English Gardener: Plants, Books and Inspiration 1560–1660* (Newhaven, 2011)

Woodward, F., *Oxfordshire Parks* (Woodstock, 1982)

CHAPTER THREE

The Seventeenth Century

The Copes in Ascendency

Responsibility for any development of the house at Hanwell and its associated landscape through the sixteenth century rested with representatives of two generations of the Cope family: Anthony (1495?–1551), whom I will refer to as Anthony I, and the 1st baronet, Sir Anthony (1550–1614), whom I will refer to as Anthony II. As we have seen, Anthony I inherited and went on to bring the court action for the completion of the property against the executors of his father's will. Elizabeth Allen (*ODNB*) notes that 'Cope's desire for the rapid completion of his residence was probably strengthened by his marriage, by 1517, to Jane (d. 1569/70), daughter of Matthew Crews, of Pynne, in Stoke English parish in Devon'. Anthony may have attended Oriel College but, not unusually, does not appear to have graduated. Subsequently, according to Anthony Wood (1813, 193), he 'went into France, Germany, Italy and elsewhere; in which places visiting the universities and joining this company to the most learned men of them, became an accomplished gentleman'. Wood goes on to describe Cope's publications, two of which survive: a book on the psalms and an account, drawn from classical authors, of Hannibal and Scipio Africanus. The latter was dedicated in 1545 by its printer, Thomas Berthelet, to King Henry VIII. It is possible that while in Italy, such an accomplished traveller and scholar might have engaged with current fashions in garden making, but there is nothing in his later career that suggests such an interest. Indeed the 1525 bequest of £20 hints that he may have needed some encouragement to complete work on the gardens at Hanwell. Allen (*ODNB*) describes him as profiting from 'extensive cattle and sheep farming, and the aggressive management of tenements and cottages inherited and acquired in Banbury'. He maintained useful links with the Spencer family by obtaining, in 1534, a wardship, of Sir William Spencer's heir, that enabled him to profit from the administration of the estate. Always seen as a loyalist, he enjoyed a number of posts at court, becoming chamberlain to Katherine Parr, Henry VIII's last queen, until her death, in 1548. This may be the context for the extraordinary armorial panel found in 2014 reused in a cottage in Hanwell and since re-instated in the castle. In 1536 Anthony was granted Brooke Priory, in Rutland, and he may have been responsible for developing the elaborate terraced water gardens there (Page 1980, 159). Allen (*ODNB*) asserts, 'in July 1547 he was deeply involved in the repression of the Oxfordshire revolt against enclosures and the more protestant policies of the new government, led by both craftsmen and conservative priests. He oversaw the hanging of some of the ringleaders, and the setting of their heads atop the highest buildings in their communities.'

Upon Anthony's death, at Hanwell, in 1551, the estate was inherited by his son Edward, who purchased the property of Tangley, in Oxfordshire, favoured by later generations (Hants. CRO, 43M48/121). He in turn had passed Hanwell on to his son, Anthony II, by 1571. This Anthony, destined to become the 1st baronet, was born in 1548. After the death of his father, in 1557, his mother Elizabeth remarried, in 1561, to George Carleton, a notable puritan whose 'radical protestant influence affected Anthony'. With a base in the East Anglian fens, Carleton was 'a pioneer in the introduction of Dutch methods of mechanical drainage by windmills, engines and devices never known or used before', a fact that may also have been relevant in the education of the young Anthony (Kennedy 1983, 29). In 1588 Sir Anthony was appointed to serve on a commission of enquiry into issues affecting Carleton's interests in aspects of Fenland drainage. He began his long parliamentary career at the age of 23 and allied himself with a caucus that combined 'defence of freedom of debate in the Commons with advocacy of further church reform' (*HOP*). His adoption of a presbyterian view of church management was expressed by his appointment, in 1586, of the radical cleric John Dod (1545–1645) as Rector of Hanwell and, much later, in 1614, a similarly committed puritan, Robert Harris (1581–1658). Sir Anthony's puritan credentials were further enhanced locally by his role, in 1589, in the suppression of the Neithrop maypole and associated 'Whitsun Ales, May Games and Morris dances' (Potts 1958, 57).

On the national stage, his attempt, in 1587, following a puritan synod held early that year, to further church reform by introducing a bill to reform the Church of England and present a revised prayer book to Parliament earned him a place in the Tower of London. However, as Beesley remarks, 'The Queen's displeasure does not seem to have been lasting for she knighted him in 1590 in which year he was also appointed sheriff for Oxfordshire [...] In 1601 Sir Anthony made preparations for a visit which the Queen intended to pay him at Hanwell, but this does not seem to have taken place' (Beesley 1841, 239). Sir Anthony is mentioned as being in attendance at the wedding of one of the Queen's maids of honour, Anne Russell, to Lord Herbert, son of the Earl of Worcester, in 1600. Viscount Dillon (1915, 69) noted that he was 'a great friend of Sir Henry Lee of Ditchley', an interesting Oxfordshire connection given the later development of the Enstone Marvels. Some years earlier, in 1585, he had entertained the Earl of Leicester on a visit to Hanwell. As with most gentry of the period, Anthony was committed to improving the status of himself and his family, and in 1603, his daughter Elizabeth was married to Richard Cecil, second son of the marquess of Exeter and a nephew of Robert Cecil. In 1610 Sir Anthony received a lease of woods in Whittlewood Forest and a grant of the manor of Bruern, Oxfordshire, which became in effect a third family home, after Hanwell and Tangley. His wealth and influence were further demonstrated when he accommodated James I and his queen for an overnight stay on 20 August 1605 (Nichols 1828, 527). On 27 August 1612 the king was scheduled to 'again become the guest of Sir Anthony Cope at Hanwell', but 'this part of the gests appears to have been disarranged'. Nichols notes that 'the visits were probably paid though not according to the predetermined dates'. Some of the issues around accommodation at the time are evidenced by a letter from Sir Anthony regarding the visit of 1605.

> One of the principal causes of my joy is the hope that I shall have you at Hanwell, which the rather I presume of for that I had your promise at London, that if you continued the circuit with the King, you would satisfy my request herein. To that end I have entreated of Mr. Rolls, the gentleman usher, my gallery which I mean to divide into two rooms, for your lordship and any other nobleman that you shall make choice of. I expected my brother according to his promise the last night, but have since received a letter, that in respect of christening Sir Thomas Smith's child it will be to-morrow in the afternoon before he come. – Hanwell, this 18 August 1605. (Cope, letter to earl of Salisbury)

In June 1611, Anthony was able to purchase a baronetcy for £10,000, as part of what Katherine S. Van Eerde (1961, 137) called, the 'increasingly desperate drama of Jacobean finances'. Part of his duty as a baronet was to support the settlement of Ulster, and to that end he had some experience of castle building through the agency of his second son, also called Anthony (d. 1636). A survey from 1619 reveals the extent of his son's Irish holdings: 'Mr. Cope, 3,000 ac., called Derry-crevy and Dromullie. A bawn of lime and stone, 80 ft. sq., 14 high, 4 flankers, in 3 of them he has built very good lodgings, 3 stories high, also two watermills and one windmill; near to bawn, 14 houses of timber, inhabited with English' (Carew, Mss 613 Lambeth Palace Library). E.M. Jope (1960, 65) considers that the cruciform house Anthony built at Castleraw, County Armagh, in 1618, to be inspired by properties in Northamptonshire, including the Lyveden New Bield. The family may have genuinely seen themselves as improvers in the context of the Irish properties. Sir Anthony's approach to enclosure at home stood in marked contrast to that of his grandfather. Sir Anthony had been part of a committee charged with interrogating the instigators of the ill-fated Oxfordshire uprising of 1596, and this experience may have coloured his outlook.

> Sir Anthony Cope was among those who wanted legislation against enclosure 'violently penned'. Balked of speaking in debate, he badgered Burghley to take up in the Lords his proposals for tougher penalties and what would have amounted to a biannual commission of inquiry into depopulation. Some attributed his proposals to puritan zeal, but as member for Banbury and examiner of many of those implicated in the conspiracy Cope had recent and pressing memories to urge him on. (Walter 1985, 135)

A convergence of views may have been one of the catalysts that led to a long-term association with Francis Bacon, who, at the start of the parliament of 1597, 'initiated discussion, introducing two bills drafted by himself against depopulating enclosure and conversion to pasture. Bacon became the main protagonist for procuring legislation against enclosure, dominating the committee established and framing the bills that emerged from it' (Ibid. 133). A more balanced approach may be seen in his argument before Parliament during the 1607 debate on unifying the laws of the two kingdoms, when Cope stated that 'testimony is but to informe the Jury, who may beleave as they see cause for if they find by circumstances that a bad fellow saith true they may believe them, *et contra*' (Willson 1931, 311). His need for a London base was occasioned by his attendance at Parliament. His residence had been the Cecil property of Rutland House, on the Strand, later modified, in 1611, during the construction of Salisbury House, a project with which Sir Anthony's brother Walter was closely associated (Guerci 2009, 31). There was some question about the tenancy, as he wrote to Sir Robert Cecil in September of 1600 to explain.

> It pleased him well to be Cecil's tenant, and he would have continued so if Cecil had not disposed of it otherwise. If Cecil parts with it hereafter, he begs to have the offer of it before another. He will shortly remove the household stuff his wife left there. – Hanwell, 22 September, 1600. (Cope 1600)

The issue of a London base had not been satisfactorily resolved, because in the following year he wrote again.

> No man could have procured my removing from Cecil House had it not been your desire, so much did I hold myself satisfied to be your tenant there. I beseech you, therefore, that I may be bold to put you in mind whether you promised not in the parting from it that if Rutland House came into your hands, I should not fail to have it of you? Pardon me if I press this promise for fear that my wife should remain a banished woman from London. – From Hanwell, this 16th of September 1601. (Cope 1601)

In both cases he cited his wife's interests in having to remove some of her 'household stuff' and being forced to remain a 'banished woman'. His latter years were marred by increasing financial difficulties. Anthony died in 1614, probably at Cope Castle, later Holland House, his brother Walter's London residence. He left debts of more £20,000, responsibility for which was mainly laid at his brother's door. While some of the losses may have accrued from poorly managed finances, there is enough spending power implied in this figure for him to have undertaken garden construction on a very large scale if he had chosen to do so.

Walter Cope, three years Anthony's junior, was entered at Gray's Inn in 1570 and used this as a springboard for a career as an administrator concerned with financial affairs. He became an official for the Court of Wards in 1574, the court's feodary (representative) for Oxfordshire in 1580 and that for the City of London and Middlesex in 1601. In this role he was charged with seeking out potential royal wardships to boost the Crown's income. In addition he cultivated the company of great men, first as a gentleman usher to William Cecil, Lord Burghley, whose secretary he had become by 1593. After Burghley's death, in 1598, he grew close to Burghley's son Robert, the earl of Salisbury, and was given a number of roles, some relating to the works at the garden at Theobalds. In March of 1600 he wrote to Cecil,

> Mr. Partington attendeth to speak with you about your business. There is an outer terrace upon which no man shall be able to walk except it be set with trees to make a shade, and except your officers agree how it shall be finished, whether with brick or earth. (Cope 1601)

Significantly, another task was the oversight of the engineering works to ensure adequate water supply for the garden. The letter he wrote to Cecil on 12 September 1602 suggests Walter had considerable practical experience.

> I am glad to hear what a plentiful spring is found near your new lodge. If you mean to do anything there this summer, it is more than time it were in hand; your presence there for two hours would settle a course for all. Goffe and my man may be there: they may stake it out before your coming. (Miller 2014)

He also had an interest in a scheme to bring 'a river of water to London and Westminster from springs out of Herts and Middlesex' (Petition, May 1605). In 1605 he was called on to appraise the visual impact of a new prison on the views from gardens in the Strand, although clearly there was one standard for the aristocracy and another for the artisan.

> According to your honors pleasure wee have taken viewe of the newe erected house in Strand lane intended for a prison to punishe vagrant persons. And wee finde the same as it is now built in our opinions noe waye offensive ether to Somerset or Arundell gardens. Nether is the same anie waye prejudiciall to Holmeade, the taylor, except it be in his prospect which is verye litle hindered thereby, ffor notwithstandinge the said house he hath full prospecte over the Thames and over some parte of Somersett garden, which wee thincke to be sufficient prospecte for a man of his qualitie. (Cope 1605)

Walter was knighted in 1603, having travelled north to greet the future King James I. Thereafter he continued to run errands for the great and the good, including assisting in the investigation of treasonous activities on the part of Henry Brooke, 11th baron Cobham (1564–1619), and the subsequent arrest and questioning of his servant Richard Mellersh. The Lord Chancellor, Thomas Egerton, writing to Robert Cecil, reported that

> Sir Walter Cope desires to be speedily dispatched of this charge, his house being now otherwise disposed as you know. Mellersh carried himself very audaciously and justifies all he has done, and desires to be committed to prison. Which he has justly deserved.

Charles Nicholl (2007, 43) gives the following account of a rather more light-hearted expedition.

> There survives amongst the Cecil papers at Hatfield House a rather huffy letter from a court official, Sir Walter Cope. He writes to Lord Cecil, Lord Cranborne:

> I have sent and bene all this morning hunting for players, juglers & such kinds of creaturs, but finde them harde to finde, wherefore leavinge notes for them to seeke me, Burbage ys come, & says ther ys no new play that the Quene hath not seene,

but they have revyved an old one cawled Loves Labore Lost, which for wytt and myrthe he sayes will please her excedingly.

Cope does not date the letter, but it is endorsed '1604' by one of Cecil's secretaries, and this date is confirmed by a performance of *Love's Labours* at court in January 1605. Shakespeare would doubtless have been one of the players so fruitlessly hunted by Cope.

Walter Cope clearly was interested in other aspects of London 'wildlife', for in a letter from Ralph Gill to the earl of Salisbury in August of 1605, a visit to the Lion Tower at the Tower of London was recorded. 'Sir Walter Cope was with me last night at 7 o'clock, where he did see under the platform through the loopholes the male and female lions and by chance one of the whelps came to the mouth of the hovel.' This was not his only encounter with matters zoological, for in January 1607 we find noted in the minutes of the East India company that he requests, 'on behalf of a young man to go for parrots, monkeys, and marmosets for Lord Salisbury'. He was also able to supply Cecil with 'a pair of tortoises and a glass of balsom' (Walter Cope, letter to the earl of Salisbury, 12 August 1606).

Further advancement came in 1609, when the king made him Chamberlain of the Exchequer and, again, four years later, when he became Public Registrar General of Commerce. In 1610 he was appointed, along with Robert Cecil, to the office of Keeper of Hyde Park, in which capacity he ordered 200 lime trees, at a cost of £20. Finally, in 1612, having been made master of the Court of Wards, he promised that he would 'execute his office sincerely with clean hands' (Lord Chamberlain, letter to George Carleton, November 1612). Francis Bacon, a rival for the post, was so confident of gaining it that he had purchased new cloaks for his men, prompting the quip reported by Dr Rawley, Bacon's chaplain, that 'Sir Walter was master of the wards and Sir Francis Bacon of the Livery' (Abbott 1885, 185). While up to this stage Walter's career in public service appears to be one of continued success and rising fortunes, schemes he entered into to advance the financial interest of himself and his brother were less successful. According to Martha Hiden (1957, 64), 'He became a member of the [Virginia] Company and had paid the large sum of £215 into the Company's treasury. He was one of the leaders of his time in creating and developing England's foreign trade.' A venture begun in 1607, to buy up former church properties still held by the Crown, was disastrous for the family fortunes. His troubles multiplied, and in February of 1614, the Lord Chamberlain, writing to Dudley Carleton, remarked that 'the King has had nine petitions in five days against Sir Walter Cope, as Master of the Wards, rather for weakness of judgment than corruption'. By 1613 the market had collapsed, and Walter died in 1614, shortly after his brother Anthony, leaving around £26,000 in debts. The Lord Chamberlain, in a letter to George Carleton in February 1614, noted he was 'heart-broken at the death of his brother, and threatened loss of his place' on account of 'his want of dignity'. While we have no certain knowledge of what Sir Anthony was doing in these years at Hanwell, it is documented that in 1604 Walter began work on a new London property, which became known as

Cope Castle. The remains of this extravagant structure survive in today's Holland Park. Also constructed was his extensive and elaborate water garden, now completely lost under Kensington but studied in depth by Sally Miller (2014).

Walter Cope's Water Maze

Sir Walter's career, as documented above, demonstrates his interest in a number of topics relating to gardens. The Kensington water maze, with its complex and novel geometries, was part of the larger park associated with his new property. The design indicates links with other water gardens of the period and may have formed a blueprint for parallel developments at Hanwell. Built at a distance of around 500 m to the south-west of the house, the Cope complex was founded on the remains of an earlier square moat with possible fishponds associated with the medieval manor of West Town. The layout is pictured on a 1734 copy of an estate map originally surveyed in 1694 (Plate 10). This shows an extraordinarily intricate arrangement of ponds and peninsulas. The feature that is easiest to describe is the square moat that lies immediately to the east of the main complex. As this feature survived into the nineteenth century and was mapped by the Ordnance Survey, it is possible to be specific about its dimensions, with the central island being 40 m square. There was a causewayed approach at the south-west corner. The sequence of ponds to the west included walkways connected to islands forming peninsulas in a variety of configurations. The square moat and its surrounds, as well as areas to the north and east, are shown planted with trees, presumably orchards. The colouring on the map points to the likelihood that the causeways and peninsulas and the areas around the pools were laid to turf. Naturally the rest of the park was filled with the more conventional elements of the period – further orchards, walks, closes, terraces and non-watery parterres – but the water garden, or 'water maze' as it was labelled in 1734, remained the most distinctive feature.

It is difficult, even within the number of water gardens established early in the seventeenth century, to find a precise parallel for Sir Walter's works in Kensington. One may be initially struck by how closely his water garden resembles Sir Francis Bacon's Pondyards, at Gorhambury, near St Albans, Hertfordshire. However, the similarities are the more superficial ones of scale and general layout, and the closest example of a geometrical complex with small peninsulas is from later in the 1620s, at Tackley, in Oxfordshire. The originality of Sir Walter's creation remains something of a conundrum. The effective management of his water garden is testified to in a letter from one Adrian Gilbert to Robert Cecil, penned in September 1602.

> You will see what winter winds and frosts will do both for increase of water and for the frosts to shiver and cast down the banks; for do what you will now, you must right it once in the spring and then set bushes and what you will. And for then ponds there in the great island by your lodge will then be best ended, and against her Majestie's coming will look trim like Mr Cope's ponds. (Gilbert 1602, quoted in Miller 2014, 29)

Miller takes this to refer to the ponds at the Kensington property, and at first this seems unlikely, given that work on the house there did not start until 1604. However, an account from 1917 by a local historian, Walter Derham (1917, 71), suggests, without giving a source, that part of the property was sold 'to Sir Walter Cope of the Strand in 1591. Cope lived at West Town Manor House, which was situated in the grounds of the house lately known as Oak Lodge and now Oakwood Court.' It is possible that Walter's expertise derives from work undertaken to modify the existing, probably medieval, site at Kensington. It is also possible that he had had a hand in landscaping and introducing new water features at the family's properties at Hanwell and Bruern, given that he was semi-resident in the county, from 1580 onwards, during his time as Feodary for Oxfordshire for the Court of Wards and Livery.

Planting within Walter's garden generally was of great importance and may again provide some insight into arrangements at Hanwell. In 1608 a visitor to the Kensington garden noted, 'We had the honour to see all but touch nothing, not so much as a cherry, which are charily preserved for the Queen's coming' (Miller 2014, 23). On a plant-buying trip to the Low Countries for Robert Cecil in 1611, John Tradescant took £38 from Sir Walter to buy trees (Hatfield House Archives, Bills 51/8 V). Miller makes an important point about Walter's botanical collection and other interests.

> Cope's London house was on the Strand, where stood the palaces of the most important men of the day. It is possible that he was the Mr Cope who was visited by Thomas Platter in 1599: 'I visited his collection with Herr Lobelus, a London physician [...] this same Mr Cope inhabits a fine house in the Snecgas [sic].' Herr Lobelus was Matthias de l'Obel or Lobel, later botanist to James I. Platter described a collection of beasts, fishes, birds, insects, nature's deformities, rocks, corals, artefacts, coins, pictures and more. He stated that Mr Cope had 'spent much time in the Indies'. This seems unlikely from what is known of Cope's life, but he did invest in a number of overseas trading companies, including the Virginia and East India companies, and sea captains were always willing to carry home curiosities for the cabinets of their investors. (Miller 2014, 22)

Amongst other items in Sir Walter's pioneering collection were 'costumes, weapons, and tools from around the globe, a round horn said to have grown from an Englishwoman's forehead, a unicorn tail, a mirror "which both reflects and multiplies objects" and Chinese objects, including an "artful little box", "earthen pitchers" and porcelain' (Palmer 1995, 34). Sir Walter's cabinet seems to have been rather well known, as it features in a comic poem, 'On a Fart in the Parliament House', from the well-known anthology *Pills to Purge Melancholy*.

> Quoth Sir Walter Cope, 'twas so readily let,
> I would it were sweet enough for my cabinet. (Anonymous 1719)

He and his collecting are also mocked in John Donne's *Catalogus Librorum aulicorum incomparabilium et non vendibilium* (Catalogue of incomparable courtly books, not for sale), composed between 1603 and 1611. Donne lists

'Believe in thy havings, and thou hast them. A test for antiquities, being a great book on very small things dictated by Walter Cope, copied out by his wife and given a Latin gloss by his amanuensis John Pory'. David Quinn (1979, 139) adds the following comment, 'Cope was a great collector of curiosities, and his avidity to put into his collection all kinds of rubbish (as well as many valuable specimens) produced some ridicule. I think Donne was getting at Cope for this.' Sir Walter clearly subscribed to what Hyde (2013, 9) calls 'the culture of curiosity and collecting'. Were his collecting interests shared by his brother Anthony? Did any part of it find its way to Hanwell and were any remnants of it perhaps surviving in a forgotten cupboard somewhere to intrigue and inspire the future 4th baronet?

Sir Francis Bacon, Gardening and *The New Atlantis*

Sir Francis Bacon is a significant element in this study, not only because of Plot's later reference to *The New Atlantis,* but also because of his being part of the same social and political circle as the Cecils and therefore, somewhat tangentially, the Copes. Was there some sharing of influences and exchange of ideas, not least through Bacon's own experiences of garden making and his associated writings?

Francis Bacon (1564–1626) was the second son of Sir Nicholas Bacon and his second wife, Anne. He grew up and was educated alongside his older brother Anthony, at Gorhambury. Francis went up to Trinity College, Cambridge, in 1573, under the personal tutelage of the master, Dr John Whitgift. He entered Gray's Inn in 1578 and subsequently worked in France, for the diplomat Sir Amias Paulet, until the death of his father, in 1579. Afterwards he returned to Gray's Inn; he was admitted to the bar in 1582 and began his legal career under the patronage of his uncle William Cecil, Lord Burghley. Much of his early work was associated with concerns over a perceived resurgence in Roman Catholicism, in which he showed some puritan leanings (*ODNB*).

Bacon's profound interest in natural philosophy was first given voice in a letter from 1592, to Lord Burghley, in which he states,

> I confess that I have as vast contemplative ends, as I have moderate civil ends; for I have taken all knowledge to be my province; and if I could purge it of two sorts of rovers, whereof the one with frivolous disputations, confutations, and verbosities, the other with blind experiments and auricular traditions and impostures, hath committed so many spoils, I hope I should bring in industrious observations, grounded conclusions, and profitable inventions and discoveries. (Spedding *et al.* 1857–74, vol. 8, 109)

After incurring the displeasure of Queen Elizabeth, he failed to gain a post as the next attorney general, but plans for a contemplative life were dashed when further legal employment for the Crown came his way. However, his philosophical interests were not entirely quashed, as demonstrated by a device he presented at Gray's Inn for Christmas of 1594, where, in a foreshadowing of *The New Atlantis,* a character advocating the pursuit of philosophy called for 'the conquest of the works of nature', commending the erection of 'a most perfect and general library', 'a spacious, wonderful garden', 'a goodly huge cabinet', as well as 'a still-house, so furnished with mills, instruments, furnaces, and vessels, as may be a palace fit for a philosopher's stone' (Greg 1914, 35). Bacon maintained a strong connection with Robert Devereux, 2nd Earl of Essex, throughout the 1590s. However, his finances, rarely secure, collapsed, and he was arrested for debt in 1598. Following Essex's abortive attempt at rebellion in 1601, Bacon found himself prosecuting his former friend and patron for treason. Efforts to gain the new king's approval paid off, for in 1603 he was knighted. In 1606 Bacon married Alice, the 14-year-old daughter of a wealthy London alderman. Two years later, surviving notes reviewing his economic situation also include his plans for improving his house and gardens at Gorhambury.

In 1605 he had published his first major philosophical work, *The Two Bookes of Francis Bacon: Of the Proficience and Advancement of Learning, Divine and Humane,* which, as well as celebrating learning in all its forms, attempted to sum up the current state of human knowledge. Alongside his philosophical endeavours, Bacon also tried to reform existing institutions, in addition to proposing the founding of new ones. After considerable efforts, Bacon was finally appointed attorney general, in 1613. However, the rise of George Villiers, later earl of Buckingham, was more instrumental in advancing his career: a place on the privy council in 1616, the office of lord keeper the following year, and lord chancellor in 1618, with his elevation to baron Verulam of Verulam. In 1620 his major philosophical work, *Novum Organum,* was published, containing a plan, the *Instauratio magna,* for advancing the cause of human understanding. This programme was divided into six sections:

1. The Divisions of the Sciences.
2. The New Organon; or Directions for the Interpretation of Nature.
3. The Phenomena of the Universe; or a Natural and Experimental History for the Foundation of Philosophy.
4. The Ladder of the Intellect.
5. Forerunners, or Anticipations of Second Philosophy.
6. Second Philosophy; or Active Science.

It was in contemplating the practical implications of this programme that Bacon was led to start work on *The New Atlantis.* Following his impeachment, as part of the parliamentary attack on monopolists, and his subsequent conviction for financial irregularities, Bacon retired to Gorhambury, on a pension of £1,200 a year. Here he had ample opportunities to pursue this and other projects. He died in 1626, following a reported abortive attempt to preserve a chicken by stuffing it with snow. *The New Atlantis* was unfinished, leaving it to William Rawley to publish posthumously. Henderson (2008, 63) sums up his life with these words: 'Throughout his life, then, Bacon flirted with the idea of abandoning his political career to devote himself to the contemplative life. It is a tribute to his enormous energy and determination that he was successful at both.'

Bacon lived for much of his life at Gray's Inn, where he was instrumental in commissioning a series of walks and a mount with banqueting house, between 1597 and 1608. Indeed his championing of tree-lined alleys there was probably inspired by work done at Theobalds, where, according to Henderson (2008, 70), 'Lord Burghley is thought to have been the first in England to have planted walks.' There is some debate about the extent to which Bacon was responsible for the design of the gardens at his suburban residence at Twickenham. Bacon leased the property between 1595 and 1606, and although his successor, Lucy Harrington, countess of Bedford, was a notable gardener in her own right, it is hard to see that she could have contributed much to the garden as illustrated by Robert Smytheson around 1609. Strong (1998, 120) described the garden as an 'emblematic one based upon the familiar plan of the pre-Copernican universe' and compared it with a similar reconstructed layout at Chastleton House, in Oxfordshire. It is interesting to see Bacon commemorating a Ptolemaic view of the universe, given that Thomas Digges had published the first heliocentric account in English in 1576 (Johnson 1933, 69). If there was, indeed, an astronomical facet to this design, it would have reflected perhaps on contemporary debates rather than a particular fixed view. On the other hand, it is a design which seems to have sprung from a profound understanding of geometry and so may reflect Bacon's other interests. Tycho Brahe's garden and observatory at Uraniborg springs to mind when one looks at the layout of Twickenham.

Bacon took up occasional residence at Gorhambury in 1601, following the death of his older brother Anthony, and in 1608 resolved to 'give directions of a plot to be made to turn the pondyard into a place of pleasure' (*Works*, Spedding *et al.* 1861–74, 76–77). Unlike for Sir Walter's water maze, there are several contemporary accounts, not the least of which is Bacon's detailed memorandum, which specifies that, within a square moat,

> The grownd to be inclosed square wth a bricke wall, and frute trees plashed upon it; on the owtside of it to sett fayre straite byrches on 2 sides and lyme trees on 2 sides, some x foote distant from the wall, so that the wall may hide most of the shaft of the tree and onely the tufts appear above. (Spedding *et al.* 1861–74, 76–77)

He then gives the width of his terraced walkways as 25 feet (7.6 m) and describes 'a fyne little stream rune upon Marvell and fine peppell'.

> All the grownd within this waulk to be cast into a laque, wth a fayre raile wth Images gilt rownd about it and some low flowres violetts and strawberries. Then a fayre hedg of Tymber woorke till it towch the water, wth some glasses colored hear and there for the ey.

> In ye Middle of the laque where the howse now stands to make an Iland of 100 broad; An in the Middle thereof to build a howse for freshnes with an upper galery open upon the water, a tarace above that, and a supping roome open under that; a dynyng roome, a bedd chamber, a Cabanett, and a Roome for Musike, a garden; In this Grownd to make one waulk between trees; The galeries to cost Northwards; Nothing to be planted hear but of choyse. To sett in fitt places... An Iland where the fayre hornbeam standes with a stand in it and seats under Neath. An Iland with

a rock. An Iland with a Grott. An Iland Mounted wth flowres in ascents. An Iland paved and with picture. Every of the Ilands to have a fayre Image to keepe it, Tryten or Nymph etc. An Iland wth an arbor of Musk roses sett all wth double violetts for sent in Autumn, some gilovers wch like wise dispers sent. A fayre bridg to ye Middle great Iland onely, ye rest by bote. (Spedding *et al.* 1861–74, 76–77)

Both Henderson and Strong attempted reconstructions of this garden on the basis of Bacon's wish list. The actuality was to be rather different and we are fortunate in having John Aubrey's account of a visit in 1656, by which time the Pondyards were in decline.

> The figures of the Ponds were thus: they were pitched at the bottomes with pebbles of several colours, which were work't into several fligures, as of Fishes, etc.., which in his Lordship's time were plainly to be seen through the cleare water, now over-grown with flagges and rushes. If a poore bodie had brought his Lordship half a dozen pebbles of a curious colour, he would give them a shilling, so curious was he in perfecting his Fishponds which I guesse doe containe four acres. In the middle of the middlemost pond in the Island is a curious banquetting-house of Roman architecture paved with black and white marble covered with Cornish slate, and neatly wainscotted. (Bennett 2015, 215)

An accompanying sketch, while demonstrating something of the overall geometry of the site, appears to show, given the conventions of Aubrey's drawing, the banqueting house rising directly from the central pool surrounded by four L-shaped pools. An estate map of 1634 (Hertfordshire Record Office, D/EV P1) portrays the same configuration of surrounding ponds, with an oblong structure standing within a central, square island. Recent mapping and a site visit by this author in 2017 showed that the access from the north and south no longer exists, the causeways having been dug away or, possibly, bridges having been removed (Fig. 16). What makes the Pondyards particularly fascinating is that we have Bacon's own principles regarding the design of gardens set out in his famous essay *Of Gardens*, with its often-quoted opening lines:

> God Almighty first planted a garden. And indeed it is the purest of human pleasures. It is the greatest refreshment to the spirits of man; without which, buildings and palaces are but gross handiworks; and a man shall ever see, that when ages grow to civility and elegancy, men come to build stately sooner than to garden finely; as if gardening were the greater perfection. (Spedding *et al.* 1861–74, vol. 12, 235)

Of Gardens was the forty-sixth essay in a collection published in 1625, entitled, *The Essayes or Counsels, civill and morall, of Francis Lo. Verulam, Viscount St. Alban,* and came immediately after a parallel essay *Of Buildings.* This account of a 'princely palace' deals with the optimum location and situation for the ideal residence and offers advice on such topics as keeping a central courtyard, 'not paved, for that striketh up a great heat in summer, and much cold in winter'. The link to the surrounding gardens is made primarily through a second, arcaded court. It seems likely that the two contemporary double courtyard properties Bacon had in mind were Thomas Howard's Audley End, Essex, and Lord Burghley's Theobalds.

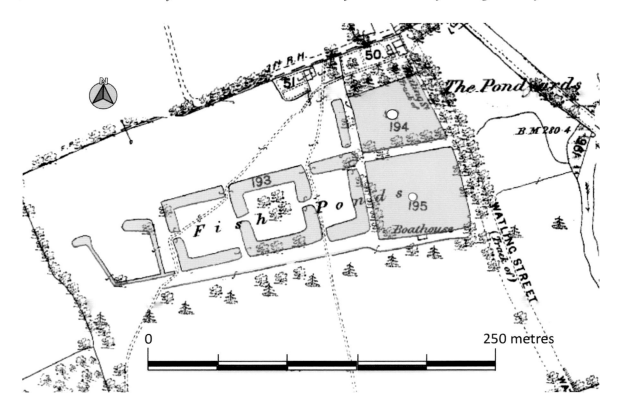

In his subsequent short essay, *Of Gardens*, after acknowledging divine precedence in their creation, Bacon moves on to practicalities, giving examples of planting to ensure what today we would call 'colour throughout the year'. Flowers are particularly praised as 'the breath of flowers is far sweeter in the air (where it comes and goes like the warbling of music) than in the hand', a reference to the practice of carrying nosegays to mask offensive odours. Bacon goes on to describe an ideal layout consisting of 'not under 30 acres of ground to be divided in three parts; a green in the entrance; a heath or desert in the going forth; and the main garden in the midst; besides alleys on both sides'. The attractiveness of a well-cut lawn is celebrated, as are shady alleys of 'carpenter's work'. Hedges and banks and mounts all have their place, but Bacon considers topiary to be 'for children'. His comments, including strictures on water in the garden, deserve quoting in full.

> For fountains, they are a great beauty and refreshment; but pools mar all, and make the garden unwholesome, and full of flies and frogs. Fountains I intend to be of two natures: the one that sprinkleth or spouteth water; the other a fair receipt of water, of some thirty or forty foot square, but without fish, or slime, or mud. For the first, the ornaments of images gilt, or of marble, which are in use, do well: but the main matter is so to convey the water, as it never stay, either in the bowls or in the cistern; that the water be never by rest discolored, green or red or the like; or gather any mossiness or putrefaction. Besides that, it is to be cleansed every day

by the hand. Also some steps up to it, and some fine pavement about it, doth well. As for the other kind of fountain, which we may call a bathing pool, it may admit much curiosity and beauty; wherewith we will not trouble ourselves: as, that the bottom be finely paved, and with images; the sides likewise; and withal embellished with colored glass, and such things of lustre; encompassed also with fine rails of low status. But the main point is the same which we mentioned in the former kind of fountain; which is, that the water be in perpetual motion, fed by a water higher than the pool, and delivered into it by fair spouts, and then discharged away under ground, by some equality of bores, that it stay little. And for fine devices, of arching water without spilling, and making it rise in several forms (of feathers, drinking glasses, canopies, and the like), they be pretty things to look on, but nothing to health and sweetness. (Spedding *et al.* 1861–74, vol. 12, 241)

The third component of the garden is that it should enjoy a 'natural wildness', although with some planting for scent and fruit. In addition, fruit trees should be cultivated against walls and within the alleys. After dismissing aviaries, he closes with an admonition to princes.

So I have made a platform [plan] of a princely garden, partly by precept, partly by drawing, not a model, but some general lines of it; and in this I have spared for no cost. But it is nothing for great princes, that for the most part taking advice with workmen, with no less cost set their things together; and sometimes add statuas and such things for state and magnificence, but nothing to the true pleasure of a garden. (Spedding *et al.* 1861–74, vol. 12, 245)

The correlation between Bacon's essay and the memorandum of 1608 on works at Gorhambury is interesting, particularly as it concerns waterworks. Bacon clearly has an aversion to still waters, which discolour and provide breeding places for frogs and flies, presumably a reaction to his experiences at the Pondyards, which could never have had a particularly vigorous flow of water. The embellishments for the bottoms of water courses as noted at the Pondyards continue to meet with approval, but it seems that Bacon was unlikely to have enjoyed fountains 'that sprinkleth or spouteth' water at this location. What is less clear is the degree to which Bacon's essay affected garden design in general. Strong labels Bacon in this context as a 'theorist', which seems a little wide of the mark given his record in commissioning works in at least three garden settings. A related publication that appeared in 1624, a year before Bacon's essay, was Wotton's *The Elements of Architecture*. Sir Henry Wotton (1568–1639), Bacon's friend and distant kinsman, was ambassador to Venice in the opening years of the seventeenth century and used his time in Italy to travel, collect and develop an interest in architecture and gardens. In the admittedly rather short section on 'Ornaments within and without the fabrique', Wotton (1624, 109) gives an account of a visit to an unnamed Italian garden.

[…] into which the first Accesse was a high walke like a Tarrace, from whence might be taken a generall view of the whole Plott below; but rather in a delightfull confusion, then with any plaine distinction of the pieces. From this the Beholder descending many steps, was afterwards conveyed againe, by several mountings and valings, to various entertainments of his sent, and sight: which I shall not neede to describe (for that were poeticall) let me onely note this, that every one of these diversities, was as if hee had beene Magically transported into a new Garden. (Wotton 1624, 109)

This strongly experiential approach to a garden chimes well with Bacon's careful detailing of routes and walkways and the variety of experiences and vistas that should be provided. Elsewhere Wotton approves the contrast between the regular and the irregular, echoing Bacon's desire to exploit the opportunity to juxtapose the formal garden with the wilderness beyond. Bacon's essay was frequently reprinted and appeared in a variety of what Henderson (2008, 59) describes as 'handsome, miniature editions, perfect for gift giving'. Despite this it is hard to discern what his influence may have been on the generations of gardeners that followed him, and the question whether one can meaningfully talk about a 'Baconian garden' remains debatable. Michael Raiger (2013, 652), in considering 'Miltonic' and 'Baconian' gardens, argues that the characteristic of a Baconian garden lies in the expression of 'mechanical power over nature'. In a more interventionist mood, Cesare Pastorino (2020, 447) emphasises the suitability of a Baconian garden for 'fructiferous experiments'. At a basic level, a Baconian garden could be identified either as one exhibiting close physical adherence to his prescriptive description of how to lay out a garden in his essay or, at a perhaps more elevated level, one in which scientific principles of organisation are made manifest and opportunities for scientific endeavour promoted. Not surprisingly, one of the key expressions of Bacon's developed view of gardens, which managed to accomplish both, was at the Enstone property of his former servant, Thomas Bushell.

A much weightier undertaking than *Of Gardens* was Bacon's Utopian vision, *The New Atlantis,* published posthumously in 1627, in 'the style of the early modern travel narrative' (Bruce 1998, x). The work is part of an extended tradition of early modern writings stretching from Thomas More's *Utopia,* from 1516, to Henry Neville's *The Isle of Pines,* from 1668. It is intriguing that *The New Atlantis*, Bacon's only work of fiction, was appended to his *Sylva Sylvarum, or a Natural History*, a curious work that was probably never meant for publication. The narrative of *The New Atlantis* begins with a voyage across the Southern Ocean and a chance encounter with the population of an unknown island called Bensalem. Access to the island was allowed once the crew had established their Christian credentials. Accommodated in the 'Strangers' House' with commendable hospitality, courtesy of the state, the travellers are allowed to enjoy an extended stay of six weeks. They meet local dignitaries, experience local customs, including a great 'feast of the family', and are introduced to the wonders of the 'House of Salomon'. Given the note in Rawley's dedicatory epistle that 'This fable my Lord devised, to the end that he might exhibit therein a model or description of a college instituted for the interpreting of Nature and the producing of great and marvellous works for the benefit of man, under the name of Salomon's House', it is not surprising that the remaining third of the book is given over to an account of this institution. The richly clad 'Father of Salomon's House' grants an audience to the narrator.

> God bless thee, my son; I will give thee the greatest jewel I have. For I will impart unto thee, for the love of God and men, a relation of the true state of Salomon's House. Son, to make you know the true state of Salomon's House, I will keep this order. First, I will set forth unto you the end of our foundation. Secondly, the preparations and instruments we have for our works. Thirdly, the several employments and functions whereto our fellows are assigned. And fourthly, the ordinances and rites which we observe. (Bruce 2008, 177)

The description of the house begins with caves that are used for a range of 'coagulations, indurations, refrigerations, and conservations' as well as accommodation for hermits. There are also great towers, 'for the view', as well as lakes and pools and 'streams and cataracts, which serve us for many motions, and likewise engines for multiplying and enforcing of winds, to set also on going diverse motions'. Artificial wells and fountains are constructed 'in imitation of the natural sources' and are used for preparing infusions. Also present are 'great and spacious houses where we imitate and demonstrate meteors; as snow, hail, rain, some artificial rains of bodies and not of water, thunders, lightnings; also generations of bodies in air; as frogs, flies, and divers others'. Bathing is clearly desirable, as 'We have also fair and large baths, of several mixtures, for the cure of diseases, and the restoring of mans body from arefaction: and others for the confirming of it in strength of sinewes, vital parts, and the very juice and substance of the body'. In addition there are the elements that one would expect to find in a park or garden but that are elevated to a higher purpose. In a prescient account of genetic modification, Bacon wrote, 'we make them also by art greater much than their nature, and their fruit greater and sweeter and of differing taste, smell, colour and figure, from their nature'. Elsewhere are kitchens, dispensaries and workshops. Resembling something more obviously recognisable as a laboratory facility are the 'perspective-houses', where optical principles are demonstrated and where artificial rainbows can be created. Associated with the perspective-houses are collections of 'precious stones of all kinds, […] crystals likewise, glasses of divers kinds, […] Also a number of fossils'. Further facilities include 'sound-houses, perfume-houses' and 'engine-houses', 'where are prepared engines and instruments for all sorts of motions'. The 'houses of deceits of the senses' are an intriguing part of the campus that feature a range of diversions, including 'all manner of feats of juggling, false apparitions, impostures and illusions; and their fallacies'. After this lengthy peregrination, the piece closes with a brief section on personnel, including, 'mystery-men, 'pioneers', 'compilers', 'dowry-men' and 'inoculators', all of whom are charged with various stages in the process of experimental investigation. Shortly afterwards the tale comes to a rather abrupt halt, with the line 'The rest was not perfected'.

Within the story, the narrator does not actually witness the wonders of Salomon's House for himself but is treated to an extended lecture, which he may or may not have regarded as fanciful. Indeed as an observer, the narrator is distinctly non-Baconian. As Bronwen Price (2002, 13) observes, 'He neither analyses nor interrogates the information he is given but bases his knowledge largely on the words of others rather than on a rigorous investigation of practical experience'. The work, certainly in the eyes of many modern commentators, is subject to interpretation from a variety of theoretical stand points, but Suzanne Smith's (2008, 102) summation that 'Bacon represents the scientist as something tantamount to a saviour of mankind and science as institutionalised benevolence' demonstrates the potentially inspirational component of his message.

Plot's reading of the text led him to identify the house at Hanwell with *The New Atlantis*. In doing so, he was not the first to make comparisons. Walter Charleton (1619–1707), former physician to Charles I, wrote in 1657 of the London College of Physicians, founded in 1518, that it was 'Solomon's House in reality' (quoted in Webster 1975, 315). Susan Bruce suggests that the work was influential in the 1640s on the thinking of Samuel Hartlib (c. 1600–62), 'the great intelligencer of Europe', and Mark Greengrass (*ODNB*) notes that he favoured 'the establishment of a model college of learning, a "Solomon's House" as envisaged in Bacon's *New Atlantis*. Hartlib saw Chelsea College, whose reform was a matter of current debate before the Long Parliament, as a possible institution.' When the Czech educationalist John Comenius (1592–1670) visited England in 1641 'nothing seemed more certain than that the plan of the great Verulam respecting the opening somewhere of a universal college, wholly devoted to the advancement of the sciences could be carried out' (quoted in MacGregor 1987, 207). That certainty was misplaced, as the Civil War broke out a few months later. Bacon's work undoubtedly was enormously important to the thinking behind the later development of the Royal Society and its founding in 1662, to say nothing of the success of Gresham College, whose origins go back even further, to 1597 (Johnson 1940). However, one of the individuals who at various times and in various ways did seek to recreate aspects of Bacon's vision was, as we shall see, his former servant Thomas Bushell.

Continental Engineers and Their Influence

While Bacon's ideas about gardens were not overly concerned with technological wizardry, those of others, including Bushell, most decidedly were. The impressive and technically accomplished gardens of Italy were, perhaps to a rather more limited extent than generally recognised, to have an impact on elements of garden design for the period. In considering the ways in which local ingenuity was enhanced by imported ideas and expertise, it is useful to determine how this may have happened. A major factor in the development of gardens later in the seventeenth century, and particularly into the eighteenth century, was 'the grand tour'. As Edward Chancy and Timothy Wilks remarked of continental travel early in the seventeenth century, every Jacobean tour at some point in its conception was charged by an impulse to travel engendered by England's long period of isolation from Catholic Europe. While late-Elizabethan England had drawn heavily upon its native inventiveness in the arts it had largely escaped the new stimulus being provided [by events in Europe]. (Chancy and Wilks 2014, 1)

This had limited the amount of personal contact with early continental developments. Elizabeth Hyde (2013, 9) makes the point that 'The Renaissance garden was, like so many other aspects of Renaissance culture, shaped by the appearance of the printed book.' In the context of water gardens, without a doubt the most important works were those published by the De Caus family, early in the seventeenth century. Other volumes, from the sixteenth century, were in circulation. *A Brief Treatyse of Gardening,* of around 1560, by Thomas Hill (c. 1528–74), was the first printed book in English on the subject. It was followed by *The Profitable Arte of Gardening,* published in 1563, and *The Gardener's Labyrinth*, dedicated in 1577 to William Cecil, and all three books were hugely successful in terms of sales. Apart from the well-known illustration of a gardener using a useful piece of technology, a pump to water the beds, Hill has little to say on the subject of water as a predominantly decorative element in the garden, presumably because his publication was aimed at gentry of the middling sort. In 1568 Hans Vredeman de Vries (1527–c.1607) published in Antwerp his *Artis Perspectivae* which contained a number of illustrated examples of fountain design, a volume that the earl of Leicester was familiar with and that may have inspired the design for his fountain at Kenilworth. Another notable source of illustrative material was Jacques Androuet du Cerceau's (1510–84) book *Les Plus Excellents Bastiments de France,* printed in 1576, which featured, amongst other sites, the gardens at Blois, Fontainebleau and Gaillon mentioned above. The ceramicist and engineer Bernard Palissy's important work *Discours admirables, de la nature des eaux et fonteines,* published in Paris in 1580, exists as a manuscript translation by one Thomas Watson for Henry Percy, the 9th earl of Northumberland, but there was no English edition (Lees-Jefferies 2010, 1). It is possible, however, that some personal contacts may have resulted in the import of some of Palissy's ideas and materials for work in the 1570s on the gardens at Beddington. Illustrative material regarding the great Italian gardens does not seem to have become available until the following century. Detailed specifications for advanced water engineering in gardens by the engineer Salomon de Caus (1576–1626) may have acted as a blueprint for the Enstone Marvels and Hanwell's House of Diversion. His magnum opus, *Les Raisons des forces mouvantes. Avec diverses machines tant utilles que plaisantes ausquelles sont adjoints plusieurs desseings de grotes et fontaines,* appeared in 1615. However, De Caus's impact on the engineering of water features in England seems to have mainly come about through his employment in this country.

Salomon De Caus was probably born and raised in Dieppe, the significance of Dieppe lying in its active and innovative programme of municipal waterworks. Writing about the brothers' formative years, Paige Johnson (2009, 176) remarks that 'through the years marking the early lives of the de Caus brothers and beyond, the waterworks remained a significant source of civic pride for Dieppe and its citizens and required the regular attention of workmen and engineers. This elevation of the hydraulic arts cannot have failed to enter into the consciousness of town residents among them the young Salomon and Isaac de Caus.' Luke Morgan (2017) established that Isaac was Salomon's younger brother, one who subsequently took over the family business. Little is known of Salomon's early career, although we know that he spent time in Italy prior to 1598, where 'passing Pratolino five miles from Florence, among other grotto works with which the said house is richly ornamented, I saw a figure of a great Cyclops, in the body of which are some grottoes very artificially made' (De Caus 1615, book 2, problem 14). Designs published later in *Forces Mouvantes* suggest at least an acquaintance with the works at the Villa d'Este, Tribolo's Fountain of the Labyrinth at the Villa Medici at Petraia and possibly the *Sacro Bosco* at Bomarzo. By the turn of the century, Salomon was plying his trade at the Coudenberg Palace in Brussels, where he worked on fountains and grottoes until his departure, in 1610. This was the longest settled period in his entire career. The precise point at which he arrived in London as tutor to Henry, Prince of Wales (1594–1612), and advisor for the prince's ambitious plans to redevelop the gardens at Richmond Palace is unknown. However, he was responsible for work at Richmond in 1611 that included the installation of a large cistern, and the following year he was commissioned to design three fountains for Robert Cecil at Hatfield House, only one of which was completed. Here he could have made the acquaintance of either Sir Francis Bacon or Sir Walter Cope, but there is no evidence of his influence at two important gardens: Gorhambury and Kensington. He was also employed by Prince Henry's mother, Queen Anne of Denmark, for projects at Greenwich, where he may have been responsible for a fountain and a small grotto, and at Somerset House, where he created a mount described by a German visitor in these terms:

> On the side facing the palace it is made like a cavern. Inside it sit the Muses, and have all sorts of instruments in their hands. Uppermost at the top stands Pegasus, a golden horse with wings. On the mountain are four small arches, in each rests a naked statue of marble. They have cornucopia in their hands and under their arms jugs from which water flows into the basin about four good paces wide, and is all around the mountain. They are supposed to represent four rivers. Among others there stands above such a female figure in black marble in gold letters Tamesis. It is the river on which London lies and flows next to this garden. The water was let play. Above at the very top of the crag it sprang up as thick as an arm, and to and fro out of the mountain as well. It is thus a very beautiful work and far surpasses the Mount Parnassus in the Pratolino near Florence. (quoted in Strong 1998, 96)

There was also a fountain representing 'a female figure [which] gives water out of a cornucopia [and] was gilded all over'.

After the death of his patron, Prince Henry, Salomon remained in London until late in 1613, when he left to take service with Frederick V, the Elector Palatine, who had married Henry's sister, the Princess Elizabeth. By 1614 he had established himself in Heidelberg, where he began work on his masterpiece, the *Hortus Palatinus*, attached to Heidelberg Castle (Plate 11). This featured extensive waterworks, and although construction was brought to a halt in 1619 by the outbreak of the Thirty Years' War, there are several significant surviving elements. Following his return to Paris, in 1619, he focused on his writings and brought out an account of the gardens at Heidelberg, as well as works on perspective, time keeping, sanitation and cartography, before his death, in 1626. If we consider the state of English gardens at the end of the first quarter of the seventeenth century from an archaeological perspective, it is clear that while architecture was well set on a course towards closer conformity with continental classicism, the gardens themselves were still in the local traditions of earth and water works. Although Salomon de Caus had brought ideas and expertise relating to fountains and grottoes, they were largely the province of the elite and were no doubt bracketed together as wonders and marvels rather than everyday components of a working estate, all of which invites the question what such features are doing in the gardens of the impecunious Thomas Bushell of Enstone and the virtuoso Sir Anthony Cope of Hanwell.

Thomas Bushell and the Enstone Marvels

In Plot's *Natural History,* his account of Hanwell's House of Diversion is immediately followed by a careful description, with accompanying plates, of 'the waterworks that surpass all others of the county', at Enstone (Plot 1705, 241). This piece about the 'Enstone Marvels' is the most detailed surviving account of water engineering in a seventeenth-century English garden and has been much discussed in books on garden history. The moving spirit behind these works was the engineer, mystic, confidence trickster and protégé of Sir Francis Bacon, Thomas Bushell Esquire. Sources for Bushell's life include his own 1628 account of his early years, *The First part of Youths Errors: Written by Thomas Bushell the Superlative Prodigall.* This is a slender volume that is 'crammed with lamentation and self-accusation, but thin in factual corroboration' (Thacker 1982, 28). Bushell attracted the attention of John Aubrey, not always the most dispassionate of observers, who said that he was 'the greatest master of the art of running into debt (perhaps) in the world' and that 'his tongue was a chain and drew in so many to be bound for him and to be engaged in his designs that he ruined a number' (Fig. 17). A detailed modern biography, *The Superlative Prodigall: A Life of Thomas Bushel,* was published in Bristol in 1932, by John Gough. Bushell was born sometime before 1600 to a family of minor gentry from Cleeve Prior, near Evesham. He had a chequered childhood, with little education and a certain amount of wayward behaviour, before, around the age of fifteen, he entered the service of Sir Francis Bacon. There is no direct evidence of the nature of his relationship with Bacon, but Bacon seems to have taken the young man under his wing and attempted to remedy the evident defects in his education to the point where they could share an interest in, and enthusiasm for, a variety of technological innovations, several of them associated with

FIGURE 17. Thomas
Bushell, from his 1628
autobiography, *The First
Part of Youths Errors.*

mining. Bushell's movements in Bacon's latter years and immediately after this
death are difficult to discern. He may at some point have gone into self-imposed
exile on the Isle of Wight or the Calf of Man and lived on wild herbs. He was
apparently charged by his late master to institute what looks very much like
his own 'House of Solomon'.

> Among the MSS. in the British Museum [Cart. Antiq. Ill D, 14] is a paper entitled,
> *Instructions from the Lord Chancellor Bacon to his servant Thomas Bushell.* It relates
> to a project he had in view of establishing a corporation for exploring deserted
> mineral works. On the supposition that such a project would meet with due
> encouragement, he says, 'Let Twitnam Park, which I sold in my younger days, be
> purchased, if possible, for a residence for such deserving persons to study in, since
> I experimentally found the situation of that place much convenient for the trial of
> my philosophical conclusions, expressed in a paper sealed to the trust which I myself
> had put in practice, and settled the same by act of parliament, if the vicissitudes of
> fortune had not intervened and prevented me'. (Lysons 1796, 127)

This clearly came to nothing, for in 1626 Bushell married an heiress and took on
the management of a small estate at Enstone, in Oxfordshire. Here he, or rather
one of his servants, discovered a remarkable natural phenomenon, bubbling
from under a large rock, a petrifying well known as Goldwell. He used this as
a basis upon which to build his extraordinary banqueting house with grotto

below (Figures 29 and 42). As with everything relating to Bushell, the exact circumstances of this are hard to reconstruct. The conventional view was that works were undertaken to prepare for, or indeed even attract, a visit from King Charles I. Edward McGee (2003, 39) argued that 'Bushell's rock provided him with a splendid opportunity not only to ingratiate himself with the king and queen, but also to promote political and economic interests of moment'. However, the truth may be more labyrinthine, as Gough's researches revealed that

> The king indeed had given him very unusual support in his work at the rock itself. Bushell must have already had access to the king, very likely through his former position in Bacon's household and his other connections with prominent men in London, for it appears that the king had 'come over from Woodstock to see the rarity of nature at Enstone' shortly after it was first unearthed (this must have been around 1628) and had heartily fallen in with Bushell's design that the rock should not only be preserved but also be 'ornamented with groves, walks, fishponds, gardens and waterworks and to that end he has taken said work into his protection.' In order to make way for the groves and walks, instructions were sent to the earl of Danby: for better enabling Bushell's endeavours ... 'To call on such as it may concern for disposing the highway to some other place which may be most convenient to his Majesty's design, trusting he will find no man so refractory as he should have cause to certify his obstinacy to the King.' Nevertheless, there were persons who did object to the proposed diversion of the highway and we read that some of the copyholders of the manor: out of a malignant disposition the next court day fined Bushell for having turned the said highway, some have cut down trees for beautifying the said rock and others have presumed to forbid his workmen employed in setting up the wall for preserving the groves and walks not at all regarding his Majesty's directions. (Gough 1932, 67)

As well as being an early instance of 'not in my backyard', this suggests much greater levels of engagement with the project by the king. The end result became justly famed, although there were plenty of detractors. Lieutenant Hammond, who visited in 1635, remarked that 'a gentleman should be so strangely conceited and humoured as to disburse and lay out so much money as he has done in planting, framing, contriving and building upon another man's freehold', it was all 'a mad gim-cracke sure'. The poet Robert Southey, visiting more than a century later, was equally dismissive. 'I learnt that the great amusement consists in getting women there and streaming up water from the ground. The maker must have been some fool who had more money than wit and more wit than charity for half the expense would have fed the hungry and clothed the naked' (Southey 1793). Despite querying Bushell's sanity, Hammond recorded further details of his visit:

> On the side of a hill is a Rocke of some 11 or 12 Foote high, from the bottom whereof (by turning of a Cocke) riseth and spouts vp about 9 foote high, a Streame which riseth vp on her top a Siluer Ball, and as the sand Streame riseth or falleth to any pitch or distance, so doth the Ball, with playing, tossing and keeping continually at the top of sayd ascending stream [...] a wall of jets like a plash'd Fence, whereby sometimes faire ladies cannot fence the crossing, flashing and dashing their smooth, soft and tender thighs and knees, by a sudden inclosing them in it.

[…] There were many strange forces of Beasts, Fishes and Fowles do appeare; and with the pretty murmuring of the Springs, the gentle running, falling and playing of the waters; the beating of a Drum; the chirping of a Nightingale, and many strange rare and audible sounds and noises doth highly worke upon any Mans Fancy. […] In the chamber is a natural Rocke, like into the head of a Beare; on the top thereof, the water rises and spouts forth, falling in the Rocke […] from about the middle of this Chamber, they make a Canopy of Raine, which […] a man […] may stand dry, which with the reflection of the Sunn at high No-one, makes appeare to our fancies Rainbows and flashing like Lightening. (Hammond 1635, 82)

Plot, visiting after the restoration by Edward Henry Lee, earl of Lichfield, in 1674, saw and heard many of the same effects. His description of the water works in the grotto is worth quoting in full, both for its very specific details and for the insights it may offer into the operation of Hanwell's House of Diversion (Plot 1705, 242). It should be read together with a close examination of Plot's illustration (Fig. 18).

Being now come down into the *Grot* by the Passage 18, *Tab.* 11 and landing at the Bottom of the *Stairs, Tab. 12. a.* on a large *half pace* before it. The *Rock* presents itself made up of large craggy *Stones* with great *Cavities* between them, *ccc & c* out of which flows *Water* perpetually Night and Day, dashing against the *Rocks* below, and that in great plenty in the driest Seasons, though fed only with a single *Spring* rising in a piece of ground call'd *Ramsall*, between *Enston* and *Ludston.* The natural *Rock* is about 10 Foot high, and so many in Bredth; some few *Shelves* of Lead *dd*, and the Top-stones only having been added (easily to be distinguish'd bob their *Dryness*) which have advanced it in all about 14 Foot high.

54. In the *half pace* just before the *Compartment eee*, upon turning one of the *Cocks* at *f* rises a *chequer Hedge* of *Water*, as they call it, *gggg*; and upon turning *another*, the two side *Columns* of *Water hh*, which rise not above the height of the natural *Rock*; and of a *third*, the middle *Column i* which ascending into the *turn* of the *Arch*, and returning not again, is received into hidden *Pipes* provided for that purpose: into *one* whereof, terminated in a very small *Cistern* of *Water* behind a *Stone* of the *Rock*, and having a *Mouth* and *Languet* just above its Surface, the *Air* being forced into it by the Approaches of the *Water*, a Noise is made near resembling the *Notes* of a *Nightingale*: But when that *Pipe* is filled there is then no more singing, till the *Water* has past away by another *Pipe* in the lower part of the *Rock*, which when almost done, there is heard a *Noise* somewhat like the Sound of a *Drum*, performed by the rushing in of *Air* into the hollow of the *Pipe*, which is large, and of *Copper*, to supply the place of the *Water* now almost gone out; which done, the *Nightingale* may be made to sing again.

55. From the turned *Roof* of the *Rock*, by help of the brass *Instrument k*, and turn off a Cock in one of the *Closets* above, they can let down a *Canopy* of *Water ll*; from the Top also they can throw *arched Spouts* of *Water* crossing one another, and dashing against the *Walls*, opposite to those of their rise, as at *m n* and *o p*; and *others* that rise out, and enter in again to the *Roof* at some Distance, never falling down at all at *q r* and *s t*. Which Falls of *Water* may be also delicately seen, turning the back upon them as well as looking forward, by help of a Looking-glass placed in the Wall opposite to them, which could not possibly be represented in the *Cut*. And some of these *Waters* (I must not say which) being often used by way of *Sport* to wet the

FIGURE 18.
Enstone, Thomas
Bushell's Grotto,
from *Plot's
Natural History*,
Tab. 12.

> *Visitants* of the *Grot*, that they might not avoid it by running up the *Stairs*, and so out into the *Grove*, by turning a Cock in another of the *Closets*, they can let fall water so plentifully in the *Door u u*, that most *People* rather cause to stay where they are, than pass through it: which is all concerning the inner *Prospect* of the *Rock*; what remains being only a Representation of the *Arch* of Stone *w w* built over it, with two *Niches x y* one of each side, and the *Grate z* at the Top, through which they look down out of the *Banqueting-room* into the *Grot*. Of which no more, but that behind the Rock there is a *Cellar* for keeping *Liquors* cool, or placing *Musick* to surprise the *Auditors*; and behind that the *Receivers* of Water to supply the *Pipes &c*. (Plot 1705, 242-244)

The attached pool and island would have been brand new at the time of Plot's visit. However, there was one other significant feature. In front of the grotto was '*A* Cistern *of Stone with five Spouts of* Water *issuing out of a Ball of Brass, in which a small* Spaniel *hunts a* Duck*, both diving after one another, and having their Motion from the Waters*' (Ibid., 232). This cistern was also noted by Aubrey after a visit in 1643, when he wrote, 'I made a drawing of the little pond opposite the grotto: there stood Neptune on a scallop shell, with his trident in his hand, aiming at a duck that swam perpetually round chased by a spaniel. The statue is of wood and about three quarters of a yard high. It looks very pretty.' Astonishingly, this element alone of the Enstone Marvels remains and was rediscovered, documented and published by the author in 2017.

The banqueting house above the grotto was initially tricked out as a habitation for a hermit, a pursuit close to Bushell's heart, with such appurtenances as an Egyptian mummy, a stuffed crocodile and a hammock all enveloped in black drapes. Bushell's main family residence must have been elsewhere yet connected to the Marvels by a series of 'groves and walks'. The likely site of his house lies some 500 m to the north-north-east, where the well-preserved earthwork remains of a formal garden of the period survived until quite recently. Constructed as a series of terraces and walkways symmetrically arranged to flank a set of formal gardens, laid out with a pattern of overlapping lozenges, all overlooking a body of water and with a wilderness beyond, the location can be tied in quite closely with Bacon's visions of the ideal garden (Plate 12). The Enstone Marvels are probably best known because of the royal visit made in 1636 by King Charles and his Queen, Henrietta Maria. While probably a little more elaborate than the festivities laid on at Hanwell for James I and later for Charles I, it certainly gives a flavour for how such an event would have been managed. Plot gives an account 30 years after the event:

> Whereupon he made *Cisterns*, and laid divers *Pipes* between the *Rocks*, and built a House over them, containing one fair *Room* for *Banqueting*, and several other small *Closets* for divers Uses, beside the *Rooms* above, which when finish't in the Year 1636, together with the *Rock, Grove, Walks*, and all other the Appurtenances, were all on the 23rd. of *Augus*t, by the said *Tho. Bushell* Esq; presented to the then *Queen's* excellent *Majesty*, who in company with the *King* himself, was graciously pleased to honour the *Rock*, not only with her *Royal* Presence, but commanded the same to be called after her own *Princely* Name, HENRIETTA: At which time as they were

entering it, there arose a *Hermite* out of the ground, and entertain'd them with a *Speech*; returning again in the close down to his peaceful *Urn*. Then was the *Rock* presented in a *Song* answer'd by an *Echo*, and after that a *Banquet* presented also in a *Sonnet*, within the Pillar of the Table; with some other songs, all set by *Simon Ive*. (Plot 1705, 241)

The whole event was set up, according to some commentators, to gain the king's support for Bushell's acquisition of mining rights for silver in Wales. In fact, he went so far as to serve the banquet on silver plates made from metal he claimed to have quarried and extracted himself. As it happened, Bushell had plenty of opportunities to mine for the king, as he went on to mint coins in Aberystwyth, from 1637 to 1642, before moving to Shrewsbury and then Oxford, in 1643 (*ODNB*). After the war, Bushell was left with a huge amount of debt, from which his fortunes never recovered. In some sense he still saw himself as the inheritor of Bacon's wishes, as in the 1650s he revisited the idea of creating "'a foundation or building, which is designed for the execution of my Lord Verulam's New Atlantis" in Lambeth Marsh and later to build, "Solomon's House in all its dimensions" in the city of Wells'. None of this materialised. While as a character Bushell remains elusive, with the Enstone Marvels he produced what Mowl (2007, 36) describes as 'a triumph of applied hydraulic engineering', ascribing the technical expertise to his readings of Salomon de Caus's *Les Raisons des Forces Mouvantes*. We shall consider developments at Enstone post–Civil War and their connections with Hanwell below.

Other Early Seventeenth-Century Water Gardens

After James I took a liking to the Cecil's property at Theobalds, an exchange was arranged such that Robert Cecil was granted the slightly decrepit Tudor Palace at Hatfield, in 1607. As Lawrence Stone (1955, 102) puts it, 'James I's increasing predilection for Theobalds as a hunting lodge made it prudent and, it was hoped, profitable, to offer the house and parks to the Crown'. Work on a new house at Hatfield began immediately, under the close personal supervision of Cecil, but with a variety of contractors employed, including in the latter stages the designer and architect Inigo Jones. Similarly, a host of gardeners and engineers were recruited to work on the gardens. In 1611 a Thomas Chaundler, together with a Dutch engineer, Simon Sturtevant, managed operations in Hatfield's East Garden, where a rock-based fountain of Neptune, with issuing stream, had been installed. It can be surmised that there were technical problems with these water works as, late in the same year, Salomon de Caus was brought in to work on the fountain and associated cisterns. Stone sums up the work in these terms:

All this was altered during the winter of 1611–12 in accordance with the new plans of de Caus, who designed a grand new central fountain. In the huge marble basin, made by the Dutch tomb-carver, Garrett Johnson, was a great artificial rock on an iron-work core. On this stood a metal statue, cast by another Dutch tomb-carver, Garret Christmas, and painted to resemble copper by Rowland Bucket. From this elaborate centre-piece ran a shallow meandering little river, in imitation of one at the Earl of Exeter's (presumably at Burghley House). This item also gave a good deal of trouble, and was altered several times. The bottom of the winding stream was paved with coloured pebbles and sea-shells. Winkles and stones were collected in England, and Tradescant shipped back from Paris one chest and eight boxes of shells. In addition, little leaden leaves, snakes and fishes were scattered about the face of the rock and the bottom of the stream. (Ibid., 127)

Earlier the same year came the first reference to a water feature known as 'The Dell'. Work here was supervised by Mountain Jennings, Cecil's gardener from Theobalds, and it is likely that Jennings was responsible for the well-known drawing of the site (*TNA, Cecil Papers, S. P.* 14/6). This shows, in slightly diagrammatic form, a stream running, corner to corner, through the centre of a square, moated enclosure at the middle of which is an arcaded pavilion with a tower at one end overlooking a balcony (Fig. 19). This structure is flanked by what appear to be hippocampus, or seahorses, that may represent fountains. Upstream is shown a water wheel at the base of a tower that must have held a header tank into which water could be pumped for the fountains. The remaining two corners are marked by what may be another pavilion and a grotto. The effect on the ground was captured by a French visitor, Samuel de Sorbière, in 1663, who remarked on

a small River which as it were forms the Compartments of a large *Parterre*, and rises and secretly looses itself in an hundred places, and whose Banks are all Lined or Boarded [...] We Dined in a Hall that looked into a Greenplot with Two Fountains

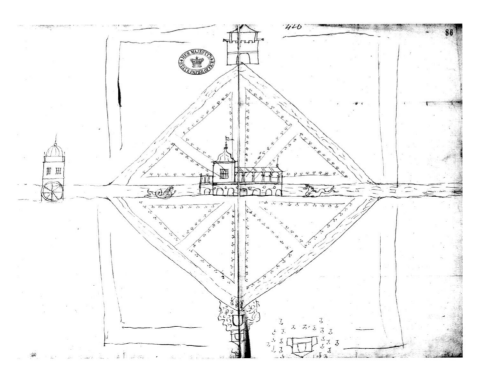

FIGURE 19. Sketch of works at the Dell, Hatfield House. © TNA Cecil papers.

in it, and having Espaliers on the sides, but a bilister before it, upon which are Flower-Pots and Statues; From this Paterre there is a way down by Two Pair of Stairs of about Twelve or Fifteen Steps to another, and from the Second to the Third: From this Terass you have a Prospect of the great Water Parterre […] You have also in those places where the River enters into and comes out of the Parterre, open Sorts of Boxes with Seats round where you may see a vast Number of Fish pass too and fro in the Water. (De Sorbière 1709, 64)

Strong (1998, 107) was of the opinion that 'Hatfield, with its walled, terraced gardens falling away from the house, was new in 1612 and destined to have probably a very considerable influence on the development of a particular garden type which was to run on into the post-Restoration period'. However, the gardens that Baptist Hicks had laid out at Chipping Campden were an equal to those at Hatfield and certainly a close contemporary.

One of six sons born to a London mercer, Baptist Hicks (1551–1629) continued in the trade and made his fortune, being knighted in 1603. His brother Michael was secretary to William Cecil, Lord Burghley, and from 1610 onwards, Hicks built himself a grand house in Kensington, next door to Cope Castle. Having purchased the manor of Chipping Campden around 1609, he began a massive programme of building there, too (*ODNB*). Following the burning of the house in 1645, the gardens reverted to pasture, and they exist today as one of the finest sets of garden earthworks in the country (Plate 13). The house stood on the edge of a large terrace with banqueting houses, which survive, to either side. It overlooked a large parterre flanked by raised banks. Below this area were a series of terraces, probably planted up as an orchard and running down the hill to a long, canal-like pool at the bottom, with a stream beyond. At the eastern end of the terracing was a small water parterre consisting of a square pool with internal banks dividing it up to create an inner pool, possibly originally lozenge-shaped. Farther to the east was a prospect mound. The strong symmetry of the site was lost at its south-east corner. Where a parterre should have been there was a much larger earthwork known as the 'The Great Sink'. This has the appearance of having originated as a medieval moated site. The garden may have remained unfinished at this point. Everson (1989, 113) stresses how 'Their careful siting allowed them to take advantage of and enhance the natural topography through a series of descending terraces while also exploiting the potential for water features.' This is a situation that was exploited in a similar way with the great east terrace at Hanwell. Excavations between 2014 and 2018 revealed traces of paths and a central fountain in the main parterre, as well as the vast scale of earth moving needed to create the terracing for the house and garden (Rigg 2018).

A number of other, smaller gentry gardens in the area were likely to have been influenced by the great works at Campden, notably Saltwood, Swinbrook and Church Enstone, all in Oxfordshire. Farther afield there were similar layouts at Harrington, where the house lies beyond the pool at the foot of the slope, and at Wakerley, both in Northamptonshire. Similarities are also seen at

Brooke Priory, Rutland, purchased for the sum of £845/10/- in 1535 by the 1st baronet, Sir Anthony Cope, and later the home of Baptist Hicks's in-laws (Walcott 1876, 342). The situation here was complicated, with the garden being laid over earlier monastic works. Such terraced gardens overlooking water courses could only work where the landform was appropriate. A good instance of a fully developed garden after this pattern is the now-vanished Massey's Court, Llannerch, painted in 1662 (Plate 14). Particularly striking is the sheer amount of architectural detailing packed into the garden, and although there may be an element of wishful thinking embodied in the painting, it remains a pointed reminder of just how 'built up' gardens of the period could be.

A site that is certainly more building than garden is Bolsover Castle, in Derbyshire. The layout here is very much conditioned by the buildings of the pre-existing medieval castle that was used as a framework for the chivalric fantasia of William Cavendish, 1st duke of Newcastle (1593–1676), from around 1612 onwards. Although the garden is not well documented, there is some evidence of terracing on the slopes to the south of the castle, possibly the remains of a formal garden or vineyard. The most remarkable survival is the Venus Fountain in the centre of the Fountain Garden, defined by the rebuilt wall of the medieval inner bailey. Dating from the early 1630s, it is described in the Historic England in these terms: 'It has a deep octagonal well with a crenellated parapet and niches in the inner walls and a central pedestal with four cylindrical projections supports a life-size statue of Venus emerging from her bath'. Other embellishments included lion masks, busts of Roman emperors (a set of recently commissioned replacements now exist), and four replica *puer mingens*, or 'pissing boys', not an uncommon motif for the period. James Campbell and Amy Boyington (2019, 7) wrote of the figures, 'The *puer mingens* motif for this fountain appears to symbolise the lustful intentions and erotic desire of the satyrs towards Venus'. Lucy Worsley (2005, 83) picks up on the idea already embodied in our consideration of the development of water gardens in assessing what she calls its 'artisan mannerist style', in 'both its classical and native influences', and concludes, 'It becomes clear that he [William Cavendish] was a well-informed patron, making a deliberate choice to turn away from the art of the continent to produce a more personal, local version: a blend of classicism and sexual pleasure'. She also considers and dismisses the suggestion that the fountain doubled as a cold plunge bath. The most interesting aspect of the work is the measures undertaken to supply water to the fountain. This was gathered in a number of conduit houses, known locally as cundy houses, and piped, in one instance across a valley, over a distance of 220 m, to the cistern tower. Here a horse gin was used to pump the water into a tank at the top of the tower, from where it was piped a short distance to the fountain. In this context it is worth reviewing the supply of water to the fountain at Kenilworth, where, in a 1609 valuation, 'all ye pipes for carriage of ye water fro ye pundit head being 3 qrters of a mile distant' were recorded, a distance subsequently confirmed by field work (Demidowicz 2013, 184).

One of the most remarkable examples of a complex of pools constructed to geometric principles can be seen at Tackley, in Oxfordshire. In 1612 the manor of Tackley was sold to John Harborne (1582–1651) of the Middle Temple, who moved there shortly afterwards and began establishing his status as a country gentleman with the aid of his steward, Rowley Ward. He became the high sheriff of Oxfordshire in 1632. Work on a new manor house, since demolished, began around 1615, and terraced formal gardens were laid out to the west of the house. Just over 350 m to the east of the house, near a spring known as the Tackwell, Harborne constructed his water garden. Whittle and Taylor (1995, 40) make a convincing case for the works being undertaken between 1620 and 1623. They cite, amongst other evidence, the publication in 1623 of the third edition of *Cheape and good husbandry for well-ordering of all beasts, and fowls, and for the generall cure of their Diseases* by Harborne's friend Gervase Markham. The section on fishing and fishponds features a plan nearly identical to Harborne's Tackley complex except for the fact that his is obviously unfinished (Fig. 20). This was probably because of difficulties acquiring a portion of additional land. After Harborne's death, in 1652, further improvements to the property were precluded by the fact that both his sons were drunkards, a family tragedy that ensured a feature surviving that might have been swept away by more prosperous descendants. In terms of its function, there can be no doubt that the cultivation of fish as a food stuff was foremost in the mind, and angling was well known as a popular pastime. In that context it is interesting that Markham deals primarily with recipes to attract different types of fish, which can then be netted. However, the layout of such ponds is well known, and complex arrangements of pools for fish breeding can be seen at Lyddington, in Leicestershire, and Charwelton, in Northamptonshire, although in both places the existence of raised terraced walks suggests an ornamental function, too. A simple arrangement of six rectangular ponds in a descending sequence with accompanying terraces may be seen at Walcot, near Charlbury, Oxfordshire. Although undated, these are assumed to have been constructed by the Jenkinson family at some point in the seventeenth century. Such features are rarely illustrated, although an example at Esher Palace, Surrey, was depicted in 1707.

Plot appears to be unaware of the ponds at Tackley, although he is familiar with similar if less geometric works elsewhere in the county.

> Not impertinent hereunto is a Contrivance for *Fish-ponds*, that I met with at the Right Worshipful Sir *Philip Harcourt's* at *Stanton Harcourt*, where they *Stews* not only feed one another, as the *Ponds* of the Right Honourable the Earl of *Clarendon* at *Cornbury*, the Learned *James Tyrril's* Esq; at *Shotover Forrest*, and Mr. *Whorwood's* at *Holton,* &c. and many may be *sewed* by letting the Water of the upper Ponds out into the lower; but by a *side Ditch* cut along by them, and *Sluces* out of each, may be any of them emptied, without letting the *Water* into, or giving the least Disturbance to the rest: which being a Convenience that I never met with before, and perhaps unknown to many, I thought good to mention. (Plot 1705, 239)

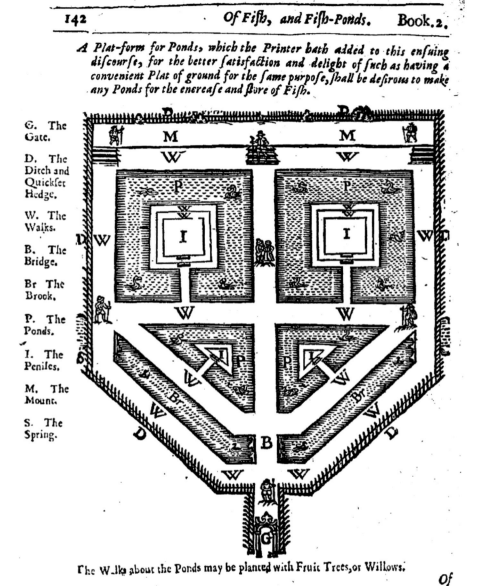

142   *Of Fish, and Fish-Ponds.*   Book. 2.

A Plat-form for Ponds, which the Printer hath added to this enfuing difcourfe, for the better fatisfaction and delight of fuch as having a convenient Plat of ground for the fame purpofe, fhall be defirous to make any Ponds for the encreafe and ftore of Fifh.

G. The Gate.

D. The Ditch and Quickfet Hedge.

W. The Walks.

B. The Bridge.

Br The Brook.

P. The Ponds.

I. The Peniles.

M. The Mount.

S. The Spring.

The W_lks about the Ponds may be planted with Fruit Trees, or Willows.

Of

FIGURE 20. *A Plat-form for Ponds*, Gervase Markham, 1623.

The form of the works at Tackley is altogether more complex and regular and, in its use of angular peninsulas, reflects aspects of Sir Walter Cope's water maze at Kensington. The extended use of triangles as a motif has been seen as possibly referring back to aspects of military engineering, as we see in the use of bastion-like features in later gardens. The possibility also exists that, as with Tresham at the Triangular Lodge, Rushden, in Northamptonshire, there was a religious dimension to the shaping. In the final analysis, Whittle and Taylor state that 'the layout of the Tackley water gardens has no exact parallel elsewhere'. Whatever the case, in Strong's opinion,

> By then such a feature was becoming old-fashioned, but John Harborne its creator was heir to a City fortune and legging his way up the social scale. Harborne was in fact upstaging the taste of his superiors from a decade before. The fact that the design for it was printed in the 1623 edition of Gervase Markham's *Cheape and Good Husbandry* catches the slippage down the social scale. (Strong 1998, 7)

The point is emphasised by Whittle and Taylor (1995, 57). 'The reason may be that few if any ornamental water gardens of this kind were made after the 1620s. After the Civil War ideas of baroque grandeur and axial planning filtered into Britain from France. Simpler layouts of canals and avenues replaced the earlier, fussier arrangement.' If Oxfordshire was lagging behind in matters of fashionable garden design, the future was being expressed in such gardens as Wilton, in Wiltshire, with its early phase of Palladianism seen in both house and garden in the early 1630s.

Although Salomon de Caus was involved early in the century in a few very prestigious projects, the fact that some of them were not brought to completion while others had a comparatively short life contributes to the notion that the more influential figure may have been his younger brother, Isaac de Caus (1590–1648). Dianne Duggan (2009, 152) notes that he was first recorded working in England in 1623, when he 'was being paid for, "making a Rocke in the vault under the banqueting house", the banqueting house in question being that designed by Inigo Jones in Whitehall.' In 1626 he may have designed a grotto for Henry, Lord Clifford, the future 5th earl of Cumberland, at Skipton Castle, in Yorkshire, before moving on to Bedford House, in Covent Garden, and Woburn Abbey, in Bedfordshire, both for Francis Russell, the 4th earl of Bedford. The grotto at Woburn is a remarkable survival and provides a useful reference point when considering other grottoes of the period known only from contemporary illustrations. Writing of it Strong (1998, 141) says, 'De Caus must have been greatly in demand but he did not begin on his most famous work at Wilton House, Wiltshire, until 1632. What was this astonishing man doing during the preceding decade?' He is of the opinion that De Caus may have had a hand in the design of Moor Park, Hertfordshire, where Lucy Harrington moved in 1617. Describing the now-vanished garden, levelled by Lancelot 'Capability' Brown, Strong (1998, 145) thought that it was 'the earliest, most spectacular evidence of Italian Renaissance gardening in England'. This is perhaps stretching a point, as essentially the gardens as described by Sir William Temple in the 1670s are similar to those at Holdenby from late in the sixteenth century and the broadly contemporary garden at Chipping Campden. Of course De Caus may have assisted Thomas Bushell with the engineering at Enstone, especially if the project was, in some sense, sponsored by Charles I. Unfortunately, there is no evidence for this.

Philip Herbert, 4th earl of Pembroke (1584–1650), courtier and advisor to both James I and, later, Charles I, inherited the property at Wilton in 1630.

John Bold (1988, 25) notes that 'According to Aubrey, Philip the 4th earl was following a suggestion of Charles when he embarked upon the alteration and enlargement of Wilton House and the laying out of the gardens in the 1630s, the works being carried out under the direction of Isaac de Caus with the detailed advice of Inigo Jones'. An earlier garden from the 1560s onwards included a pond garden to the west of the house, where a contemporary survey recorded that 'there are five pools newly made in the past year at the walks around the aforesaid' (Whitaker 2014, 146). These pools survived into the eighteenth century. The year 1632 saw the start of work on the new garden, with expenditure reaching a peak two years later. The initial design, proposed by De Caus and done 'in the Italian manner' according to Aubrey's account, was for a large strictly symmetrical garden placed against a vastly extended south front of the house. The extension to the building was never achieved, leaving the central axis of the scheme aligned on the south-west corner of the house. Such was the desire for a regular scheme of planting that the line of the River Nadder, which runs at an angle across the garden from west to east, was all but ignored. De Caus's special expertise with water was expressed in a grotto and several fountains. Celia Fiennes visited sometime before 1682, and her detailed account creates a picture of one of the last great expressions of the art of *giochi d'acqua* in England.

> The Gardens are very fine with many gravel walkes with grass squaires set with fine brass and stone statues-fish ponds and basons with ffigures in the middle spouting out water-dwarfe trees of all sorts and a fine flower garden-much wall fruite. The river runs through the garden that easeily conveys by pipes water to all Parts. A Grottoe is att the end of the garden just the middle off the house-its garnished with many fine ffigures of the Goddesses, and about 2 yards off the doore is severall pipes in a line that with a sluce spoutts water up to wett the strangers-in the middle roome is a round table and a large Pipe in the midst, on which they put a Crown or Gun or a branch, and so yt spouts the water through the Carvings and poynts all round the roome at the Artists pleasure to wet the Company-there are figures at Each corner of the roome that Can weep water on the beholders and by a straight pipe on the table they force up the water into the hollow carving of the rooff like a Crown or Coronet to appearance but is hollow within to retaine the water fforced into it in great quantetyes yt disperses in the hollow Cavity over the roome and descends in a Shower of raine all about the roome-on each side is two little roomes which by the turning their wires the water runnes in the rockes-you see and hear it and also it is so contrived in one room yt it makes the melody of Nightingerlls and all sorts of birds wch engages the Curiosity of the Strangers to go in to see, but at the Entrance off each room is a line of pipes that appear not till by a Sluce moved – it washes the spectators designed for diversion.
>
> The Grottoe is leaded on the top where are fish ponds, and just without the grottoe is a wooden bridge over the river. The barristers are set out wth Lyons set thick on Either Side wth their mouths open, and by a sluce spout out water each to other in a perfect arch the length of the bridge. There are fine woods beyond the house and a large parke walled in. (quoted in Morris 1982, 38)

Fiennes perhaps missed the technical detail of how the water was supplied to the grotto. John Aubrey (1847, 91), however, had noticed that 'by the kitchen gardens a stream which turns a wheel that moves the engine to raise water to the top of the cisterns at the corner of the great garden, to serve the water works of the grotto'. Aubrey also commented on the fact that 'Monsieur de Caus had here a contrivance, by the turning of a cocke, to shew three rainbowes, the secret whereof he did keep to himself; he would not let the gardener, show to strangers, know how to doe it; and so, upon his death, it is lost.' Apart from demonstrating a certain level of commercial acumen, the installation of a 'rainbow' fountain was, according to Johnson (2007, 51), 'a unique combination of myth and mechanics; a nexus of cultural emblems, personal iconography, and scientific advances in an ornament'. Other fountains with accompanying statues raised less-elevating thoughts in the mind of a least one visitor. Lieutenant Hammond, whose comments on the Enstone Marvels have already been quoted, had

> the privilege of being taken around by Isaac de Caus in person. He describes him as 'the fat Dutch keeper thereof, a rare Artist'. [...] Hammond gives the impression of being in a state of lecherous excitement. In each of the parterre squares was a fountain with a nude statue of a woman. He reported gleefully: 'on one is Venus with her son Cupid in her Armes; in another Diana with her bathing sheeting a third is Susanna pulling a thorn out of her Foote; and in the fourth Cleopatra with the Serpent'. He added lustfully that 'with the turning of Cockes' there was 'a washing and dashing the Eyes and Thighs of faire Venus and Diana'. (quoted in Mowl 2004, 35)

Remarkably, these statues, by the Dutch-trained sculptor Nicholas Stone, remain extant and are illustrated with photographs by Strong (1998, 150). Also present is one of the columns that were the basis for the two 'coronet' fountains, where a crown was made to rise and fall by the pressure of the water. According to De Caus's own publication from around 1645, *Le Jardin de Wilton*, the design of the garden also included a cascade and an elaborate water parterre, although its precise location has never been identified, and it may not have been built. The gardens had a brief heyday and were largely swept away by the process whereby, as Mowl (2004, 86) puts it, 'Wilton Gardens re-invents itself least once every hundred years.' Isaac de Caus died in 1648, and it is notable that his particular brand of elaborate waterworks was far less popular in the decades after the Civil War. Amy Bovington and James Campbell (2019, 57) believed that 'If it was not for the advent of the English Civil War in 1642 and its consequent political instability, it is likely that there would have been many more such ornate gardens, grottoes, fountains and automata in England.' A final flourishing of garden design before the vicissitudes of the Civil War and the Commonwealth can be seen at Hunstanton Hall, in Norfolk. Here a modest house began with a brick gatehouse around 1490 and was added to in 1578 and in the 1630s. It belonged to the Le Strange family. The gardens around the hall were based on a series of interconnecting moats not dissimilar to Theobalds but perhaps not on quite such a grand scale (Fig. 21). Dating from the 1640s

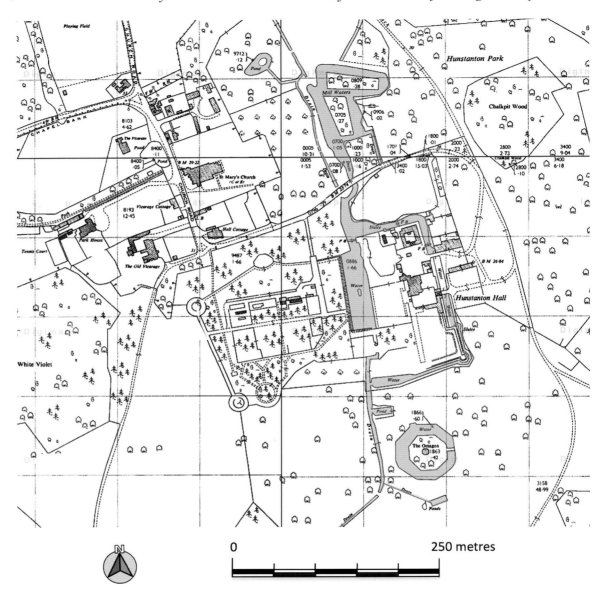

FIGURE 21. Hunstanton Hall, plan of water features. © Crown Copyright and Landmark Information Group Limited (2021). All rights reserved.

is the Octagon. The Historic England listing describes it and its environs in the following terms:

> approximately 200 m south of the Hall is the octagonal carstone and brick banqueting house known as The Octagon (listed grade II*), constructed on an island surrounded by an octagonal moat and reached by a small brick and stone footbridge. Some 30m south of this is a small rectangular pool lined with tiles known as 'Grandfather's Bath', which feeds the octagonal pool that in turn feeds the Hall moats. (Historic England)

This is a particularly interesting combination in view of the octagonal island and House of Diversion at Hanwell, a garden in which one can also find 'Sir Anthony's Bath'. A possible connection exists through family ties recorded by Francis Blomefield. 'Sir Nicholas L'Estrange's second wife was Anne, daughter of Sir William Paston, by whom he had no issue: she was widow of Sir George Chaworth, of Nottinghamshire, and married a third husband, Sir Anthony Cope' (Blomefield 1809, 312).

The gardens so far examined in this book were designed for a combination of pleasure and profit, in varying proportions. However, even more significant for the study of the gardens at Hanwell is a garden with an avowedly 'scientific' purpose established at Wadham College, Oxford. The college was founded in 1609 by Dorothy Wadham, on land which was part of an Augustinian priory. A framework of medieval walls delineated the boundary and gave some structure to the gardens (Mandelbrote 2017, 199). The garden itself was rather conservative in form, with a central mount surrounded by four plots, further cast into quarters and hedged (Fig. 22). What made it special were the additions commissioned by John Wilkins (1614–72) from 1651, in what Mavis Batey (1982, 43) describes as 'a manner to please the distinguished set of natural scientists who made the college their home at Dr. Wilkins's invitation'. Wilkins had come to

FIGURE 22. Wadham College and gardens, from David Loggan's *Oxford Illustrata*, of 1675.

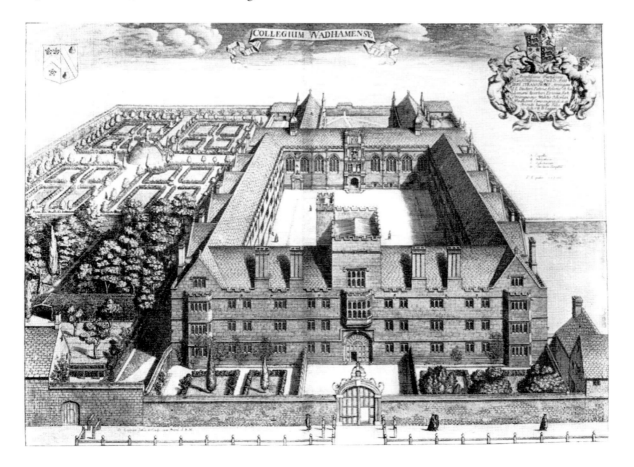

Wadham as warden, as a parliamentary appointee, in 1648, the same year that he published his *Mathematical Magick, or, The Wonders that may be Performed by Mechanical Geometry,* which included notes on the effects of simple mechanisms as well as more complex machines, such as submarines, aircraft and automata *(ODNB).* As Blair Worden (1997, 738) describes it, Wilkins's influence at Oxford in defining a separation between intellectual and political pursuits did much to maintain the university's standing in the eyes of parliamentarians and royalists alike. More specifically, he gathered together a community of like-minded individuals, such as Seth Ward, John Wallis, William Petty, Ralph Bathurst, Robert Boyle, Robert Hooke and Christopher Wren, and managed cultural and social events. Given Cope's later interests as recorded by Plot, the young Anthony Cope would almost certainly have participated in some of these assemblies. The other element, very much in the tradition of Bacon's *New Atlantis,* was the provision of suitable facilities for the study of natural philosophy. Oxford was no stranger to such advances; the university's botanic garden had been opened in 1621, 'to promote the furtherance of learning and to glorify nature' (Bowdler 2018, 20). However, the marvels assembled at Wadham were particularly worthy of comment. Aubrey, Evelyn and Plot all reported on them. Aubrey said of Wilkins, 'He was the principal reviver of experimental philosophy (in the spirit of Lord Bacon) at Oxford, where he had weekly an experimental philosophical [scientific] club, which began 1649, and was the cradle of the Royal Society. When he came to London, they met at the Bull-head tavern in Cheapside, till it grew too big for a club, and so they came to Gresham College parlour.' Evelyn visited in 1654 and recorded the following in his diary:

> We all dined at that most obliging and universally-curious Dr. Wilkins's, at Wadham. He was the first who showed me the transparent apiaries, which he had built like castles and palaces, and so ordered them one upon another, as to take the honey without destroying the bees. These were adorned with a variety of dials, little statues, vanes, etc.; and, he was so abundantly civil, finding me pleased with them, to present me with one of the hives which he had empty, and which I afterward had in my garden at Sayes Court, where it continued many years, and which his Majesty came on purpose to see and contemplate with much satisfaction. He had also contrived a hollow statue, which gave a voice and uttered words by a long, concealed pipe that went to its mouth, while one speaks through it at a good distance. He had, above in his lodgings and gallery, variety of shadows, dials, perspectives, and many other artificial, mathematical, and magical curiosities, a waywiser, a thermometer, a monstrous magnet, conic, and other sections, a balance on a demi-circle; most of them of his own, and that prodigious young scholar Mr. Christopher Wren, who presented me with a piece of white marble, which he had stained with a lively red, very deep, as beautiful as if it had been natural. (Evelyn 1955, 307)

As well as having serious intentions, Wilkins was not above the occasional practical joke, and one wonders what the impact may have been of the prank he played on George Ashwell, later to be Sir Anthony Cope's chaplain and rector of Hanwell. Fellow of Jesus College, Cambridge, Thomas Woodcock (d. 1695) told the story.

> Of Mr. Ashwell abused by Dr. Wilkins – When the Dr. was warden of Wadham Colledge he had the statue of Flora in his Garden; into which he had contrived a pipe, thro' which to speak. At that time Oliver Cromwell had sent to the University if any would go to preach the Gospel in Virginia, they should have good incouragement. One Mr. Ashwell was walking towards the statue, when Dr. Wilkins sat conveniently to whisper and said, Ashwell goe preach the Gospel in Virginia. The voice amazed him, and at the next return, it repeated the same words. At another return it said, Ashwell, for the 3rd and last time, goe preach the Gospel in Virginia. He going off amazed, the Dr. wheeled about and meet him:asked him what ayled him to look so affrighted: He said if ever man heard a voice from heaven I did; the Dr. said you have always derided such fancyes; but he persisted in it, til the Dr. unridled all to him, that he might have a quiet in his mind and suffer no harm by a delusion. (Moore Smith 1907, 81)

Anthony Turner (2007, 340) considered the joke to be 'harmless except that Ashwell was convinced that he had heard heavenly instruction'. But the fact that, as a story, it was being passed around Cambridge suggests that Ashwell may have not been quite so amused.

Following Wilkins's departure for Cambridge in 1659, the garden may have gone into something of a decline. Plot (1705, 240) describes a rainbow fountain, presumably similar to that at Wilton, by repute only.

> Amongst the *Water-work*s of Pleasure, we must not forget an *Engine* contrived by the Right Reverend Father in God, *John Wilkins*, late Lord Bishop of *Chester*, when he was *Warden* of *Wadham College*, though long since taken thence; whereby but few Galons of *Water* forced through a narrow *Fissure*, he could raise a *Mist* in his *Garden*, wherein a Person placed at a due Distance between the *Sun* and the *Mist*, might see an exquisite *Rainbow* in all its proper *Colours*: which Distance I conceive was the same with that assigned by *Des Cartes*, *viz.* where the Eye of the Beholder is placed in an Angle of 42 Degrees, made by the *Decussation* of the Line of *Vision*, and the Rays of the *Sun*; and the *Fissure* such another as in his *Diagram*. But what kind of *Instrument* it was that forced the *Water*, I dare not venture to relate, the Description given me of it being but lame and imperfect. (Plot 1705, 240)

Of all this there is scarcely a trace remaining. The speaking statue of Atlas fell in a storm, and then the mount was demolished in 1753 and replaced by a pond, which was in turn filled in and given over to the typical grassy expanse of an Oxford college lawn.

The acquisition by John Evelyn (1620–1706) of one of the transparent bee-hives from Wadham for his own garden at Sayes Court, in Kent, is significant. Strong (1998, 221) views Evelyn in these terms: 'John Evelyn takes us firmly on into the world of the Royal Society. We are witnessing the shedding of the old hieroglyphic and analogic readings of the gardens in favour of empirical study.' Evelyn matriculated at Balliol College, Oxford, in 1637, and from 1641 he travelled extensively on the continent, partly to avoid the rigours of the English Civil War. He spent considerable time in Italy, where he documented visits to some of the great gardens of the day. In 1647 he returned to England and took over the management of his family's holdings, including his main residence, Sayes Court, before finally moving to his brother George's property at Wotton House, in Surrey, in 1694. Although the gardens at Wotton still exist, only the barest outline belongs to John Evelyn's era; the surviving grottoes and fountains are primarily nineteenth century. The development of these gardens was very much a family affair, with his brother George in residence and his cousin George supervising the works. John's role may have initially been one of offering advice and encouragement. The garden itself was fairly conventional, with a parterre plus fountain, two grottoes and a mount; however, the wider estate was notable because of the extent to which water was utilised to run the family's gunpowder mills. Evelyn took on a Baconian project, the idea being, according to Juliet Odgers (2011, 238), that 'the workshops of tradesmen, the kitchen, brewhouse and gardens would serve as the sources of relevant "facts". In these places, "nature" was subjected to all sorts of revealing transformations and tradesmen were consequently in possession of a large amount of knowledge, which, if subjected to informed scrutiny, could further the natural philosopher's understanding.'

Like many of Evelyn's undertakings this did not get far beyond the note-taking stage, but aspects of the work did find their way into the programme of the Royal Society. He was a prolific writer, and his vast project on gardening, *Elysium Britannicum,* remained subject to constant revision and was ultimately unfinished. However, it is possible to chart the different strands of his thinking about water. Chapter VI of Book 1 dealt with water in its philosophical and spiritual dimension, for example for gardening: '*Raine* is best and especially that which hath been reserved at the *equinoxes* […] as being most all impregnat with the *universal Spirit*'. The practical and comprehensive nature of Book 2 is shown by some of the chapter headings:

Chapter 9, Of Fountains, Cascades, Rivulets, Piscenas, Canales and Water-works
Chapter 10, Of Rocks, Grots, Crypto's, Mounts, Precipices, Porticos, Venti-ducts, and other Hortulan refreshments
Chapter 11, Of Statues, Obeliscs, Columns, Dyals, Pots, Vasas, Perspectives, Paintings and other Ornaments
Chapter 12, Of Artificial Echoes, Automats and Hydraulic motions.

Such a publication would have served the young Sir Anthony Cope admirably as a manual to have had in hand as he prepared his garden of wonders in the early 1660s, and it is not inconceivable that he could have seen parts of it in manuscript form. Unfortunately it did not find its way into print until 2001. The practice of creating water gardens in the opening decades of the seventeenth century, with varying degrees of technical accomplishment and ambition, sets the scene for the works at Hanwell that belong to later decades. These further developments in the years before the outbreak of the Civil War give us a context within which the young Sir Anthony Cope developed his passion for natural philosophy and found ways to express that within his garden.

Bibliography

Abbott, E.A., *Francis Bacon: An Account of His Life and Works* (London, 1885)

Anonymous, 'On a Fart in the Parliament House', in *Wit and Mirth: or Pills to Purge Melancholy* (London, 1719)

Aubrey, J., *Memoirs of Natural Remarques in the County of Wiltshire*, ed. Britton, J. (London, 1847)

Aubrey, J., *John Aubrey Brief Lives*, ed. Bennett, K. (Oxford, 2015)

Bacon, F., *Instauratio magna* [Novum organum] (London, 1620).

Bacon, F., *Works of Francis Bacon*, vol. 12, ed. Spedding, J., Ellis, R. and Heath, D. (London, 1857–74).

Bacon, F., *Gesta Grayorum*, ed. Greg, W. (Oxford, 1914)

Bacon, F., *The New Atlantis* (originally published London, 1627), in Bruce, S. (ed.) *Three Early Modern Utopias: Utopia, New Atlantis and The Island of Pines* (Oxford, 2008)

Batey, M., *Oxford Gardens: The University's Influence on Garden History* (Oxford, 1982)

Bennett, K. (ed.), *John Aubrey Brief Lives* (Oxford, 2015)

Blomefield, F., 'Smethdon Hundred: Hunstanton Lordship', in *An Essay Towards a Topographical History of the County of Norfolk* 10 (London, 1809)

Bold, J., *Wilton House and English Palladianism* (London, 1988)

Bowdler, R., 'Landscapes of Learning: Gardens and Grounds at England's Older Universities 1550–1800', *Baltic Journal of Art History* 16 (2018)

Bowyer, R., *The Parliamentary Diary of Robert Bowyer, 1606–1607*, ed. Willson, D. (Minneapolis, 1931)

Boyington, A. and Campbell, J., 'The Influence of the de Caus brothers on Hydraulic Engineering and Fountain Design in Seventeenth-Century England', in Campbell, J. *et al.* (eds) *Water, Doors and Buildings: Studies in the History of Construction* (Cambridge, 2019)

Bushell, T., *The First part of Youths Errors: Written by Thomas Bushell the Superlative Prodigall* (London, 1628)

Campbell, J. and Boyington, A., 'The Problems of Meaning and Use of the puer mingens Motif in Fountain Design 1400–1700', *Studies in the History of Gardens and Designed Landscape* 40(2) (2019)

Carew, N., A Book of the Plantation of Ulster, Lambeth Palace Library, Mss 613, https://discovery.nationalarchives.gov.uk/details/r/9517ab48-f8e1-4321-82e2-499ccbcfe810, accessed 14 March 2020

Chaney, E. and Wilks, T., *The Jacobean Grand Tour: Early Stuart Travellers in Europe* (London, 2014)

Cope, A., letter to Sir Robert Cecil (September 1600), http://www.british-history.ac.uk/cal-cecil-papers/vol10/pp315-335, accessed 11 January 2021

Cope, A., letter to Sir Robert Cecil (September 1601), http://www.british-history.ac.uk/cal-cecil-papers/vol11/pp374-401, accessed 11 January 2021

Cope, A., letter to earl of Salisbury (August 1605), http://www.british-history.ac.uk/cal-cecil-papers/vol17/pp374-409, accessed 11 January 2021

Cope, W., letter to Sir Robert Cecil (March 1601), http://www.british-history.ac.uk/cal-cecil-papers/vol11/pp100-119, accessed 17 January 2021

Cope, W., letter to Sir John Fortescue (December 1605), http://www.british-history.ac.uk/cal-cecil-papers/vol24/pp36-57, accessed 17 January 2021.

Cope, W., letter to the earl of Salisbury (12 August 1606), http://www.british-history.ac.uk/cal-cecil-papers/vol18/pp220-235, accessed 17 January 2021

De Caus, I., *Wilton Garden*, facsimile edition (London, 1895)

De Caus, S., *Les Raisons des forces mouvantes. Avec diverses machines tant utilles que plaisantes ausquelles sont adjoints plusieurs desseings de grotes et fontaines* (Frankfurt, 1615)

Demidowicz, G., 'Appendix 2, the Water Supply for Leicester's Fountain', in Keay, A. and Watkins, J. (eds) *The Elizabethan Garden at Kenilworth Castle* (Swindon, 2013)

Derham, W., 'Holland House and Earl's Court: Their History and Topography', *Journal of the British Archaeological Association* 23(1) (1917)

Dillon (Viscount), 'A Procession of Queen Elizabeth to Blackfriars', *Archaeological Journal* 72(1) (1915)

Duggan, D., 'Isaac de Caus: Surveyor, Grotto and Garden designer', *Studies in the History of Gardens and Designed Landscapes* 29(3) (2009)

East India Company, court minutes (January 1607), //www.british-history.ac.uk/cal-state-papers/colonial/east-indies-china-japan/vol2/pp145-148, accessed 17 January 2021.

Evelyn, J., *Diary: Introduction and De Vita Propria*, ed. De Beer, E., vol. 1 (Oxford, 1955)

Evelyn, J., *Elysium Britannicum or The Royal Gardens*, ed. Ingram, J.E. (Philadelphia, 2001)

Everson, P., 'The Gardens of Campden House, Chipping Campden, Gloucestershire', *Garden History* 17(2) (1989)

Gill, R., letter to the earl of Salisbury, http://www.british-history.ac.uk/cal-cecil-papers/vol17/pp344-374, accessed 11 January 2021.

Gough, J., *The Superlative Prodigall: A Life of Thomas Bushell* (Bristol, 1932)

Grant to the earl of Salisbury and Sir Walter Cope, of the office of Keepers of Hyde Park (16 November 1610), http://www.british-history.ac.uk/cal-state-papers/domestic/jas1/1603-10/pp640-655, accessed 17 January 2021

Guerci, M., 'Salisbury House in London, 1599–1694: The Strand Palace of Sir Robert Cecil', *Architectural History* 52 (2009)

Hammond, W., *A Relation of a Short Survey of the Western Counties, Made by a Lieutenant of the Military Company in Norwich in 1635*, Camden Miscellany, 3rd series (London, 1936)

Hants. CRO, 43M48/121 (conveyance of Teyngle or Tyngle [Tangley] Grange, Oxon, 1551)

Hatfield House Archives, Bills 51/8 V

Henderson, P., 'Sir Francis Bacon's Essay "Of Gardens" in Context', *Garden History* 36(1) (2008)

Hiden, M., 'A Voyage of Fishing and Discovery, 1609', *Virginia Magazine of History and Biography* 65(1) (1957)

HOP. 1558–1603, Haster, P.W., 'Carleton, George (1529–90)'

Hyde, E., 'Introduction', in Hyde, E. (ed.) *A Cultural History of Gardens the Renaissance* (London, 2013)

Johnson, F., 'Thomas Digges, the Copernican System, and the Idea of the Infinity of the Universe in 1576', *Huntington Library Bulletin* 5 (1934)

Johnson, F., 'Gresham College Precursor of the Royal Society', *Journal of the History of Ideas* 1(4) (1940)

Johnson, P., 'Proof of the Heavenly Iris: The Fountain of Three Rainbows at Wilton House, Wiltshire', *Garden History* 35(1) (2007)

Johnson, P., 'Producing Pleasantness: The Waterworks of Isaac de Caus, Outlandish Engineer', *Studies in the History of Gardens and Designed Landscapes* 29(3) (2009)

Jope, E.M., 'Moyry, Charlemont, Castleraw, and Richhill: Fortification to Architecture in the North of Ireland 1570–1700', *Ulster Journal of Archaeology* 23 (1960)

Kennedy, M., 'Fen Drainage, the Central Government, and Local Interest: Carleton and the Gentlemen of South Holland', *Historical Journal* 26(1) (1983)

Lees-Jeffries, H., 'An Elizabethan Translation of Bernard Palissy's "On Waters and Fountains"', *Studies in the History of Gardens and Designed Landscapes* 30(1) (2010)

Lord Chancellor, letter to Robert Cecil (October 1603), http://www.british-history.ac.uk/cal-cecil-papers/vol15/pp253-277, accessed 17 January 2021

Lord Chamberlain, letter to George Carleton (November 1612), http://www.british-history.ac.uk/cal-state-papers/domestic/jas1/1611-18/pp154-160, accessed 17 January 2021

Lord Chamberlain, letter to George Carleton (February 1614), http://www.british-history.ac.uk/cal-state-papers/domestic/jas1/1611-18/pp222-225 accessed, 17 January 2021

Lord Chamberlain, letter to George Carleton (August 1614), http://www.british-history.ac.uk/cal-state-papers/domestic/jas1/1611-18/pp250-252, accessed 17 January 2021

Lysons, D., *Environs of London, Being an Historical Account of the Towns, Villages and Hamlets, within Twelve Miles of That Capital* (London, 1796)

MacGregor, A., '"A Magazin of All Manner of Inventions", Museums in the Quest for "Salomon's House" in Seventeenth-Century England', *Journal of the History of Collections* 1(2) (1987)

Mandelbrote, S., 'John Wilkins and the Gardens of Wadham College', in Poole, W. (ed.) *John Wilkins and the Gardens of Wadham College* (Leiden, 2017)

Markham, G., *Cheape and Good Husbandry for Well-Ordering of All Beasts, and Fowls, and for the Generall Cure of Their Diseases* (London, 1623)

McGee, T., '"The Presentment of Bushell's Rock": Place, Politics, and Theatrical Self-Promotion', *Medieval and Renaissance Drama in England* 16 (2003)

Miller, S., *The Pleasure Grounds of Holland House* (London, 2014)

Miller, S., '"The Ponds or Water Maze": An Early Seventeenth-Century Water Garden at Cope Castle in Kensington', *Garden History* 42(1) (2014)

Moore Smith, G.C. (ed.), *Extracts from the papers of Thomas Woodcock (Ob. 1695)* (London, 1907)

Morgan, L., *Nature as Model: Salomon de Caus and Early Seventeenth-Century Landscape Design* (Philadelphia, 2017)

Morris, C. (ed.), *The Illustrated Journeys of Celia Fiennes 1685–1712* (London, 1982)

Mowl, T., *Historic Gardens of Wiltshire* (Stroud, 2004)

Mowl, T., *The Historic Gardens of England: Oxfordshire* (Stroud, 2007)

Nicholl, C., *The Lodger: Shakespeare on Silver Street* (London, 2007)

Nichols, J., *The Progresses, Processions, and Magnificent Festivities, of King James I,* vol. 1 (London, 1828)

Odgers, J., 'Water in Use and Philosophy at Wotton House: John Evelyn and the History of the Trades', *Architectural Research Quarterly* 15(3) (2011)

ODNB, Allen, E., 'Cope, Sir Anthony (1495/6–1551)'

ODNB, Allen, E., 'Cope, Sir Anthony, first baronet (1548–1614)'

ODNB, Ashton, A. 'Hicks, Baptist, first Viscount Campden (1551?–1629)'

ODNB, Boon, G., 'Bushell, Thomas (b. before 1600, d. 1674)'

ODNB, Greengrass, M., 'Hartlib, Samuel (c. 1600–1662)'

ODNB, Henry, J., 'Wilkins, John (1614–1672)'

ODNB, Peltonen, M., 'Bacon, Francis, Viscount St. Albans (1551–1626)'.

Page, W., 'House of Austin Canons: Priory of Brooke', in *Victoria History of the County of Rutland,* vol. 1 (London, 1908)

Pastorino, C., 'Beyond Recipes: The Baconian Natural and Experimental Histories as an Epistemic Genre', *Centaurus* 62(3) (2020)

Petition (May 1605), http://www.british-history.ac.uk/cal-cecil-papers/vol17/pp167-206, accessed 17 January 2021

Platter, T., *The Journals of Two Travellers in Elizabethan and Early Stuart England* (London, 1995)

Plot, R., *The Natural History of Oxfordshire* (London, 1705)

Potts, W., *A History of Banbury* (Banbury, 1958)

Price, B., 'Introduction', in Price, B. (ed.) *Francis Bacon's* New Atlantis*: New Interdisciplinary Essays* (Manchester, 2002)

Quinn, D., 'Reviewed Work: John Pory, 1572–1636: The Life and Letters of a Man of Many Parts by William S. Powell', *William and Mary Quarterly* 36(1) (1979)

Raiger, M., 'Fancy, Dreams, and Paradise: Miltonic and Baconian Garden Imagery in Coleridge's "Kubla Khan"', *Studies in Philology* 110(3) (2013)

Rigg, V. (ed.), *The Howse Which Was so Faire: Discovering Campden House and Gardens* (Chipping Campden, 2018)

Smith, D., Payne, M. and Marshall, M., 'Rediscovering John Donne's *Catalogus librorum satyricus*', *Review of English Studies* 69(290) (2018)

Smith, S., 'The New Atlantis: Francis Bacon's Theological-Political Utopia?', *Harvard Theological Review* 101(1) (2008)

Sorbière, S., *A Voyage to England* (London, 1709)

Southey, R., letter to Charles Collins (31 March 1793) quoted in Baughman, R., 'Southey the Schoolboy', *Huntington Library Quarterly* 7 (1944)

Spedding, J., *The Letters and Life of Francis Bacon*, 7 vols. (London, 1861-74)

Stone, L., 'The Building of Hatfield House', *Archaeological Journal* 112(1) (1955)

Thacker, C., 'An Extraordinary Solitude', in Butler, S., Ross, S. and Smith, A. (eds) *Of Oxfordshire Gardens* (Oxford, 1982)

Turner, A., 'Stagecraft and Mathematical Magic in Early Modern London', *Nuncius: Journal of the Material and Visual History of Science* 22(2) (2007)

Van Eerde, K., 'The Jacobean Baronets: An Issue between King and Parliament', *Journal of Modern History* 33(2) (1961)

Walcott, M., 'The Benedictine Abbey of St. Mary, Pershore', *Journal of the British Archaeological Association,* First Series 32(3) (1876)

Walter, J., '"Rising of the People"? The Oxfordshire Rising of 1596', *Past and Present* 107 (1985)

Wass, S., 'The Enstone Marvels Rediscovered', *Garden History* 45(2) (2017)

Webster, C., *The Great Instauration: Science, Medicine and Reform 1626–1660* (London, 1975)

Whitaker, J., 'An Old Arcadia: The Gardens of William Herbert, 1st. Earl of Pembroke, Wilton, Wiltshire', *Garden History* 42(2) (2014)

Whittle, E. and Taylor, C., 'The Early Seventeenth-Century Gardens of Tackley, Oxfordshire', *Garden History* 22(1) (1995)

Wood, A., *Athenae Oxonienses: An Exact History of Writers and Bishops Who Have Had Their Education in the University of Oxford*, vol. 1 (Oxford, 1813)

Woodcock, T., *Extracts from the Papers of Thomas Woodcock (Ob. 1695)*, ed. Moore Smith, G.C. (London, 1907)

Worden, B., 'Cromwellian Oxford', in Tyacke, N. (ed.) *The History of the University of Oxford, Volume IV: Seventeenth-Century Oxford* (Oxford, 1997)

Worsley, L., 'The "Artisan Mannerist" Style in British Sculpture: A Bawdy Fountain at Bolsover Castle', *Renaissance Studies* 19(1) (2005)

Wotton, H., *The Elements of Architecture, Collected by Sir Henry Wotton, Kt., from the Best Authors and Examples* (London, 1624)

CHAPTER FOUR

The Copes of Hanwell House

Sir Anthony Cope, the 4th Baronet

After the deaths, in 1614, of Sir Anthony, the 1st baronet, and his brother Sir Walter, both of whom were in considerable debt, the family must have struggled to rebuild its finances. This task went to Sir Anthony's heir, William (1577?–1637), and William's wife, Elizabeth Chaworth, whom he had married in 1602. They had been living on the other side of the River Cherwell, in the small property at Hardwick. He was an M.P. for Banbury for parliaments called from 1604 onwards, and he was an active participant, frequently taking opportunities to pursue his family's interest. Despite having inherited debts, William had also borrowed heavily to acquire further local properties. His lack of financial liquidity led into an almost continual round of litigation, a not uncommon state of affairs for many members of the gentry of the time. In an attempt to raise some income, William became part of a syndicate selling export licences for wool and invested in further schemes relating to pipe staves and sea coal. None of these investments made much of a contribution to clearing his debts, and after the close of parliament in 1624, he was arrested because he owed money. A drama ensued:

> Just over a month after the prorogation Cope was arrested at the suit of Lady Coppyn for a debt of £3,000 'and for seeking to escape from the sheriff who had used him kindly, upon his word and promise to be true prisoner', and was imprisoned in Oxford Castle. After transfer to the Fleet he was temporarily released in August 1624 to entertain King James at Hanwell for three days. He was removed from the commission of the peace, but was still at liberty 'by *habeas corpus*' when Charles I summoned his first Parliament in 1625. (*HOP*)

Accommodating the king could hardly have eased his financial difficulties. In May 1626 William was attempting, unsuccessfully, to approach the East India Company 'for their dividends, and had returned without money or good words' (East India Company, Court Minutes, May 1626). Further attempts were made to arrest him, and in 1629 his debts were finally settled by him surrendering his estate to a panel of trustees headed by viscount Saye and Sele, of nearby Broughton Castle. William's sense of obligation to Lord Saye may have led him to oppose Ship Money, a tax that could be levied at time of war without the permission of Parliament, despite having played host to King Charles and his queen in August of 1636, although equally it may have been a matter of principle. One wonders if the subject of the Enstone Marvels, which the royal couple had visited that same month, figured in their conversation at all and if the ears of the four-year-old Anthony heard anything of the wonders to be experienced there.

William died in 1637, acknowledging the family's long-term support of the puritan clerics John Dod and Robert Harris by leaving them £20 each in his will (TNA, PROB 11/175/196). He was succeeded by his eldest son, John, who in 1631 had married Lady Elizabeth Fane, a daughter of the earl of Westmorland. She gave birth to Anthony in 1632 and John in 1634. In 1638 Sir John took out a loan for £150 from the poet John Milton (1608–74). The fact that Sir John died shortly afterwards, also in 1638, led to a series of court actions that prompted Joseph French (1939, 124) to describe the Copes as 'one of the most litigious families in England'. The death of their father must have been around the time that a portrait was painted of the two boys (Plate 15). It is probable that Lady Elizabeth initially had some oversight of the estate, during the minority of her sons. In an incident after the start of the Civil War, it was reported that on 8 August 1642 some royalist hotheads attacked

> the grave and reverend Mr. Harris (of Hanwell neer Banbury) […] they outed him and his family, took possession of his house on Sunday night, and made him wander for his lodging, and took possession of the Lady Copes house there, and of all the armes, and ammunition they could meet with in the town. (Anonymous 1642)

While this account, no doubt, is coloured by the propaganda of the time, this must have been an alarming incident for the family, including the 10-year-old Anthony, and perhaps provided the impetus for his mother to remarry, in 1643. Her second husband was Colonel William Cope, a cousin of her former husband (Plate 16). This was followed by a move to Bruern, which would have allowed her to get away from the conflict in the area immediately around Banbury, where the castle was periodically besieged. In 1654 Colonel Cope took on the manor of Icomb, formerly in Worcestershire and now in Gloucestershire. The somewhat peripatetic nature of family life at the time is demonstrated by an extraordinary note in a commonplace book discovered in Herefordshire in 1874 and evidently written by Lady Elizabeth at some point post-1653, possibly after the move to Icomb.

> John Cope and Elizabeth Fane were maried upon shrouf tewsday in ye year 1631 at Westminster by ye Bishop of Lincolne, it being Valentine's day ye 14 of Feb.
>
> My sonne Anthony was born at Abthorpe ye 16 day of Nouemb. being friday in ye year 1632 between 3 & 4 a clock in ye morning, he was Christened on ye 6 day of Decemb. by my mother ye Countes of Westmoreland, my brother the Earle of Westmoreland, & Sir William Cope, but Sir Gui Palmes was deputy for him.
>
> My second sonne William was borne at Hanwell ye 3 d day of Decem. being tewsday 1633 betweene 9 & 10 a clock in ye morning, he was Christened on ye 17th day, by my Grand: ye old Lady Cope, my Lord Say & my Lord Gerard. he dyed on ye 13th of Sept. 1634.
>
> My sonne John was borne at Hanwell, ye 19th of Nouemb. being Wednesday, 1634 betweene 9 & 10 a clock at night, he was christened on ye 31 day by my mother ye Countes of Westmoreland, my brother Lee and my cossin Knightly.

My daughter Mary was borne at Brewerne ye 28th of Noue. being Monday in ye year 1636 betweene 2 & 3 a clock in ye morning she was christened on ye 9th of Decem. by my sister Rachell Fane, my sister Lee, & Sir Robert Jenkinson She dyed upon ye 10 Oct. 1639.

My daughter Elizabeth was borne at Brewerne ye 3rd of June being Sunday in ye year 1638, betweene 2 & 3 a clock in ye morning she was baptised on ye 10th day by my sister Lee, my sister Mary Cope & my cousin William Cope.

My dear husband Sr John Cope changed this life for a better upon Saterday morning ye 13th of October 1638.

William Cope & Elizabeth Cope were maryed ye 3rd day of January 1643 in ye chappell at Brewerne by Mr Robert Harris of Hanwell.

My sonne Henery was borne at Brewerne ye 23 Octob. being Wedensday in ye yeare 1644, betweene 3 & 4 a clock in ye afternoone, he was baptised on ye 12th of November by my Lady Wilmott, the Earle of Bath & Sir Thomas Pope (my son Ant'was deputy for my Lord of Bathe).

My sonne William was borne at Brewerne ye 12th of Febr. being thursday in ye year 1645 betweene 7 & 8 in ye morning, he dyed ye Wednesday following &was buried in ye chapel at Brewerne upon thursday.

My daughter Elizabeth was borne at Tangly ye 18th of Nouemb. being satterday in ye yeare 1647 betweene 6 & 7 in ye morning, she was baptised on ye 30th of November by Sir Edmond Bray, ye Lady Lacy & ye Lady Jenkinson

My sonne Richard was born at Tangly ye 30th Decem. being satterday in ye yeare 1648 betweene 4 & 5 in ye morning. he dyed ye friday seuenight after & was buried in ye chapel at Brewerne upon satterday ye 18th of January.

My daughter Rachell was borne at Tangly ye 18th of June being thursday in ye yeare 1650 betweene 5 & 6 in ye morning, she was baptised on ye 5th of Jully by the Countesse of Bath, ye Lady Darcy & ye Earle of Westmoreland.

My sonne William was borne at Brewerne ye 4th of Sept. being Thursday in ye year 1651 about 12 a clock at night, he was baptised on ye 28 of Sept. ye witnesses were Mis Childe, my son Anthony Cope & Sr William Walter. (*Miscellanea Genealogica et Heraldica* 1874, 240)

Apart from being a dreadful testimony to the rate of child mortality, possibly even higher amongst the well-to-do because of their use of wet nurses, and offering useful insights into the family connections enjoyed by Lady Elizabeth, it also provides information about the family's movements before, during and after the Civil War. Abthorpe was the home of her father, Francis, earl of Westmoreland, and so it seems a suitable setting for the birth of her first son. The Cope family seat at Hanwell was equally appropriate as a family residence in the early 1630s, but she was at Bruern for the birth of her subsequent children, from 1636 until 1645, although she must have returned to Hanwell, perhaps upon the death of her first husband, where she may well have stayed until her marriage took her back to Bruern in 1643.

During his formative years, Anthony would have travelled between a variety of family properties. He went up to Oxford probably late in 1648, aged 15, to attend Oriel College. The college may have seemed to him to be the epitome of modernity, as it was effectively rebuilt between 1620 and 1642. His great-great-great-grandfather Anthony Cope may have started a family connection with the college, and Blair Worden (1997, 767) notes that 'only one other house preserved so distinctly royalist a character: Oriel [...] where the proportion of sons of royalists was even higher than at Queen's. The royalist provosts Richard [John] Sanders [provost 1644–53] and Robert Saye [1653–91] resisted all visitatorial efforts to puritanize their house with obstinacy, even with insolence.' Given the family's ongoing connection with the puritan divines John Dod and Robert Harris, this could have put the young Sir Anthony in a difficult position, especially in view of the febrile atmosphere that must have existed in Oxford around the time of King Charles's execution, in January 1649. A further family connection in the city at the time, although one which may not have sat well with the young Sir Anthony, was Lady Isabella Thynne (b. 1623), granddaughter of Sir Walter Cope, who was the brother of Sir Anthony's great-grandfather. Aubrey captures and possibly embellishes her colourful presence in his account of Ralph Kettle, president of Trinity College.

> Our grove was the Daphne for the Ladies and their Gallants to walke in, and many times my lady Isabella Thynne would make her Entreys with a Theorbo or lute played before her. I have heard her play on it in the Grove myselfe, which she did rarely; for which Mr. Edmund Waller hath in his Poems for ever made her famous. One may say of her as Tacitus sayd of Agrippina, *Cuncta alia illi adfuere, praeter animum honestum.* She was most beautifull, most humble, charitable, etc. but she could not subdue one thing. I remember one time this lady and fine Mrs. Fenshawe *(her great and intimate friend, who lay at our college), would have a frolick to make a visitt to the President. The old Dr. quickly percieved that they came to abuse him; he addresses his discourse to Mrs. Fenshawe, saying, 'Madam, your husband and father I bred up here, and I knew your grandfather; I know you to be a gentlewoman, I will not say you are a whore; but gett you gonne for a very woman.'
>
> *She was wont, and my lady Thynne, to come to our Chapell, mornings, halfe dressd, like angells. (Aubrey 2015, 181)

Antonia Fraser (1984, 35) adds, 'She became the mistress of the Royalist leader, the Marquess of Ormonde [...] Later she became involved in Royalist plotting, her father the Earl of Holland having been executed for his part in the second Civil War. Lady Isabella left England in 1650, finding refuge with Ormonde's sensible and charitable wife Elizabeth Desmond.' Lady Isabella's subsequent efforts on behalf of the exiled Prince Charles may well have led her into a circle of informants and agents that was to include the cleric Richard Allestree.

Dr. Saye was to be recorded in Sir Anthony's will of 1674 as his former tutor, receiving a bequest of £50, 'in remembrance of my love' (TNA, PROB 11/350/249). The college buttery book for 1648–49 shows him to have been by far the biggest spender amongst the undergraduates. As the only 'gentleman' at Oriel, he presumably had a certain level of consumption to maintain, although his pattern of spending suggests long absences from the university. For example, he seems to have been away for three weeks from St Thomas's Day to Lady

Day, in the spring of 1649, and was absent also for much of the early summer in 1650, possibly back at Tangley, preparing to greet his new half-sister, Rachell (Oriel College Archive, TF 1 E1/6). There are no entries for him from Michaelmas term 1651, at which point he presumably had entered into his majority, and in September 1651 he witnessed the baptism of his half-brother William, at Bruern. His brother John went up to Queen's College in the same year. No specific information about Sir Anthony's studies as part of his undergraduate B.A. course is available, although he would have received a sound grounding in mathematics, possibly with the support of a private tutor, as well as having the option of attending lectures from a range of specialists, some of whom embraced current thinking on natural philosophy. It is possible that he also studied astronomy, which would have necessitated the purchase of a range of instruments (Feingold 1997, 374). In describing the curriculum at Christ Church from the 1660s, E.G.W. Bill (1988, 245) noted that 'the degree of BA embraced in theory if not always in practice, logic, mathematics, natural and moral philosophy, the elements of religion and prescribed classical authors.' Despite slightly irregular attendance, he would still have been subject to a system which 'not only trained more students who made science their vocation, but provided considerable proportion of the educated public with at least a modicum of scientific knowledge, thus contributing to a relatively sizeable community of "virtuosi" who made possible the flowering of English science' (Feingold 1997, 426). While at Oxford, Anthony was very likely to have made contact with John Wilkins, who was warden at Wadham College. Wilkins was another new arrival at Oxford. His grandfather on his mother's side was John Dod, who as a minister had been supported by previous generations of Copes (Clarke 1660, 200). Given the family connection, it is reasonable to assume that Sir Anthony experienced the 'garden of curiosities' that Wilkins had assembled at Wadham and that this inspired him, together with other links to the Oxford establishment, to develop his own role as virtuoso. This familiarity with Wadham College was maintained at least into the late 1650s, when, as we shall see, one of Sir Anthony's house guests, the musician Thomas Baltzar, gave concerts there.

Sir Anthony married his cousin Mary Dutton, daughter of the 3rd Baron Gerard, of Gerard's Bromley, Staffordshire, and Mary Fane, sister to Sir Anthony's mother Elizabeth. The ceremony probably took place in 1651. His mother had also listed the births and unfortunate deaths of Anthony's children.

> My sonne Ant' Copes eldest sonne was borne at Aston in Yorkshire upon Wednesday ye 16 March 1652 about 4 a clock in ye morning, he was baptised John and dyed ye monday seuenight after.
>
> his second son was borne at Aston on Thursday ye bout a fortnight after.
>
> his 3 d sonne was borne at Tangley on Wedensday ye 13th of Decem. 1654 betweene 7 & 8 in ye morning, he was baptised Henry on Satterday ye 16. ye witnesses were Lord Vicount Faulkland, Sr Edmond Brag & my self.
>
> [Marginal Note] He dyed ye 8 of June 1662

his first daughter was borne at Tangly ye last of April 1656 & was baptised Mary, ye witnesses were ye Lord Gerard, ye Countesse of Westmoreland & ye Lady Kilmurrey. (*Miscellanea Genealogica et Heraldica* 1874, 241)

The presence of Sir Anthony and his pregnant wife at Aston Hall in Yorkshire is partially explained by the fact that his mother's sister, Catherine, had married Conyers Darcy, 2nd earl of Holderness, in 1645. Presumably family links were sufficiently strong to ensure that Sir Anthony was made welcome at one of the family seats, although why they are so far from their Oxfordshire holdings remains a puzzle. By 1654 they were back at Tangley, where their third son and first daughter, who were both to survive infancy but were to die at the ages of seven and fifteen, respectively, were born. The family had clearly at this stage adopted Tangley as their main residence, as legal documents from 1655 name him the owner as Sir Anthony Cope of Tangley. In 1658 as part of continuing litigation arising from the unpaid loan from Milton 20 years earlier, it was recorded, possibly as a ruse, that Sir Anthony 'has hired the house at Tangley to live in with his family and pays £30 a year rent for it' (French 1939, 129). As noted previously, one of the most remarkable and tantalising references to Tangley comes in Plot's *Natural History*, where, in giving an account of stones he termed *Brontiae*, he identified 'a Learned Society of *Virtuosi*, that, During the late Usurpation lived obscurely at *Tangley*'. A curious incident is recorded for 22 June 1658.

> Petition of Sir William Walter, Bart., of Sarsden, co. Oxon, to the Protector. Being bound with sureties to keep the peace, according to the general order for compounders, I was summoned by Major Crook to Oxford, and made prisoner under the marshal's custody. I went on Sunday, 6 June, to Carfax church, and was placed where the mayor and aldermen sit. After service, Sir Ant. Cope, Bart., of Tangley, came up and said to me – 'Sir Wm. Walter, if I were not a good Christian, I would cudgel you; you are an unworthy fellow.' I made no reply, but appeal to you for relief. (petition of Sir William Walter)

Walter was a disaffected cavalier, who, in 1646, had paid a fine of £1,430 for 'deserting his Habitation, and assisting the Forces raised against the Parliament' (Fine, Sir William Walter). In 1655, following a failed royalist uprising led by John Penruddock, he had narrowly escaped arrest by Captain Unton Croke and Henry Smith when it was decided to purge Oxfordshire of a number of those who were considered undesirable. Writing to the Protector, Croke reported:

> In pursuance of your instructions, wee have seized the persons of the lord Lovelace' sir John Burlacie, sir Thomas Pope, John Osbaldiston, esq; who were included in the list sent us from your highnesse. Sir William Walter and col. Sands are, as wee heare, at London, and soe out of our reache. Wee have alsoe secured the lord of Falkland, George Nappier, Thomas Whorwood, Esq; who are dangerous and disaffected persons. (Croke, letter to the Protector)

It is unclear what Sir Anthony's grudge was about, but it is plausible that the dispute was linked to issues arising out of the operation of the royalist underground at the time.

One wonders if the arrival of their daughter Mary marked the final attempt at a large family. As both parents were still young, there may have been some medical reason for the lack of further births. Perhaps from 1656 onwards Sir Anthony's thoughts turned back to Hanwell and its grounds – and the consolations of natural philosophy. Certainly he had at least two remarkable individuals resident at Hanwell towards the end of the 1650s. One of them, Richard Allestree, was a royalist agent, so it is not surprising that Sir Anthony was signatory to a *Declaration of the County of Oxon* calling for the restitution of Members of Parliament who were expelled in 1648. Indeed he was part of the delegation that presented it to General Monck, in London, on 15 February, as was his step-father, William Cope (Beesley 1841, 474). During the course of Booth's rising, late in 1659, Sir Anthony further pledged his support for a 'free parliament'.

> The presenters of Oxfordshire's declaration, too, included names that the exiled court would have been glad to see. Lord Falkland, son of a famous royalist statesman and himself in close contact with the crown and regarded as a friend by it, headed the deputation to Monck. He and another of the presenters, Sir Anthony Cope, had worked together to promote the rising of 1659 (after which Falkland was imprisoned, though he was alleged to have 'betrayed' the conspiracy). (Worden 2020, 189)

Soon afterwards Sir Anthony was elected the member for Banbury to the Convention Parliament, which met in April that year and voted for the restoration of the monarchy. He was what M.W. Helms, Leonard Naylor and Geoffrey Jagger described as a 'moderately active member of the Cavalier Parliament' that was elected in 1661 (*HOP*). There is little evidence in his parliamentary career of the kind of interests that earned him the epithet of virtuoso. Sir Anthony was a captain of Foot in the regiment of Lord Falkland between 1661 and 1662 and may have served in Dunkirk along with his younger brother John. His later membership of Parliament was not without incident, and in August of 1671, the house was informed of another apparently unprovoked assault.

> [...] that Sir Anthony Cope, a Member of this House, was Yesterday in the Evening, stopt and assaulted by one Landisdall; who expressed contemptuous Words, in Breach of the Privilege of this House; viz. That, because he was a Member of this House, he would send him to the Compter.

> Ordered, That Landisdall the Beadle of Billingsgate Ward, living in the Parish of St. Mary Hill, in the City of London, be sent for in Custody of the Serjeant at Arms attending this House, for his Breach of Privilege of this House, in affronting Sir Anthony Cope, a Member of this House; and for contemptuous Words against this House. (Assault on Sir Anthony Cope)

One of his last public acts in London, which took place in 1673, on the anniversary of the Gunpowder Plot, was to lead a procession to burn, in effigy, the pope, a major event presented in the context of anti-Catholic sentiment at the time. In the aftermath of the Test Act, of 1673, the outing of the Duke of York as a Catholic, and the duke's recent remarriage to an Italian Catholic, Mary of Modena, Sir Anthony chose to align himself with what was to become the Whig faction, which supported constitutional monarchy and Parliament. The family's ownership of property associated with the Wool Quay in London involved them in the rebuilding of the Customs House after the Great Fire in 1666.

> the site of the new building was considerably larger than that occupied by its predecessor. Additional land was taken for the extension from Sir Anthony Cope, but it is to be noted that the building did not, as did its successor, extend northwards to Thames Street. A considerable strip of land was left on the north side, which was later occupied by two rebuilt taverns and a large warehouse owned by Sir Anthony. (Gater and Godfrey 1934, 31)

> Work was undertaken between 1668 and 1671 to a design by Christopher Wren, as his first major project within the city. There is some evidence of a collaboration between Cope and Wren, as the Treasury Minute book for 1667 notes that 'Sir Anthony Cope called in with Dr. Wrenne about building the new Custom House [London port], Sir John Wolstenholme being present. The matter in difference to be stated by Sir Robert Long et al. to-morrow.'

Things did not go altogether smoothly, for in January 1673 a letter was sent from the Treasury indicating an ongoing connection with Wren.

> Entry of the reference to Sir C. Harbord of the petition of Sir Anthony Cope for recompense for damage done him by the new building of the Custom House. Said Harbord is to examine what the King's right of building upon the old and new Wool Quay is and how far both the legality and equity of it does extend and to take a strict survey of the buildings and measures of ground, joining Dr. Wren with him herein. (Entry Book (January 1673), http://www.british-history.ac.uk/cal-treasury-books/vol4/pp37-55, accessed 14 January 2021)

Sir Anthony died in 1675, as Plot was compiling his *Natural History,* a work which may have bought him some small degree of posthumous fame. The cause of Sir Anthony's death is not recorded, but both his demise and his wife's descent into madness were much later ascribed, by the Rev. Leslie Ahrendt, rector of Hanwell, to grief at the loss of their children. In 1941 Ahrendt recorded translations from the Latin of the inscriptions on the tombs of two of Sir Anthony's offspring.

> Here lies a boy of high qualities and higher hope, Henry Cope, darling only son of the most noble Sir Anthony Cope, Baronet, and of Mary his wife. Seven years he lived here, and then he rested in the Lord to enjoy the eternal Seventh Day. During his eighth year the Lord took him on the Lord's day itself, June 8th, A.D.1662.

> Here at the feet of a beloved brother in death untimely to her family, yet timely to her, lies mistress Mary Cope, only begotten daughter of these same parents and their only hope. A virgin, she passed to the choir of virgins on the eve of the Annunciation of the Blessed Virgin Mary whose name she bore. She reached within a year of the same limit of life as her brother, and the same day of the week on which he died before her namely the Lord's Day, A.D.1671. (A/TC, Ahrendt 1941, 13)

These touching words with their emphasis on the loss of hope and the almost obsessive attention to the timing of their deaths suggests deep grief. Ahrendt goes on to write, 'Four years later, at the age of only forty three, their father

PLATE 1. The initial 'Voyage to the House of Diversion', approaching the island in the lake for the first time, on a foggy day, 15 March 2012.

PLATE 2. A team assembles. From left to right: Stephen Day, the author, Samuel Phipps, Verna Wass, Brenda Day, Rowena Archer and Christopher Taylor, 2 January 2013.

PLATE 3. Portrait of the antiquary Robert Plot, by Sylvester Harding.

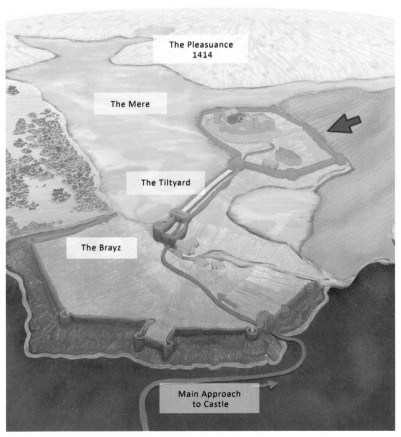

The Pleasuance
1414

The Mere

The Tiltyard

The Brayz

Main Approach
to Castle

PLATE 4. Kenilworth, the landscape, showing direction of attack in 1266. Background image by Lizzie Robertson.

PLATE 5. Domaine de Villarceaux, 17th-century water garden looking north.

PLATE 6. Giardino di Castelli, Florence, the fountain of Hercules by Ammannati.

PLATE 7. Giardino di Castelli, Florence, pipework above the Grotto of the Animals.

PLATE 8. Trinity College, Cambridge, fountain built in 1601.

PLATE 9. Armorial panel from Hanwell.

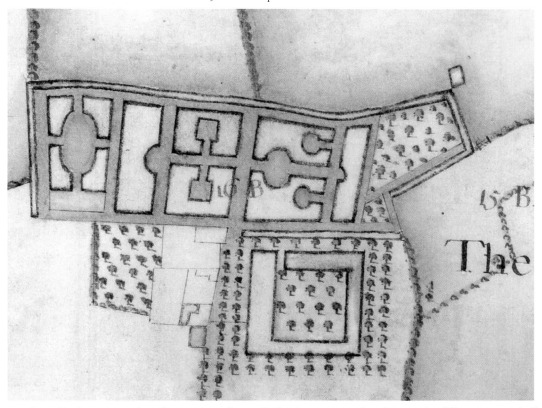

PLATE 10. Cope Castle, water gardens from survey of 1694. By kind permission, Royal Borough of Kensington and Chelsea Libraries.

PLATE 11. Heidelberg, painting of the *Hortus Palatinus,* by Jacques Fouquier, 1620.

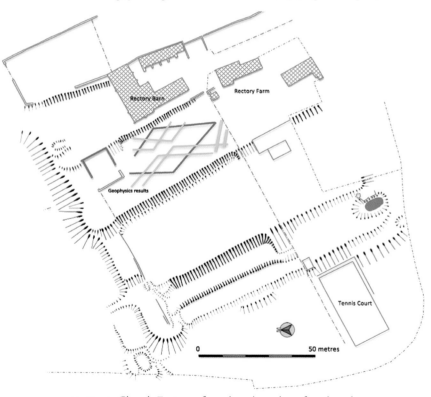

PLATE 12. Church Enstone, formal garden, plan of earthworks.

PLATE 13. Chipping Campden, view of garden earthworks and banqueting house looking north.

PLATE 14. Gardens of Masseys Court, Llannerch, painting of 1662. By kind permission, Yale Center for British Art, Paul Mellon Collection, USA.

PLATE 15. Portrait of the young Anthony and John Cope, probably painted around 1638. By kind permission of Bruern Abbey.

PLATE 16. Col. Wm. Cope of Icomb and Duck End, by kind permission of Phillip Mould.

PLATE 17. *The Crimson Bedchamber,* by Sir John Baptist de Medina; the seated figure to the left may be Baltzar. © NPL-DeA Picture Library/Bridgeman Images.

PLATE 18. Hanwell, the lake (Pond B) looking west towards the island.

PLATE 19. Hanwell, HANH 15, the lake (Pond B) side wall looking south.

PLATE 20. Hanwell, steps in north-west corner of Sunken Garden looking west.

PLATE 21. Hanwell, dam (Pond F) at south-east end of park looking west.

PLATE 22. Hanwell, HANA 13, 'Sir Anthony's Bath', looking north-east.

PLATE 23. Hanwell, HANB13, the cascade after excavation, looking south-west.

PLATE 24. Hanwell, HANK19, north wall of octagon with setting out trench, looking south-west.

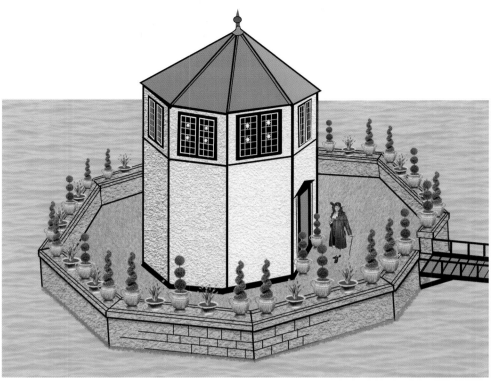

PLATE 25. Hanwell, reconstruction of the House of Diversion.

PLATE 26. Hanwell, HANK20, an intact example of pot type 2 being lifted in October 2020.

PLATE 27. Hanwell, garden urn P10 showing 'pancake' effect of impact.

PLATE 28. Reconstructed pots of types 3 and 4 on display in our pop-up museum, September 2021 open weekend.

PLATE 29. Pierrepont House, Nottingham, *c.* 1705. By kind permission, Yale Center for British Art, Paul Mellon Collection, USA.

PLATE 30. Pots depicted on embroidery from Stoke Edith, 1710–1720, © Victoria and Albert Museum, London.

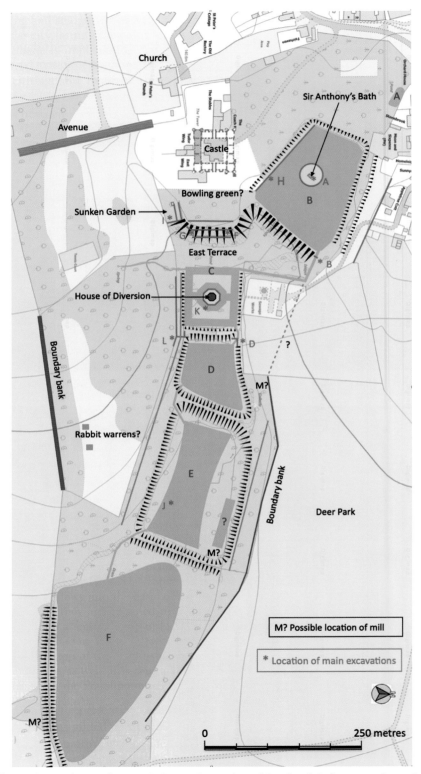

died of a broken heart. Their mother went out of her mind through grief and lived for another forty years. Perhaps it was she who caused the legend of the ghost of Hanwell Castle' (A/TC, Ahrendt 1941, 13). No sources are quoted by Ahrendt in support of his views. Ghost stories apart, it would not be surprising if, after the death of his last surviving son, in 1662, Sir Anthony threw himself into the development of his gardens over the next decade or so. What is puzzling is how few accounts or reports there are, apart from Plot's, of Sir Anthony's activities at Hanwell between the Restoration, in 1660, and his death, in 1675. As Roderick Floud (2019, 4) put it, 'The restoration of Charles II […] meant that there was spending of large amounts of public money on gardens and, by that means and through his own personal interest, gave a crucial boost to gardening by the wealthy and aristocratic.' Presumably Sir Anthony fits into this demographic.

Hanwell, Cope and Plot

Robert Plot was born near Sittingborne, in Kent, and matriculated at Magdalen College, Oxford, in 1658. He remained there until 1676, when he moved to University College, where he remained until his marriage, in 1690. Early in the 1670s he conceived the idea of continuing in the vein of Leland and Camp-den, 'being studious to make search after the Rarities both of Nature and Arts afforded in the Kingdome for the Information of the Curious and in order to produce an Historical account of the same' (Anonymous 1674). His method was to circulate a series of questionnaires to interested parties, many of whom were members of the Royal Society, with John Aubrey in Wiltshire being one of his first respondents. Added to this was a commitment to what today we would call field work. Beginning in the village of Cropredy, in the north of Oxfordshire, he systematically toured the county, which he had divided into sectors mainly on the basis of using rivers as boundaries (Mendyk 1985, 161). Plot defined his mission in the following terms:

> I shall consider, first, *Natural Things*, such as […] Animals, Plants, and the universal *Furniture of the World*. Secondly, her *extravagancies* and *defects*, occasioned either by the Exuberancy of Matter, or Obstinacy of Impediments, as in *Monsters*. And then lastly, as she is restrained, forced, fashioned, or determined, by Artificial Operations. All which, without Absurdity, may fall under the general Notation of a *Natural History*, things of *Art* (as the Lord *Bacon* well observeth) not differing from those of *Nature* in *form* and *essence*, but in the *efficient* only; Man having no Power over *Nature*, but in her Matter and Motion, *i.e.*, to put together, separate, or fashion Natural Bodies – and sometimes to alter their ordinary Course. (Plot 1705, 1)

Graham Parry (1995, 300) describes this as his 'attempt to produce a new style county history written in conformity with the Baconian values of the Royal Society'. Plot had become a member of the Royal Society and, from 1683, was its secretary and also editor of the society's *Philosophical Transactions*. This placed him, according to Mendyk (1985, 164), 'in direct contact with many of the leading British experimentalists'.

Plot wrote of Sir Anthony in uniformly positive tones. He was given the title 'naturalist' once and 'artist' twice. In this context, the term artist may have had a number of connotations in the seventeenth century: 'a person who pursues a craft or trade; a craftsperson, an artisan', 'a person skilled or proficient at a particular task or occupation; an expert', or, most intriguingly, 'A person skilled in magic arts or occult sciences; an astrologer, an alchemist' (*OED*). He was named 'virtuoso' twice and was described as 'great and eminent' on two occasions, but the most frequently used term was 'ingenious', which was employed three times. Ingenious is by far the most common term Plot used to express his appreciation of those he picked out to acknowledge some practical achievement. However, there are only two other instances of the use of virtuoso in Plot's *Natural History*. One refers to 'those Eminent virtuosi, Mr. Hook and Mr. Ray' (Plot 1705, 112). John Ray (1627–1705) was a well-known naturalist, whom Plot mentions on several occasions and who was noted, on 15 March 1675, as being in London with 'Hooke and Sir John Cope' (Raven 1950, xviii). This was just three months before the death of Sir Anthony. There is no information about what business they were conducting, so the reference remains a curious one. Plot (1705, 233) wrote of the two Roberts – Boyle and Hooke – in these terms: '[…] the most Learned and Ingenious, the Honourable *Robert Boyle* Esq. with the concurrent Help of that exquisite Contriver; Mr. *Robert Hook*'. The other virtuoso listed by Plot was Sir Thomas Pennyston. Plot (1705, 68), in describing investigations into a curious heavy white earth, wrote, 'We tried it also at *Cornwel*, in Sir *Thomas Pennyston's Laboratory*, because of its Weight with divers *fluxing Salts*, in hopes of some kind of *metalline* Substance, but all (as before) to little Purpose.' Clearly, in Plot's mind, virtuosi are characterised, to a certain extent, by their hands-on approach to scientific investigations, a viewpoint shared by his contemporaries. For example, writing in 1663 of Robert Boyle, Scottish physicist George Sinclair described him as 'so worthy and learned a virtuoso' (quoted in Craik 2018, 242). In looking at the totality of Sir Anthony's interests, as charted by Plot, we see that a slightly acerbic analysis of what it means to be a virtuoso, by Judith Drake, writing in 1696, could apply to both men.

> A Box or two of Pebbles or Shells, and a dozen of Wasps, Spiders and Caterpillers are his Cargoe. He values a Camelion, or Salamander's Egg, above all the Sugars and Spices of the West and East-Indies.... He visits Mines, Cole-pits, and Quarries frequently but not for that sordid end that other Men usually do, viz. gain; but for the sake of the fossile Shells and Teeth that are sometime found there […]

> To what purpose is it, that these Gentlemen ransack all Parts both of Earth and Sea to procure these Triffles? [...] I know that the desire of knowledge and the discovery of things yet unknown is the Pretence; but what Knowledge is it? What Discoveries do we owe to their Labours? It is only the Discovery of some few unheeded Varieties of Plants, Shells, or Insects, unheeded only because useless; and the Knowledge they boast so much of, is no more than a Register of their Names, and Marks of Distinction. (Drake 1696)

A more elevated view of a virtuoso, which could have been Sir Anthony's own guiding light, was voiced by Bacon almost a century earlier, in his *Advancement of Learning*.

> [...] men have entered into a desire of learning and knowledge sometime upon a natural curiosity and inquisitive appetite; sometime to entertain their minds with variety and delight; sometime for ornament and reputation; as if there were sought in knowledge a couch, where upon to rest a searching and restless spirit; or a terrace for a wandering and variable mind to walk up and down with a fair prospect; or a tower of state, for a proud mind to raise itself upon. (Spedding *et al.* 1857, 134)

Walter Houghton, in his early study of English virtuosi in the seventeenth century, argued that 'the virtuoso stops at the very point where the genuine scientist really begins'. He sums up his view that virtuosity was in some ways a brake on scientific progress.

> Wilkins, indeed, was called 'the principall reviver of experimental philosophy (secundum mentem domini Baconi);' and the master's lodgings at Wadham College was, I think, consciously associated with Solomon's House. Yet when we examine their study of automata and of optics, as compared with Bacon's in the New Atlantis, we find the clearest evidence for that dilution and distortion of the scientific mind which this essay has traced more than once to the spirit of virtuosity. (Houghton 1942, 194)

This would appear to be a little harsh in Sir Anthony's case, especially if we accept Plot's verdict that he had achieved a semblance of *The New Atlantis* at Hanwell, building on the activities of his 'Learned Society of Virtuosi' at Tangley.

The New Atlantis continued to be a concept to draw inspiration from throughout the latter part of the seventeenth century. Plot would certainly have been aware of R.H.'s (Robert Hooke's?) continuation of *The New Atlantis* and, even more topically, of Joseph Glanvill's (1636–80) essay of 1676. Glanvill, from a puritan household and an Oxford graduate, was described as 'the most skillful apologist of the virtuosi' (Westfall 1973, 18). His *Antifanatickal Religion and Free Philosophy* was sub-titled *Continuation of the New Atlantis* and offered 'an intellectual history and encomium of the Cambridge Platonists and latitudinarians' (*ODNB*). An instance of a practical attempt to realise *The New Atlantis* was documented by Andrew Agha (2020, v), who suggested that Anthony Ashley Cooper, 1st earl of Shaftesbury (1621–83) used the labour of enslaved people to develop 'his 12,000-acre Carolina estate, as the material manifestation of a Royal Society influenced laboratory'. Although Sir Anthony Cope of Hanwell was perhaps not widely recognised as such, Plot obviously thought that Cope had figured highly amongst such company.

Plot mentions Hanwell and the works of Sir Anthony eleven times in his *Natural History*, more than any other location outside the city of Oxford. However, there is a note of sadness tinting these references, as it is clear that, during the compilation of the book, Sir Anthony had died. Although Plot never explicitly states it, it is a fair assumption that Plot knew Hanwell well and probably visited several times. We can now examine these entries in more detail. in the order in which they appear in Plot's work.

Sir Anthony's Pebble

It can be assumed that, during the course of a visit to Hanwell, Plot was treated to a view of Sir Anthony's collection of rocks and minerals, presumably held in something like the cabinet of curiosities for which his great-great-uncle Sir Walter had been known, and possibly located in the House of Diversion.

> Of Pebbles there are some also *transparent* to be had around *Finstock* and *Nuneham-Courtney*; I found them also in the way between *New-Yate* and *Ensham*, but none comparable to what was shown me by that great *Virtuoso*, the Right Worshipful Sir *Anthony Cope* of *Hanwell*, [...] The *Pebble*, I remember, was about the Breadth off one's Hand, off a flat Form, and yet not much less than an Inch in Thickness, so clear and pellucid, that no *Chrystal*, that I ever saw yet, excelled it; so that had not its *Master*, the cautious *Artist*, took care to leave on it part of its outward Coat, few would have believed it had ever been a *Pebble*. (Plot 1705, 73)

The pebble on view was a sample of rock crystal. It is interesting, particularly in the context of the report that Sir Anthony's mill was capable of cutting stone, 'after the manner of lapidaries', that Plot credits him with a hands-on approach to preparing this specimen. Plot goes on to comment on the use of such materials in glass making and compares some Oxfordshire pebbles to those used by the glass-makers of Murano. He later describes George Ravenscroft's glassworks at Henley-on-Thames and the fact that some analysis of the materials used was undertaken by 'the Ingenious Dr. *Ludwell* formerly Fellow of *Wadham College*' (Plot 1705, 258). There is an important point here about the dating of some of the glassware excavated at Hanwell, explained by Christine MacLeod:

> In the spring of 1674 George Ravenscroft, a London merchant trading with Venice in currants, lace, and glassware, took out a patent for 'cristaline glass'. The patent covered his attempt to produce a closer imitation of Venetian glassware. Unfortunately, his new glass, because it contained an excess of alkaline salts (which salts gave such glass its name of 'soda glass'), was found to 'crizzle', that is, to become opaque and gray through countless hairline cracks. In the course of correcting the problem, in 1675–76, Ravenscroft chanced on lead oxide as an alternative to a large part of the salts. This produced the lustrous glass substance, lead crystal, that became the distinctive feature of high-quality English glass. (MacLeod 1987, 777)

Although the precise terms and dates of this innovation have been questioned, the fact that samples of both crizzled and uncrizzled glass have been excavated from amongst the debris of the House of Diversion reinforces data from other finds regarding the date of the building.

Sir Anthony's Cutlery

Shortly after his report of the translucent pebble, Plot notes that, in comparing some local conglomerates

> with the best *Jasper* and *Achat* [Agate] I have seen such as these, found about *Hampstead*, curiously wrought into Handles of Knives by that eminent Artist Sir *Anthony Cope*; to which few *Achats* might be compared, perhaps none preferred, either in the Polish, or variety of Colours. (Plot 1705, 74)

Whether these were on show or were wielded by Plot himself, perhaps in the course of dinner at Hanwell, is uncertain, but again it reveals Sir Anthony's special interest in geology. And clearly these items were produced at Hanwell rather than purchased elsewhere. Examples of cutlery of the period in the collection of the V & A offer some insight into the appearance of these knives and their usage.

> In the 17th century, sets of matching cutlery were still a novelty, and highly prized. The culture of the day demanded that they 'should not be merely polished and abundant but also rare and distinct.' It was the sign of a gentleman that he possessed cutlery made of unusual and valuable materials, and many knives, forks and spoons of this period have handles of agate, ivory, or other precious materials. (V & A Online catalogue)

Knife handles in agate, chalcedony and cornelian were part of the original collection at the Ashmolean Museum curated by Plot, but nothing is recorded of their origin (MacGregor 1983, 265). A similar collection was curated by Sir John Soane and is now on display in the Enlightenment gallery at the British Museum.

Sir Anthony's Fossil

Writing of a type of stone he termed '*Bucardites* our *Stones* like *Bull's Hearts*', Plot tells the following story:

> Of these I had one sent me by my worthy Friend *Robert Perrot* Esq; from *North-Leigh*, ten Inches round and near ten Pounds in Weight, which is the biggest of the kind that I have yet saw, except one that I found at Shutford, going up a little Hill East-ward of the *Town*, about 20 Pounds in Weight, though broken half away, curiously reticulated with a White spar-colour'd *Stone*, as in *Tab. 7 Fig. 4* which being much too heavy for my Horse-portage, was afterward upon my direction, fetch'd away by the Ingenious Sir *Anthony Cope*, since whose Decease it is come I suppose into the hands of his equally Ingenious Brother Sir *John Cope*, the Heir of his Virtues as well as Estate. (Plot 1705, 128)

Here we have further evidence of the interest, shared by the two virtuosi, in rocks, minerals and fossils, although Plot maintained that they were the product of mineral salts crystallising within rocks rather than relics of anything that had once been alive. We have no record of how Sir Anthony viewed these curiously shaped stones and even less of what his brother John made of what he inherited. Plot was able to have the fossil drawn, for it is ably illustrated in his *Natural History*, to the point where modern palaeontologists have been able to identify it as an example of *Homomya gibbosa* (Oxford Museum of Natural History, *Robert Plot*, exhibition leaflet (No date), p. 8), probably from a deposit of inferior oolite from the Middle Jurassic (Fig. 23). The fossil supposedly remained in the hands

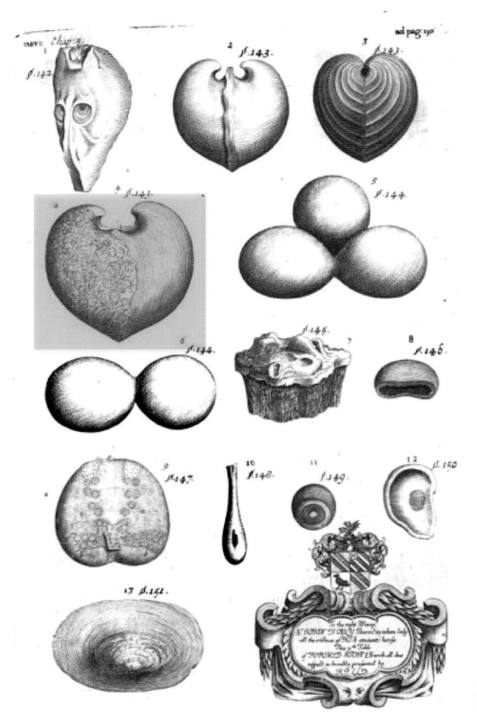

FIGURE 23. Plot's *Natural History*, Tab. VII, showing the Shutford fossil shaded.

of his brother John. This element of continuity is borne out by the dedication of the engraving 'TAB II':

> To the right Worshipfull
> The learned and curious
> Artist SIR JOHN COPE Baronet
> This Second Table
> of formed STONES whereof the 9th.
> and 10th. are found in his own grounds
> is humbly dedicated (Plot 1705, facing 93)

If Plot had recovered the Shutford specimen, one wonders if he might have also taken other items from Sir Anthony's collection, including the two specimens collected at Hanwell. However, writing in 1692, he makes it clear that he hopes one of his prize specimens is still in the custody of Lady Cope at Hanwell, so it appears that the collection was not passed on (Plot, letter to Edward Lloyd). Plot also records examples of a fossil he terms a 'selenite' from Hanwell, a further instance of Sir Anthony's collecting interests (Plot 1705, 84). The reference to the study of fossil sea urchins by the 'Learned Society of *Virtuosi*', which presumably included Sir Anthony, at the Cope property at Tangley is instructive.

> The *Center* of these *Rays,* by *Pliny* called *Modiolus,* by Aristotle, Umbilicus, is never placed on the Top of the Stone, but always inclining to one side, as that at the Bottom does to the other; the *Axis* lying obliquely to the *Horizon* of the Stone. Which gave Occasion to a Learned Society of *Virtuosi*, that, during the late Usurpation, lived obscurely at *Tangley*, and had then time to think of so mean a Subject, by consent to term it the *Polar-Stone,* having ingeniously found out, by clapping two of them together […] that they made up a *Globe.* (Plot 1705, 92)

Being at leisure contributed to their being free to study a subject that may have been viewed as comparatively trivial. Even so there is a measure of discussion resulting in the group being confident enough to offer their own nomenclature to the stones. Indeed it can be assumed that they are actively involved in searching for fossils in the area, as Plot also notes specimens of Brontiae being recovered from Tangley (Plot 1705, 91).

Sir Anthony's Elm

Writing of a particularly distinctive variety of narrow, small-leaved elm, Plot says,

> Of those there are plenty in the *Avenues* to the House of the Honourable the Lady *Cope,* the Relict of the most Ingenious Sir *Anthony Cope* of *Hanwell,* where there is a whole Walk of them planted in order beside others that grow wild in the *Coppices* of the *Park.* (Plot 1705, 161)

As well as simply noting the trees' presence, Plot also collected specimens, because, according to J.V. Armstrong and P.D. Sell (1996, 39), 'Robert Plot, an

Oxford antiquarian, discovered an elm at Hanwell Oxfordshire which he named *Ulmusfolio angustoglabro.* A specimen collected by Plot is in the British Museum and shows that it is a distinct species of small-leaved elm still found in northern Oxfordshire today.' Further investigations by C. Jarvis (2013) revealed that 'The Plot specimens that Peter Sell refers to appear to have come into Soane's herbarium comparatively early where they occupy one of the bound volumes (HS 113, ff. 1–186) held within the Natural History Museum's Botany Collections.' Given that a variety of small-leaved elm (*Ulmus plotii*) can still be seen in the park at Hanwell, the question whether or not these are descendants of the elms Plot collected from is an interesting one. Botanist M.A. Spencer (2013 pers. comm.) considered that this was certainly possible. Another vegetative curiosity still to be found within the garden is a colony of the rare broad-leaved ragwort (*Senecio sarracenicus*). Peter Llewellyn comments,

> Also known as Saracen's Woundwort and until recently known as *Senecio fluviatilis*, this European plant was introduced from the Netherlands or Germany around the 16th century when it was known as Saracen's Confound or Saracen's Comfrey. Like many of the *Senecio* genus it flowers in mid or late summer but this plant stands over 2 m tall. The flowers are obviously typically Ragwort and it usually grows in damp or wet areas. (Llewellyn 2020)

Again the possibility exists that this is maybe a long-term survival from a much earlier planting.

Sir Anthony's Mollusc

It easy enough to see how Plot would have become familiar with the Hanwell elms; however, it is a testimony to his diligence and systematic approach to gathering information for his book that he also busied himself identifying molluscs in the ponds.

> I found also in Ponds at *Bradwell, Hanwell,* and *Shotover-Forest,* as well as in *Rivers,* the *Mytilus flaminum maximus subviridis,* whereof I examined several in hopes of the *Pearls* to be found in them, mentioned by Sir *Hugh Plat* in the *Appendix* to his *Jewel-house* of *Art* and *Nature*; but I could not meet with any with *craggy rough* outsides, in which it seems they are only found (*ours* being all of them *smooth*) and so lost my Labour. (Plot 1705, 190)

The disappointed Plot was probably referring to the swan mussel (*Anodonta cygnea*), which as well as turning up in water-laid silts during excavations at Hanwell also maintains a healthy population in the lake to this day. His search would have been better directed towards the freshwater pearl mussel (*Margaritifera margaritifera*), a species of growing rarity and protected under the Wildlife and Countryside Act of 1981.

Sir Anthony's Clock

Plot was obviously very taken by Sir Anthony's water clock, or clepsydra, and includes a lengthy and detailed description of the mechanism and its workings.

The account follows on from his report on Wilkins's rainbow fountain at Wadham College.

> Nor can I pass by unmentioned, a *Clock* that I met with at *Hanwell*, at the house of the Right Worshipful Sir *Anthony Cope*, that moves by Water, and shews the *Hours*, by the rise of a new gilded *Sun* for every *Hour*, moving in a small *Hemisphere* of Wood, each carrying in their *Centers* the Number of some *Hour* depicted *black*; as suppose of *one* a clock, which ascending half way to the *Zenith* of the *Arch*, shews it a quarter past *one*, at the *Zenith* half *Hour*; whence descending again half way towards the *Horizon*, three quarters past *one*; and at last absconding under it, there presently arises another gilded *Sun* above the *Horizon* at the other side of the *Arch*, carrying in its *Center* the Figure *two*: and so of the rest. Which ingenious Device, though taken out of *Bettinus*, who calls it, *aquaria Automatis ingeniosissimi horarium operationem*: yet being since improved by that *ingenious Person*, and applied to other Uses, particularly of a *Pseudo-perpetual Motion* made by the descent of several gilt *Bullets* upon an *indented* Declivity, successively delivered by a Wheel much of the same Fabrick with the *Typanum* of the *Water-clock*, so that they seem still the *same*: I could not but in Justice take notice of it. (Plot 1705, 240)

The work Plot is referring to is *Aerarium philosophiae mathematicae,* by Mario Bettini (1582–1657), published in 1648. Bettini was part of what Mordechai Feingold (2003, vii) called 'the complex Jesuit encounter with the mathematical sciences during the seventeenth century'. However, the clock mechanism appears to be a design by a Jesuit professor, P. Francesco Eschinardi, who probably copied the idea from one Attilio Parisio, who had published details in Venice in 1598. It is contained in *Appendix Ad Exodium De Tympano,* attached as a supplement to Bettini's original work. While noting that water clocks are of a very ancient lineage, Silvio Bedini (1962, 115) comments that, in the seventeenth century, 'During the period of scientific exploration a "new" type was apparently introduced, consisting of a compartmented metal cylinder which rotated by the displacement of a contained fluid through one or more small openings in the partitions between the compartments.' Instead of the timing of the clock being regulated by an escapement, it was controlled by the rate at which the water was permitted to flow between compartments (Fig. 24). One of the most striking features of this clock, compared with other, contemporary time pieces, was that it would have operated smoothly and fairly silently, a fact celebrated in 1656 by the creation of such a timepiece by the Campari brothers for a sleepless Pope Alexander VII (Ibid. 128).

One slightly puzzling feature of Plot's account is the phrase 'that moves by water'. This is not the case with clocks modelled after the Bettinus/Eschinardi pattern. Although there are several water-powered designs described by the De Caus brothers, there are no accounts of any of them actually having been constructed in England. Evelyn also describes and illustrates a variety of water-powered timepieces and includes an observation about such an instrument in the possession of a Mr Greatorex (Evelyn 2001, 247). This is likely to be Ralph Greatorex (c. 1625–75), who was a well-known mathematical and

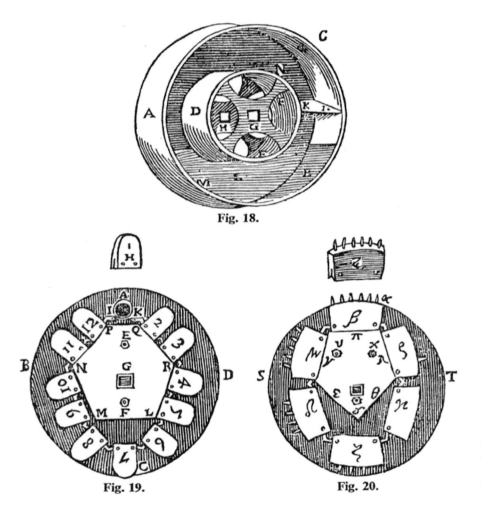

Fig. 18.

Fig. 19.   Fig. 20.

FIGURE 24. Eschinardi's *Appendix ad Exodium de Tympano,* figures showing internal workings of water clock.

scientific instrument maker with many contacts amongst the Oxford experimentalists (*ODNB*). A further design, published by the Royal Society in 1746, is unlikely to have been following the pattern of the Hanwell clock. Given that the *Appendix* actually specifies in considerable detail exactly how to produce such a timepiece, it is possible that Sir Anthony commissioned a local craftsman to make the clock based on the published material. In that connection it may be significant that in 1671 Sir Anthony presented a conventional mechanical clock to the village church, made by George Harris of Fritwell (Fig. 25). Cyril Beeson (1989, 39) noted, without giving his source, that Cope owned a copy of G. da Capriglia's *Misura del Tempo* of 1665, 'the earliest treatise on clocks, which describes and illustrates turret clocks'. The possibility exists that Sir Anthony may have also purchased one of Harris's lantern clocks. The finial on an example sold in 2006 bears a strong resemblance to an example excavated

FIGURE 25. Hanwell church, clock of 1671, by George Harris.

on the site of the House of Diversion in 2019. It is unclear who 'the ingenious person' was who generated 'pseudo-perpetual motion'. As we are still presumably in the realm of time keeping, this may be a reference to an early type of rolling-ball clock observed by Evelyn in 1655 (quoted in Ord-Hume 2005, 186). In what seems like a fortuitous survival, in *The Beauties of England,* published in 1764, Philip Luccombe states (1764, 139) that 'Hanwell-park, near Banbury; the Seat of Sir Jonathan Cope, Bart. where is a Clock that moves by water....', but the author then quotes Plot almost verbatim, so this is probably simply an instance of lazy reporting.

Sir Anthony's Net

Immediately after his account of John Wilkins's well-known transparent bee-hives, as installed in the gardens at Wadham College, Plot goes on to record, perhaps prompted by association, Sir Anthony's prowess at fishing.

> For *Fish,* I was shewed the model of a net contrived by the ingenious Sir *Anthony Cope,* that seemed likely to catch all found within such a compass. (Plot 1705, 263)

Fishing with nets was certainly the most common form of fishing as employed throughout the Middle Ages and into the early modern period for the large-scale exploitation of fish as a food resource. Markham (1657, 145) recommends the use of a 'shove net' when harvesting fish. Shove-, or push-, net fishing is still widely employed today, especially when collecting shrimps, and features a large net typically suspended on an arrangement of two or three poles. In the literature of the time, netting is seen as the poor commercial relation to the noble pastime of angling, as documented in such works as Tomas Barker's *The Art of Angling,* from 1659, and of course Isaak Walton's *The Compleat Angler,* of 1653. The authors of *The Countrey Farme,* published in London in 1616, celebrated the taking of fish 'by the angle, which is the most generous and best kind of all other, and may truly be called the Emperor of all exercises'. It is perhaps significant that, in turning his attention to the production of a net, Sir Anthony was demonstrating his concern with the technical and economic aspects of fishing above the pursuit of leisure.

Sir Anthony's House of Diversion

Plot's account of the 'Water-works' at Hanwell follows the report on the water clock.

> There are some other *Water-works* at the same Sir *Anthony Cope's, in* a House of *Diversion* built in a small *Island* on one of the *Fish-ponds,* Eastward of his House, where a *Ball* is tost by a *Column* of *Water* and artificial *Showers* descend at pleasure; within which they can yet so place a *Candle,* that though one would think it must needs be overwhelmed with *Water,* it shall not be extinguish'd &c. (Plot 1705, 240)

It is difficult not to associate this account with Plot's well-known engraving of the Enstone Marvels, which appears just a couple of pages later (Fig. 26). It is an image that is both useful and distracting. Here we undoubtedly have a small island in a pool, revetted in stone and approached by a timber bridge. Playing upon it are a variety of water jets, operated by a gardener and soaking a visitor. To what extent this image provides clues as to the appearance of Hanwell's near equivalent is debatable. After giving an account of the king's visit to Enstone, Plot writes:

> Which *Structure* with all the Ingenious Contrivances about it, continued in a flourishing Condition for some few Years, till the last unhappy *Wars* coming on, it became wholly neglected, and so sensibly decayed, till at last it lapsed (being next door to Ruine) into the Hands of the Right Honourable and truly *Noble Lord, Edward Henry* Earl of Lichfield, Lord of the *Soil;* who in the Year 1674 not only repaired the broken *Cisterns* and *Pipes,* but made a fair Addition to it, in a small *Island* situate in the Passage of a *Rivulet.* just before the Building set over the *Rock;* which though the last interaction, is yet the first that presents itself in then exterior *Prospect* of the whole Work *Tab. II* wherein the Figures

> 2. 2. *The* Island *in the middle of it.*
> 3. 3. *The* Pales *round it standing on a stone Wall.*
> 4. *An artificial* Rock *erected in the middle of the* Island *covered with living aqueous* Plants.
> 5. *The* Keeper *of the Water-work that turns the* Cocks.
> 6. *A* Canopy *of water cast over the* Rock, *by*
> 7. *an* Instrument *of* Brass *for that purpose.*
> 8. *A* Column *of* Water *rising about 14 Foot, designed to toss a* Ball.

FIGURE 26. The restored Enstone Marvels, from Plot's *Natural History*, Tab. 12.

9. *The Streams of Water from about 30* Pipes *set round the* Rock, *that water the whole* Island, *and Sportively wet and* Persons *within it; which most* People *striving to avoid, get behind the* Man *that turns the* Cocks *whom he wets with*

10. a Spout *of* Water *that he lets fly over his Head; or else if they endeavour to run out of the* Island *over the Bridge, with*

11. 12. *which are two other* Spouts, *whereof that represented at a 11, strikes the* Legs, *and that at 12 the* Reins *of the* Back.

13. *The* Bridge *over the Water lying on two* Trestles.

14. *The* Steps *leading into the* Grove, *and toward the* House, *where you pass by*

15. a Table *of black* Marble.

16. A Cistern *of Stone, with five Spouts of* Water *issuing out of a Ball off Brass, in which a small* Spaniel *hunts a* Duck, *both diving after one another, and having their Motion from the Water.*

17. *The way up into the* Banqueting-room *over the* Rock, *and other* Closets &c.

18. *The Passage between the* Cistern *and* Building.

19. *The iron* Grate *that gives Light to the Grot within.*

20. *The Passage down to the* Grot.

21. *The Windows of the* Banqueting-room.

22. *The* Grove *and* Walks *behind and on each End of the* Building. (Plot 1705, 241)

These new works at Enstone are likely to be a near contemporary to the construction of Hanwell's lesser wonders, yet the whole business of their recreation is a little perplexing. The 'truly *Noble Lord, Edward Henry* Earl of Lichfield, Lord of the *Soil*', born in 1663, was just eleven years old when he is said to have commissioned repairs to the site. This same year, 1674, he was created earl of Lichfield upon his betrothal to Charlotte Fitzroy, an illegitimate daughter of Charles II. Perhaps the refurbishment of the Enstone Marvels was thought to be an appropriate gesture towards the future nuptials of the two children. Edward Henry's father, Sir Francis Henry Lee, was 4th baronet of Quarrendon, a location where, as we saw, there was an extensive water garden. He died in 1667. His mother, Lady Elizabeth Pope, came from Wroxton, just 3 miles (5 km) from Hanwell. There must have been at least an acquaintanceship with the Copes, and perhaps even friendship with Sir Anthony's wife, Mary, who would have been of a similar age. Elizabeth's father, Thomas, was, as noted earlier, present at the christening of Sir Anthony's half-brother, Henry, at Bruern, in 1644. Presumably a senior member of the Lichfield household was responsible for actually overseeing the design and construction of the new island, but it is possible that his mother provided the guiding hand and may have been influenced by Sir Anthony's enthusiasms and the developments at Hanwell. Whatever the case, there was something distinctly old-fashioned about extending the range of *giochi d'acqua* available in Oxfordshire in the 1670s, but again, bearing in mind Charles II's close involvement with his daughter, there could also have been a sense of paying tribute to Charles I's patronage of the original works.

In comparing and contrasting the set-up at Hanwell and Enstone, we see that the common element is that of an island enhanced with significant amounts of plumbing. Both enjoyed the distinction of having a column of water which tossed a ball in the air, a common enough feature of earlier water works. The fact that at Hanwell 'showers could be made to descend at pleasure' without extinguishing a lit candle and that at Enstone the entire island could be watered argues for an extensive network of pipes, stopcocks and nozzles. What Plot's account of Hanwell conspicuously lacks is any sense that visitors could expect to get 'sportively wet'.

Plot's naming of the House of Diversion presumably repeated Sir Anthony's own usage, and indeed the term 'diversion' is used later, in brother John's will of 1713, in connection with the pursuit of scientific interests. There is also something of an echo of Bacon's 'House of Deceit' in *The New Atlantis*. As we have already seen in the case of the 'House of Salomon', the term house can mean more than a simple single structure; however, here, the context strongly suggests an enclosed, roofed space, a conjecture supported by the archaeological evidence. In the second half of the seventeenth century (*OED*), the word diversion refers to both 'The turning away of the thoughts, attention, etc. from fatiguing or sad occupations, with implication of pleasurable excitement' and 'an amusement, entertainment, sport, pastime'. A more succinct, modern definition is particularly helpful: 'making amusement out of study' (Domingo 2016, 1). Evelyn's comment in the opening paragraph in *Elysium Britannicum, Cap. IX, Of Fountaines, Cascad's, Rivulets, Camales, Piscina's and Water-workes* provides a suitably watery context for the use of the word.

> There is none comparable to Water, and of that especially which proceedes from the Living Fountaine, to refresh and irrigate the thirsty plants, to dispose and elevate into Fountaines, Girandolas, Cascades, Piscinas, and other innumerable pleasant and magnificent diversions. (Evelyn 2001, 169)

With this in mind, one might expect the phrase 'House of Diversion' to have been in common use in the seventeenth century, but in fact instances of usage of the term are extremely rare. In the archive *Early Modern Letters Online*, its searchable collection of more than 150,000 letters contains not a single instance of the words, nor, apart from references to Plot, does *Early English Books Online*. Two of the key references from the eighteenth century put a distinctly dubious gloss on the phrase. A sermon preached in London by Ferdinand Fina (1704, 5) to merchants trading with Spain used the term as synonymous with a play house: '*An Assembly and Conventicle of Atheists, of Lyars, and Deceivers, full of Iniquity and Vanity*'. In a farce by Isaac Bickerstaff, a character named Goose re-emphasises the seedy nature of such an establishment.

> You must learn to think more advantagiously, if you expect Prosperity here – But that I may not be tedious in my first Lectures, we'll quit this Conversation, and retire to a House of Diversion in the Hundreds of Drury; we'll drink 'till we rival the Sun with our ruddy Complexions; set up all Night with the Moon; lye with half a Dozen Virgins; break all the Windows of the Mansion; and then, like true Sons of Parnassus, make a hasty Escape, and pay no Reckoning, but leave that to be accounted for by the Gods. (Bickerstaff 1732, 5)

The closest usage for what we may imagine to be Plot's intention was published more than a century later, in 1787, in the memoires of the Italian playwright Carlo Goldoni, whose Masonic lodge was judged to be a

> 'little house of diversion', where one 'passes time tranquil all that gives pleasure […] honestly', but also, a cultural institution, a type of academy reserved for the 'bourgeoisie.' Two requirements of the conversation provided that each one has to apply himself to some art or science communicating to the others the insights he will have learned from his reading and that every meeting day one of the company would have propose some doubtful point, either economic, or mercantile, or scientific on which each one would give his opinion. (quoted in Del Negro 2003, 168)

The House of Diversion can, from Plot's account, be envisaged as an enclosed space within which Sir Anthony's waterworks were displayed, but it seems likely that it would also have functioned in a similar way to the many banqueting halls or houses incorporated into gardens of the period. Here one might expect to appreciate good conversation while admiring perhaps objects of natural curiosity and enjoying a range of food and drink served from a buffet.

Sir Anthony's Mill

Possibly an even more ambitious construction than the House of Diversion was an elaborately engineered water mill.

> At *Hanwell* in the Park, there its also a *Mill* erected by the ingenious Sir *Anthony Cope*, of wonderful contrivance, where-with that great *Virtuoso* did not only grind the *Corn* for his House, but with the same motion turned a very large *Engine* for cutting the hardest Stone, after the manner of *Lapidaries*; and another for boaring of *Guns*: and there, as in the *Mill* at *Tusmore*, either severally or all together, at pleasure. (Plot 1705, 269)

An early mill at Hanwell, known as Moor Mill, whose traces can be seen just under 1 km to the west, was in the hands of the Copes from 1538 until late in the eighteenth century. The mill had closed by 1895 (*VCH*). This cannot have been the extraordinary piece of engineering described by Plot, as it lay well outside the park. Both a sawmill for timber and a boring mill, to create water pipes from logs of elm, are illustrated in the Isaac de Caus volume *New and Rare Inventions of Water-works,* published in London, in 1659. These images may well have been the starting point for the construction of Sir Anthony's 'large Engine', although for cutting stone and boring guns one would imagine a further degree of robustness.

While water wheels for pumping water to garden features were not uncommon (they were used for this purpose at Hatfield and Wilton), such an overtly 'industrial' application is very unusual in a garden setting. Seemingly a slightly eccentric addition to one's garden, the siting of this mill, of such extraordinary capabilities, chimes well with the view taken by Bacon and later by Evelyn that there is knowledge to be had at the hands of those who, as artisans and craftspersons, pursue a trade. This view is also reflected in Evelyn's approach to the complex of mills at his family's own property at Wotton House, described by P.F. Brandon (1984, 76) as an 'archetypal rural workshop'. There is a clear echo here of Bacon's celebration of mechanisms in *The New Atlantis*:

> We have also engine-houses, where are prepared engines and instruments for all sorts of motions. There we imitate and practise to make swifter motions than any you have, either out of your muskets or any engine that you have: and to make them and multiply them more easily, and with small force, by wheels and other means.

At the time of writing, the position of this mill has yet to be located.

Sir Anthony's Structure

After identifying stately buildings in private hands, Plot makes a list, starting with Hanwell, writing,

> Whereunto might be added several *Structures* of the *minor Nobility*, that shew a great deal either of past or present Magnificence, such as that of the Right Worshipful Sir *Anthony Cope* late of *Hanwell*, of Sir *John Cope* at *Bruern* Abbey, the Lady *Spencer* at *Yarnton*. (Plot 1705, 271)

Sir Anthony's Paintings

In an almost throw-away comment, Plot draws attention to

> […] some remarkable Pieces of *Paintings* that we have here at *Oxon*; amongst which (to omit the *Deformation* of a *Caesar's* Head to be seen in the *Schools*), brought into Shape by a *metalline Cylinder*, and several others of the kind at *Sir John Cope's*. (Plot 1705, 279)

Although it is possible that Sir John purchased them himself, it is more likely that they were in the house at Hanwell. Sir John presumably inherited them from his brother. Such images, known as anamorphs, have a long history, dating back to the sixteenth century, and were often to be found in cabinets of curiosity. James Hunt (2000, 232) defines these as 'images of objects which have been distorted in some way so that only by viewing them from some particular direction or in some particular optical surface do they become recognisable'. Salomon de Caus touched briefly on these images in his *La Perspective avec la Raison des Ombres et Miroirs,* from 1612. Amongst the many books published on optics and perspective was a volume by Jean-François Niceron (1613–46) from 1638, which included detailed instructions for preparing anamorphs. The German scholar Athanasius Kircher (1602–80) produced a text in 1646 on experiments on geometry and illusion in his *Ars magna lucid et umbra*, which was studied at Oxford. In 1651 John Lydall (1623–57), a fellow of Trinity College, exhorted Aubrey to investigate, on the basis of Kircher's publication,

> how to draw pictures upon a cone so that to the eye rightly placed at one set distance they shall appear in a due proportion, at all others in a deformed. So like-wise how to draw them unlike upon a plaine, that being reflected from a cylindricall glasse, they may answer in a just symmetry & resemblance. (quoted in Frank 1973, 215)

In a further publication by Bettini, *Recreationum mathematicarum apiara novissima duodecim,* from 1642, which may have been known to Sir Anthony, there is a section on the creation of anamorphic images, including an illustration showing the head of Caesar brought into shape by a polished cone (Fig. 27).

The only other near-contemporary reference to Sir Anthony's interests comes post-mortem, in the minutes of a meeting of the Royal Society for 25 May 1681. Unsurprisingly, Robert Plot was in attendance.

> It was by several affirmed, that there were some English flints, which when polished, would be as beautiful as East-India stones: that Sir ANTHONY COPE had some such stones, which he took up at Bishops-Stortford, which being cut and polished seemed in the beauty, hardness and polish even to exceed the India Stones
>
> Mr. HENSHAW mentioned the stones of the same nature, which he had formerly brought from St. Alban's, and which were of as great a redness and beauty as those of Sir ANTHONY COPE, and were to be had of any desirable size. (Birch 1757, 88)

It is interesting that some six years after his death, at least some memory of his collection lingered on, presumably partly kept alive by Plot, although not exclusively so, as the 'affirmation' of Sir Anthony's polished stones comes from a number of people at the meeting. Plot appears to have maintained cordial relations with Sir John Cope after Sir Anthony's death, and it may be significant that when, in the late 1670s, he commenced work on his *Natural History of Staffordshire,* it was dedicated to the 'Right Honourable the Virtuous and most accomplished Lady, Jane Lady Gerard Baroness Gerard of Gerards Bromley, the first actual encourager of this design'. Jane Gerard was sister-in-law to Sir Anthony's widow, Mary.

FIGURE 27. Anamorphic image from Bettini's *Recreationum Mathematicarum.*

Sir Anthony's Companions

In order to make a successful claim that Hanwell at least shared some of the attributes of Bacon's *The New Atlantis,* it is necessary to populate the house and garden with Bacon's cast of potential 'mystery-men', 'pioneers', 'compilers', 'dowry-men' and, of course, 'inoculators'. Although the term was not used at the time, these individuals might usefully be called 'New Atlanteans'. One such man, Richard Allestree (1619?–81), was born 'the son of a decayed Derbyshire gentleman', as Beesley (1841, 471) rather engagingly puts it, in Uppington, Shropshire (Fig. 28). He entered Christ Church College, Oxford,

FIGURE 28. Richard Allestree, 1684 engraving by David Loggan.

as a commoner in 1636. In a rather congratulatory paragraph, in what John Spurr (*ODNB*) describes as 'the hagiographic biography', John Fell, Samuel's son, notes that

> Six months after his settlement in the University, Dr. Samuel Fell, the dean, observing his parts and industry, made him student of the college, which title he readily answered by great and happy application to study, wherein he made remarkable improvement; as a testimony and encouragement of which, so soon as he had taken the degree of Bachelor of Arts, he was chosen Moderator in Philosophy, and had the employment renewed year by year, till the disturbances of the kingdom interrupted the studies and repose of the University, putting them into arms. (Fell 1848, 2)

In 1642 Allestree enlisted in the royalist army, and he may have taken part in an early skirmish or two before returning to Oxford.

> According to his later biographers Allestree distinguished himself by his daring at this juncture. Saye's troops were seizing the treasure of the colleges and had locked the valuables found in the deanery at Christ Church in a chamber. Allestree, who had a key to the chamber, secretly removed these spoils overnight and would have been punished had not the parliamentarian forces left to join the earl of Essex's army. (*ODNB*)

Allestree returned to the army and fought at the battle of Edgehill, in October of that year. He was arrested by parliamentarian forces from Broughton Castle while on his way back to Oxford. Beesley (1841, 473) records that 'on the garrison of Broughton surrendering to the king's forces on the following Thursday, Allestree gained his liberty'. It is not clear how much time he spent serving under the royalist flag, but he was back in Oxford the following year and undertaking more teaching. All this came to an end in 1648, when he was disqualified, along with some 190 other fellows, from teaching, having refused to submit to the parliamentarian visitation. After a period as chaplain to Francis Newport, 1st earl of Bradford, participating in the ill-fated Battle of Worcester, in 1651 and lodging for a time in Oxford and associating with other royalist clerics, Samuel Fell and John Dolben, Allestree took on new accommodation.

> Sir Anthony Cope, a loyal young gentleman of considerable quality and fortune in the county of Oxford, prevailed upon him to live in his family; which he did for several years, having liberty to go or stay as his occasions required, whereby he was enabled to step aside without notice upon messages from the King's friends; which service he managed with great courage and dexterity. (Fell 1848, 11)

It is unclear exactly when Allestree moved to Hanwell. A letter dated 12 January 1656 from Elias Ashmole (1617–92) shows him to be abroad, as it requests him to seek out material on a former alchemist.

> Now if your Retourne lye neere any of the places before menconed (which I guess to lie in Tyrole, but our Maps aford us not the place) pray enquire after St Michaells Hermitage & take notice neere what Towne of Note the said Hermitage lyes (for further then Inspurge our Mapps will not enable me to trace it) as also enquire whether there be any (& what) remembrance of such an old man, or what storyes

the people thereabout haue left of him, or if you meete with any booke of Paracelsus that has the tytle of Cœna Domini, let it be conveyd hither for me, & I shall count my selfe much beholding to you. (Ashmole 1656)

This not only indicates, at the very least, a friendly acquaintance between the two men, but also presumably reflects on Allestree's own interest in alchemy. During the late 1650s it appears that he was using Hanwell as something of a safe house during the campaign to restore the future Charles II to the throne. Intriguingly, his occasional code name seems to have been 'Little Richard' (Routledge 1932, 135). One assumes he was collecting financial contributions from royalist sympathisers, smuggling them across the channel to the court in exile and returning with instructions and messages of thanks and encouragement. Beesley, referring to 'King James the Second's Papers', indicates something of the risks that all parties were running:

> The proceedings which were carried on from Hanwell were conducted with the strictest privacy. Indeed such was Cromwell's vigilance, that both Allestree and Sir Anthony Cope had good reason to exercise the utmost caution, lest the movements of the former should be traced. It is however certain that Allestree performed several difficult journeys to the King while in his exile. (Beesley 1841, 473)

That the dangers were real is borne out by events, in what Julian Whitehead (2009, 192) called 'uncertain and giddy times', when in 1658, ex-royalist commander Sir Henry Slingsby; a minister, the Reverend John Hewett; and three others taken at the Mermaid Tavern in London's Cheapside were executed for treason for doing little more than making ill-judged comments. On one occasion, during the winter of 1659, Allestree was arrested, in Dover, and imprisoned for several weeks, but the climate was changing rapidly, and a number of royalist friends were able to organise his release. He would almost certainly have been aware of the growing number of royalist conspirators in Oxford, one of whom was Sir Anthony's former tutor, Robert Saye, who made the quadrangle at Oriel College available for mustering should armed revolt break out in the city (Beddard 1997, 810). After the Restoration of Charles II, Allestree was made a canon of Christ Church Cathedral, and in 1663 he became a chaplain-in-ordinary to the king and later that year Regius Professor of Divinity. Finally, in August of 1665, he was appointed provost of Eton College (*ODNB*).

Allestree's theology as a churchman is characterised by Mark Purcell (1999, 126) as being 'whole-heartedly Arminian ['following the doctrines of Jacobus Arminius (1560–1609), a Dutch Protestant theologian, who rejected the Calvinist doctrine of predestination' (*OED*)]; he rejected the episcopalian Calvinism of the first half of the seventeenth century and clearly saw himself as a spiritual successor of the martyred (and Oxonian) Archbishop Laud'. There is no doubt at all that Allestree was also, when required to be, what today we might call 'a man of action'. As Fell (1848, 6) says, 'he thought it no disgrace to carry a musket and perform all duties of a common soldier, forward upon all occasions to put himself into action'. Allestree was responsible for a number of devotional works, of which the best known publication is *The Whole Duty of*

Man, published anonymously in 1657, a text that he may have been working on during his time at Hanwell. Paul Elmen (1951, 19) remarks that 'the authorship has been concealed with surprising success', although the writing of it could perhaps have provided Allestree with a good cover story if he had ever needed to explain his absence from Oxford. However, it was not simply as a theologian that Allestree excelled. The admittedly biased John Fell praises his

> deeper insight into all the parts of learning – the modern and learned languages, rhetoric, philosophy, mathematics, history, antiquity, moral and polemical divinity, all of which was not to be pumped up, or ransacked out of commonplace books, but was ready at hand, digested for his own use and communication in discourse to others. (Fell 1848, 19)

His library, now administered as part of the collection at Christ Church College, contains a number of his journals, which reveal in particular Allestree's expertise and interest in mathematics and include many detailed notes based on his study of astrology. This is something of a family speciality, as his uncle, also named Richard Allestree, was an almanac maker and mathematician, who published almanacs from 1617 until he died, in 1643 (*ODNB*). Another significant family connection was with the publisher James Allestree, who was probably a cousin, and who became, from 1663, an appointed printer to the Royal Society (Rivington 1984, 1). Allestree's subsequent devotion to the cause of learning seems wholly characteristic of the man, but what remains mysterious is that we have no record of visits to, or correspondence with, Sir Anthony once Allestree's time at Hanwell had come to a close. Nor has a careful examination of his hand-written notebooks revealed anything that could be viewed as a reference to Hanwell or any studies that may have been conducted there. Perhaps the habit of secrecy was a hard one to lose.

It was noted of Allestree by Fell (1848, 22) that 'To render himself secure from inordination of intemperance, he frequently abstained from lawful satisfactions, by the stated returns of fasting and abstinence, and continent in celibacy during his whole life.' Given this fact, one wonders how he got on with Sir Anthony's other known house guest for the period, the musician Thomas Baltzar, one whose career could surely be summed up in modern parlance as one of 'sex and drugs and rock and roll'. Thomas Baltzar (1631–63), a celebrated violinist, was, according to Evelyn, 'the most famous artist for the violin that the world had yet produced'. Born in Lubeck, Germany, from a family of musicians, he was briefly a performer at the court of Queen Christina of Sweden, before being recruited to come to England, possibly by Nathaniel Ingelo, a fellow of Eton College and a member of Bulstrode Whitelocke's 1654 embassy to Sweden (Holman 1984, 3). The first record of his performing in England comes in a diary entry for 4 March 1656 by Evelyn.

> This night I was invited by Mr. *Rog: L'Estrange* to heare the incomperable *Lubicer* on the Violin, his variety upon a few notes & plaine ground with that wonderfull dexterity, as was admirable, & though a very young man, yet so perfect & skillfull

as there was nothing so crosse & perplext, which being by our Artists, brought to him, which he did not at first sight, with ravishing sweetenesse, & improvements, play off, to the astonishment of our best Masters: In Summ, he plaid on that single Instrument a full Consort, so as the rest, flung-downe their Instruments, as acknowledging a victory: As to my owne particular, I stand to this houre amaz'd that God should give so great perfection to so young a person: There were at that time as excellent in that profession as any were thought in Europ: *Paule Wheeler, Mr. Mell* and others, 'til this prodigie appeared & then they vanish'd; nor can I any longer question, the effects we read of in *Davids* harp, to charm maligne spirits, & what is said some particular notes produc'd in the Passions of *Alexander* & that King of Denmark. (Evelyn 1955, 168)

This would no doubt qualify today as a five-star review, although it is obvious that some of the acknowledged professionals in the audience were less than enchanted by the performance. The violin was at the time considered to be rather a modern instrument, for which playing techniques were, in England, undergoing rapid change. As described by Mary Cyr (1995, 54), 'With the arrival of famous violinists from abroad, such as Thomas Baltzar and Nicola Matteis, the English were exposed to fresh influences. The holding of the bow (the bow grip), the placement of the instrument against the body, the kinds of sonorities used on the instrument, all underwent decisive changes.' Baltzar is listed amongst the performers for a production of the opera *The Siege of Rhodes,* by Sir William Davenant, staged in the summer of 1656 at Rutland House, in Charterhouse Yard, and Anthony Wood recorded a performance at Cambridge in 1658, the same year that Baltzar arrived in Oxford. At this point, Baltzar was, according to Wood,

entertained by Sir Anthony Cope of Hanwell House, Banbury, Bart., with whom he continued about two years; and in that time we had his company several times in Oxon where, playing in consort or division he would run up his fingers to the end of the fingerboard of his violin and run them back insensibly and all in alacrity and in very good tune which some there never saw the like before. (quoted in Holman 1984, 8)

Peter Holman suggests that for Sir Anthony, 'evidently Baltzar was a human addition to his collection of marvels'. There are no obvious reasons why Baltzar should have moved in with the Copes except that there may have been a family connection with Roger Le Strange, the promotor of the London concert, as Sir Anthony's great-grandfather had married one Anne Le Strange. The first documented performance in Oxford was on Saturday 24 July 1658, and Wood was there.

Thomas Balsar or Baltzar, a Lubecker borne, and the most famous artist for the violin that the world has yet produced, was now in Oxon: and this day A[nthony] W[ood] was with him and Mr Edward Low, lately organist of Ch[rist] church, at the meeting house of William Ellis. A. W. did then and there, to his very great astonishment, heare him play on the violin. He then saw him run up his fingers to the end of the finger board of the violin and run them back insensibly, and all with alacrity and in very good tune, which he nor any in England saw the like before. A. W. entertain'd him and Mr Low with what the house could then afford, and afterwards he invited them to the tavern; but they being engag'd to goe to other company, he could no more heare him play or see him play at that time.

Afterwards he came to one of the weekly meetings at Mr Ellis's house and he played to the wonder of all the auditory: and exercising his fingers and instrument several wayes to the utmost of his power, Wilson thereupon, the public professor (the greatest judg of musick that ever was) did, after his humoursome way, stoop downe to Baltzar's feet, to see whether he had a huff on, that is to say to see whether he was a devill or not, because he acted beyond the parts of man. (Kiessling 2009, 59)

Perhaps the most significant of the reports in connection with this study is that of a concert given at the behest of John Wilkins at Wadham College. Again Wood reports.

About that time it was that Dr John Wilkins, warden of Wadham Coll, the greatest curioso of his time, invited him and some of the musicians to his lodgings in that Coll. purposely to have a consort and to see and heare him play. The instruments and books were carried thither, but none could be perswaded to play against him in consort on the violin. At length the company perceiving A. W. standing behind, in a corner neare the door, they haled him in among them, and play forsooth he must against him. Whereupon he being not able to avoid it, he took up a violin and behaved himself as poor Troylus did against Achilles. He was abash'd at it, yet honour he got by playing with, and against such a grand master as Baltzar was. Mr Davis Mell was accounted hitherto the best for the violin in England as I have before told you; but after Baltzar came into England and shew'd his most wonderful parts on that instrument, Mell was not so admired; yet he played sweeter, and was a well bred gentleman and not given to excessive drinking as Baltzar was. (Ibid., 59)

Baltzar was living at Hanwell while giving concerts in Oxford, and accounts of attendees at his performances reveal the presence of several key players in the development of new scientific thinking and practices. Upon the Restoration of Charles II, Baltzar was appointed, in September 1660, to the King's Private Music. Less than two years later he was dead. Initially Wood recorded this as being the result of 'the French pox [syphilis] and other distempers' although he later changed his mind and noted that

This person being much admired by all lovers of musick, his company was therefore desired; and company, especially musicall company, delighting in drinking, made him drink more than ordinary which brought him to his grave. (Ibid., 96)

The household that Sir Anthony's wife, Mary, presided over in the late 1650s at Hanwell must have been a remarkable one, assuming she was indeed around and not away in one of the other family properties. It is possible that Allestree was reflecting on this *ménage* when he commented on 'The soul imprisoned in this house of clay [...] as if a fiddler should play in a dungeon' (Allestree Collection M.3.23 22).

As well as practising, and no doubt drinking, for long hours, Baltzar almost certainly composed a number of pieces during his time at Hanwell, including a set of Divisions in D minor from 1659 (Holman 1984, 16). A selection of his music is amongst the manuscripts in Christ Church Music Library and was recorded by Peter Wood in 2008. There was a painting in the possession of Lord St Oswald of Nostell Priory, in Yorkshire, entitled *The Crimson Bedchamber, portrait group of gentlemen with musical instruments,* that was traditionally said to depict the 'Cabal' Ministry of King Charles II and to have been painted by Sir John Baptist de Medina (1659–1710). Holman (1984, 33) makes a strong case that in fact this is a portrayal of the king's musicians from the early 1660s, in which case the seated figure to the left may be Baltzar (Plate 17).

However remarkable these two men were and whatever kind of relationship they may have had, they hardly constituted a community. Given that Plot was writing fifteen years after they had departed Hanwell and that he mentions neither of them in his *Natural History* rather suggests that they were not on his mind when he made his comparison to *The New Atlantis*. One individual whom Plot could possibly have been acquainted with was a shepherd from Hanwell named John Claridge, the author of a publication dating from 1670 entitled *The Shepherd's Legacy*. The pamphlet deals with his abilities in weather forecasting, wife choosing and curing sheep of such conditions as 'black-winds', 'water-canker' and 'liver-rot'. A number of his recipes appear very similar to examples noted by Allestree in some of his notebooks. Tellingly, in the preface, Claridge describes how he has been 'importuned by sundry friends (some of them being worthy persons) to make public his work'. It seems likely that, as Claridge was an inhabitant of Hanwell, one of these 'worthy persons' was Sir Anthony Cope. The fact that an individual as 'humble' as a shepherd could publish his observations on natural phenomena and indeed have them printed in London suggests local patronage and possible subsidy. However, while there are interesting echoes of Plot's observations of the weather, Claridge gets no mention in *Natural History*. Except for a pair of able-seamen from Bristol, Plot's authorities tend to be either ancient authors or university men. In tracking down the historical personage of John Claridge, we can note that in 1660 a weaver of that name is recorded as living in the adjacent parish of Bourton (Oxfordshire History Centre, Misc. Pe. V/4, 5). A memorandum in the parish register dated 31 August 1662, about the public reading of George Ashwell's certificate in connection with the Act of Uniformity, was signed by John Claridge as a church warden (Oxfordshire History Centre, PAR122). On 9 May 1693 a John Claridge is listed as a legatee in the will of William Hawtin, a weaver from Horley. 'To my brother John Claridge of Hanwell £5. If my brother John Claridge don't live it is to go to his son Samuell Claridge' (William Hawtin, will, probate, July 1697). If this Claridge is the author of the pamphlet, he must have been quite elderly. Given that the tract published in 1670 claims 40 years' 'on-the-job' experience, he was probably born around 1620. By 1841 John Claridge had become, according to Beesley (1841, 526), 'only an apocryphal person'. However, a thorough attempt to save Claridge from obscurity was made by W.E. Rye, in the 1853 edition of Notes and Queries. The work was originally published in London by John Hancock Junior, at 'The Three Bibles in Popes-head-ally next Cornhill'. A search through his other publications fails to turn up any other volumes with a possible connection to north Oxfordshire or Sir Anthony Cope. Keith Thomas (1972, 282) gives a brief account of John Claridge, suggesting that his weather predictions were aligned with 'the magician's art of fortune telling'.

A further potential member of Sir Anthony's community of 'New Atlanteans' was the royalist cleric George Ashwell (1612–94). Ashwell attended Wadham College, where he became fellow librarian and sub-warden, from 1629 to 1648, when he was probably ejected by the parliamentarian visitors. Anthony Wood (1848, 396) described him as 'a quiet and pious man […] well read in the fathers and schoolmen' and as 'a noted tutor'. It is possible that during his time at Oxford he made the acquaintance of the young Sir Anthony. After a period as curate in Westwood, Worcestershire, Ashwell succeeded Robert Harris to the living of Hanwell, in 1658. Beesley suggests that he was chaplain to Sir Anthony before his appointment. There is no doubt that Ashwell was a scholar with several works of divinity to his name, as well as a translation of *The History of Hai Eb'n Yockdan, An Indian Prince: Or, the Self-Taught Philosopher,* published in London and Banbury in 1686. Ashwell's approach to this work may be summed up in that he 'cut out most philosophical elements from the narrative to create an Orientalist easy-read. But by adding after the text a theological pamphlet entitled "The Book of Nature," Ashwell also turned Ibn Tufayl's discourse into a defence of "natural religion"' (Ferlier and Gallien 2019, 1). Since he was an advocate of natural religion, one might have expected him to have shared some of Sir Anthony's enthusiasm for natural philosophy; however, his unfortunate experience in the garden at Wadham, recorded earlier, may have made him a little reluctant to become too involved. His *Gestus Eucharisticus,* published in 1663, is dedicated to 'the Right Worshipful, His Worthily Honoured Patron, Sir Anthony Cope of Hanwell, Baronet'. In the dedicatory epistle Ashwell speaks of Sir Anthony in these terms:

> As to the choice of the Person, to whose Protection I have made bold to recommend so inconsiderable a Treatise; the very Title in the Front of this Epistle will, I hope, either defend or Excuse me to the World, though the Discourse itself be unworthy of his Acceptance. For the very name of Patron is a Sufficient Evidence of my Obligations, and may justly claime whatsoever I can do in this kind, as a Testimonial of my Gratitude; which I must shew as I can, when I cannot as I would. And your Noblenesse, I well know, looks not so much at the Greatness of the Gift, as the good will of the Giver. […] I have nothing more to adde, but what I am bound upon all good occasions to remember; my hearty prayers for a Blessing upon Your Self, your Noble Lady, and all the Branches of your Ancient Family. And more especially, at this present, that God would so prosper your counsels and endeavours for the Public Peace. (Ashwell 1663)

Clearly it is in the nature of such dedications to offer fulsome praise to one's patron, but in this instance there seems to be a particular warmth, possibly engendered by sympathy for the death of Henry, Sir Anthony's only surviving son, in 1662. Given that shortly after Ashwell's appointment we have Richard Allestree and Thomas Baltzar in residence, his incumbency as a 'quiet, unassuming fair-minded man' may, at the very least, have been a soothing presence. Further evidence of Ashwell's acquaintanceship with Allestree comes from the fact that a manuscript, 'borrowed of Mr. Ashwell', and presumably not returned, exists in the Allestree Library at Christ Church. To what extent Ashwell shared Allestree's Arminian enthusiasms is uncertain, although Daniella Bianchi (1985, 112) describes Ashwell as 'an English, Catholic controversialist' in connection with his anti-Socinian Oxford publication, *De Socino et Socinianismo Dissertatio,* of 1679. One assumes that his presence was further valued, as Sir Anthony and his family met the challenges of infant mortality, family disputes and ultimately Sir Anthony's final illness and death, together with the mental health problems that may have plagued his wife, Mary. While no doubt theological discussion and debate were a part of Sir Anthony's day-to-day contacts with Ashwell, we have no evidence to suggest that such conversations played an unusually significant part in discourses at Hanwell, unlike, for example, was the case for an earlier circle that met in the Oxfordshire village of Great Tew.

A serious issue in terms of establishing Sir Anthony's credentials as the patron of a *New Atlantis* is that, from 1660 onwards, we have no other instance of his playing host to, or even making contact with, any of the many individuals who would undoubtedly have shared his interests. Andrea Rusnock (1999, 156) notes, of the Royal Society, that 'Communications from far-flung correspondents became part of the Society's practice following Henry Oldenburg's initiative in the 1660s and 1670s.' However extensive that correspondence may have been, Sir Anthony does not appear to have participated in any of it. Indeed one might have expected him to have become an early member of the Royal Society, but he did not.

Bibliography

Agha, A., *Shaftesbury's Atlantis*, PhD thesis, University of South Carolina (2020)

Ahrendt, L.W.A., *Hanwell Heritage: Notes on the History and Architecture of the Parish* (1941), A/TC, duplicated leaflet.

Allestree Collection Christ Church, Oxford, M.3.23 22

Anonymous, *Proceedings at Banbury Since the Ordnance Went Down for the Lord Brooks to Fortify Warwick Castle* (1642), quoted in Beesley, A. *History of Banbury* (London, 1841)

Anonymous, 'Oxford Testimonial to Dr. Plot', 25 July 1674, quoted in Gunther, R., *Science in Oxford*, vol. 12 (Oxford, 1939)

Armstrong, J.V. and Sell, P.D., 'A Revision of the British Elms: The Historical Background', *Botanical Journal of the Linnean Society* 120 (1996)

Ashmole, E., letter to Richard Allestree (1656) http://emlo.bodleian.ox.ac.uk/profile/work/daa63344-8bfe-4dff-80ef-9509d19b5715?sort=date-a&rows=50&people=All-

estree&baseurl=/forms/advanced&start=1&type=advanced&numFound=6, accessed 2 February 2021

Ashwell, G., *Gestus Eucharisticu*s (Oxford, 1663)

Assault on Sir Anthony Cope (18 April 1671), http://www.british-history.ac.uk/commons-jrnl/vol9/pp236-237, accessed 11 January 2021

Aubrey, J., *Brief Lives,* ed. Bennett, K. (Oxford, 2015)

Bacon, F., *The New Atlantis* (originally published London, 1626), in Bruce, S. (ed.) *Three Early Modern Utopias: Utopia, New Atlantis and The Island of Pines* (Oxford, 2008)

Bacon, F., *The Works of Francis Bacon*, eds Spedding, J., Ellis, R. and Heath, D.D. (London, 1857–74)

Beddard, R., 'Restoration Oxford', in Tyacke, N. (ed.) *The History of the University of Oxford, Vol. IV Seventeenth-Century Oxford* (Oxford, 1997)

Bedini, S., 'The Compartmented Cylindrical Clepsydra', *Technology and Culture* 3(2) (1962)

Beeson, C., *Clockmaking in Oxfordshire 1400–1850* (Oxford, 1989)

Bettini, M., *Recreationum mathematicarum apiara novissima duodecim: Quæ continent militaria, stereometrica, conica, & novas alias jucundas praxes ac theorias, in omni mathematicarum scientarum genere* (Bologna, 1642)

Bianchi, D., 'Some Sources for a History of English Socinianism: A Bibliography of 17th Century English Socinian Writings', *Topoi* 4 (1985)

Bickerstaff, I., *The Modern Poetasters: or, Directors no Conjurers. A Farce. On the Famous Ode Writers, Satyrists, Panegyrists, &c. of the Present Times* (London, 1721)

Bill, E.G.W., *Education at Christ Church, Oxford 1660–1800* (Oxford, 1988)

Birch, T., *The History of the Royal Society of London for Improving of Natural Knowledge from Its First Rise, in Which the Most Considerable of Those Papers Communicated to the Society, Which Have Hitherto Not Been Published, Are Inserted as a Supplement to the Philosophical Transactions*, Vol. 4 (London, 1757)

Brandon, P.F., 'Land, Technology and Water Management in the Tillingbourne Valley, Surrey, 1560–1760', *Southern History* 6 (1984)

Claridge, J. *The Shepherd's Legacy* (1670), Met Office Archives, https://digital.nmla.metoffice.gov.uk/file/sdb%3AdigitalFile%7C656f7d4c-f4cc-489f-a199-8a9f16f41320/, accessed 15 March 2021

Clarke, S., *The Lives of Two and Twenty English Divines* (London, 1660)

Craik, A., 'The Hydrostatical Works of George Sinclair (c.1630–1696): Their Neglect and Criticism', *Notes and Records of the Royal Society Journal of the History of Science* 72(3) (2018)

Croke, U., letter to the Protector (1655), http://www.british-history.ac.uk/thurloe-papers/vol3/pp514-528, accessed 11 January 2021

Cyr, M., 'Violin Playing in Late Seventeenth-Century England: Baltzar, Matteis, and Purcell', *Performance Practice Review* 8(1) (1995)

De Caus, I., *New and Rare Inventions of Water-Works: Shewing the Easiest Waies to Raise Water Higher Than the Spring. By Which Invention the Perpetual Motion Is Proposed Many Hard Labours Performd and Varieties of Motions and Sounds Produced a Work Both Usefull Profitable and Delightful for All Sorts of People* (London, 1659)

De Caus, S. *La Perspective avec la Raison des Ombres et Miroirs* (London, 1612)

Del Negro, P., 'Carlo Goldoni and Venetian Freemasonry', *Italica* 80(2) (2003)

Domingo, D., *The Rhetoric of Diversion in English Literature and Culture, 1690–1760* (Cambridge, 2016)

Drake, J. (attr. Mary Astell), *An Essay in Defence of the Female Sex, in Which Are Inserted the Characters of a Pendant, a Squire, a Beau, a Vertuoso, a Poetaster, a City-Critick* (London, 1696)

East India Company, court minutes (May 1626), pp. 192–205, http://www.british-history.ac.uk/cal-state-papers/colonial/east-indies-china-japan/vol6/pp192-205, accessed 17 January 2021

Elmen, P., 'Richard Allestree and *The Whole Duty of Man*', *The Library* 5(1) (1951)

Estienne, C., Liébault, J., Markham, G. and Surflet, R., *Maison rustique, or, The Countrey Farme* (London, 1616)

Feingold, M., 'The Mathematical Sciences and New Philosophies', in Tyacke, N. (ed.) *The History of the University of Oxford, Volume IV: Seventeenth-Century Oxford* (Oxford, 1997)

Feingold, M. (ed.), 'The New Science and Jesuit Science: Seventeenth Century Perspectives, Archimedes', *New Studies in the History and Philosophy of Science and Technology* 6 (2003)

Fell, J., *The Life of Allestree* (London, reprint 1848)

Ferlier, L. and Gallien, C., '"Enthusiastick" Uses of an Oriental Tale: The English Translations of Ibn Tufayl's Hayy Ibn Yaqdhan in the Eighteenth Century', in Gallien, C. and Niayesh, L. (eds) *Eastern Resonances in Early Modern England: New Transculturalisms, 1400–1800* (London, 2019)

Fina, F., *A Sermon upon the Occasion of the Late Storm* (London, 1704)

Floud, R., *The Economic History of the English Garden* (London, 2019)

Frank, R., 'John Aubrey, F.R.S., John Lydall, and Science at Commonwealth Oxford', *Notes and Records of the Royal Society of London* 27(2) (1973)

Fraser, A., *The Weaker Vessel, Woman's Lot in Seventeenth-Century England* (London, 1984)

French, J.M., *Milton in Chancery: New Chapters* in *the Lives of the Poet and His Father* (New York, 1939)

Gater, G.H. and Godfrey, W. (eds), 'Custom House Quay and the Old Custom House', in *Survey of London: Vol. 15, All Hallows, Barking-by-the-Tower, Pt II* (1934)

Hamilton, C., 'A Description of a Clepsydra or Water-Clock', *Philosophical Transactions* 44 (1746)

Hawtin, W., will, probate (July 1697), Banbury, http://wills.oxfordshirefhs.org.uk/az/wtext/hawtin_003.html, accessed 15 March 2021

Holman, P., 'Thomas Baltzar (?1631–1663), the "Incomparable *Lubicer* on the Violin"', *Chelys: The Journal of the Viola da Gamba Society* 13 (1984)

HOP, Helms, M.W. Naylor, L. and Jagger, G., 'Sir Anthony Cope (1632–75)'

HOP, Davidson, A. and Sgroi, R., 'Cope, Sir William (1577–1637)'

Houghton, W., 'The English Virtuoso in the Seventeenth Century: Part II', *Journal of the History of Ideas* 3(2) (1942)

Hunt, J.L., Nickel, B.G. and Gigault, C., 'Anamorphic Images', *American Journal of Physics* 68(3) (2000)

Kiessling, N.K. (ed.), *The Life of Anthony Wood in His Own Words* (Oxford, 2009)

Kircher, A., *Ars magna lucid et umbra* (Rome, 1646)

Llewellyn, P., 'Senecio sarracenicus: Broad-leaved ragwort'. https://www.ukwildflowers.com/Web_pages/senecio_sarracenicus_broad_leaved_ragwort.htm, accessed 11 November 2020

Luckombe, P., *The Beauties of England: or, a Comprehensive View of the Antiquities of This Kingdom; the Seats of the Nobility and Gentry; the Chief Villages, Market Towns, and Cities; Intended as a Travelling Pocket Companion* (London, 1764)

MacGregor, A., *Antiquities from the Foundation Collection of the Ashmolean Museum*, PhD thesis, University of Durham (1983)

MacLeod, C., 'Accident or Design? George Ravenscroft's Patent and the Invention of Lead-Crystal Glass', *Technology and Culture* 28(4) (1987)

Mendyk, S., 'Robert Plot: Britain's "Genial Father of County Natural Histories"', in *Notes and Records of the Royal Society of London* 39(2) (1985)

Miscellanea Genealogica et Heraldica New Series 1 (1874)

Niceron, J., *La perspective curieuse avec l'optique et la catoptrique* (Paris, 1652)

ODNB, Bendall, S., 'Greatorex, Ralph (c. 1625–1675)'

ODNB, Burns, W., 'Glanvill [Glanville], Joseph (1636–1680)'

ODNB, Dixon, P., 'Ashwell, George (1612–1694)'

ODNB, Spurr, J., 'Allestree, Richard (1621/2–1681)'

Ord-Hume, A., *Perpetual Motion: The History of an Obsession* (Kempton, 2005)

Oriel College Archive, TF 1 E1/6, Buttery Book, 1648–49

Oxford Museum of Natural History, *Robert Plot*, exhibition leaflet (no date)

Oxfordshire History Centre, Misc. Pe. V/4, 5, Cropredy Par. Rec., tithe books

Oxfordshire History Centre, PAR122, Parish of Hanwell, church registers vol. 1 (1586–1753)

Parry, G., *The Trophies of Time: English Antiquarians of the Seventeenth Century* (Oxford, 1995)

Plot, R., letter to Edward Lloyd, quoted in Gunther, R., *Early Science in Oxford*, vol. 12 (London, 1920)

Plot, R., *The Natural History of Staffordshire* (Oxford, 1705)

Purcell, M., '"Useful Weapons for the Defence of That Cause": Richard Allestree, John Fell and the Foundation of the Allestree Library', *The Library* 6(2) (1999)

Raven, C., *John Ray: Naturalist His Life and Works* (Cambridge, 1950)

Rivington, C., 'Early Printers to the Royal Society 1663–1708', *The Royal Society Journal of the History of Science* 39 (1984)

Routledge, F., *Calendar of the Clarendon State Papers Preserved in the Bodleian Library, Vol. IV 1657–1660* (Oxford, 1932)

Rusnock, A., 'Correspondence Networks and the Royal Society, 1700–1750', *British Journal for the History of Science* 32(2) (1999)

Rye, W.B., 'The Shepherd of Banbury's Weather Rules', *Notes and Queries* 181 (1853)

Thomas, K., *Religion and the Decline of Magic* (London, 1972)

TNA, PROB 11/175/196 (will, Sir William Cope of Hanwell, Oxfordshire, 26 October 1637)

TNA, PROB 11/350/249 (will, Sir Anthony Cope)

Treasury Entry Book (January 1673), http://www.british-history.ac.uk/cal-treasury-books/vol4/pp37-55, accessed 14 January 2021

Treasury Minute Book (November 1667), http://www.british-history.ac.uk/cal-treasury-books/vol2/pp115-132, accessed 11 January 2021

Tyacke, N., 'Religious Controversy', in Tyacke, N. (ed.) *The History of the University of Oxford, Vol. IV: Seventeenth-Century Oxford* (Oxford, 1997)

V & A Museum, online catalogue, http://collections.vam.ac.uk/item/O295366/fork-unknown/, accessed 17 September 2020

Walter, W., fine (18 August 1646), http://www.british-history.ac.uk/commons-jrnl/vol4/pp645-648, accessed 11 January 2021

Walter, W., petition of Sir William Walter, Bart., of Sarsden, Co. Oxon, to the Protector (June 1658), http://www.british-history.ac.uk/cal-state-papers/domestic/interregnum/1658-9/pp69-80, accessed 11 January 2021

Westfall, R., *Science and Religion in Seventeenth-Century England* (Ann Arbor, 1973)

Whitehead, J., *Cavalier and Roundhead Spies: Intelligence in the Civil War and Commonwealth* (Barnsley, 2009)

Wood, A., *Athenae Oxonienses: An Exact History of Writers and Bishops Who Have Had Their Education in the University of Oxford* (Oxford, 1848)

Wood, P., *Baltzar: Complete Works for Unaccompanied Violin*, Msr Classics ASIN: B000XULO70 (2008)

Worden, B., 'Cromwellian Oxford', in Tyacke, N. (ed.) *The History of the University of Oxford, Vol. IV: Seventeenth-Century Oxford* (Oxford, 1997)

Worden, B., 'The Demand for a Free Parliament', in Southcombe, G. and Tapsell, G. (eds.) *Revolutionary England c. 1630–c. 1660* (London, 2020)

CHAPTER FIVE

Digging Hanwell

The Archaeology of the Gardens 1600–1660

By the end of the sixteenth century the garden and park at Hanwell are likely to have featured fishponds, probably some medieval survivors alongside the larger pool mentioned in the will of 1525. Within the wider confines of the deer park there would have been boundary banks, terraces, walkways and some formal planting, probably adjacent to the house. However, the argument put forward here is that the next major stages in the garden's development belonged to the seventeenth century. A particular difficulty in considering the gardens at Hanwell, and indeed most historic gardens, is the lack, except for one important instance, of any firm dating evidence. Most of the conclusions drawn here about sequencing within the garden are on the basis of parallels with other, contemporary gardens and the known interests and activities of members of the Cope family, especially Walter. The assumption, based on the trajectory of the family's finances, is that the bulk of the large-scale civil engineering to create the water garden was undertaken early in the seventeenth century. This produced the setting for Sir Anthony's later additions post–Civil War.

The methods used to study the garden have included looking at historic mapping evidence and LiDAR images (Fig. 29). This was complemented by ground-based survey, interspersed with selective excavation of identified features. Work extended over nearly a decade and involved around 1500 person-days on site for the author and numerous volunteers. The surviving remains of the water gardens at Hanwell cover nearly 8 ha and extend in an east–west line for just over 750 m. Although most of the valley is wooded today, early Ordnance Survey maps show that in the nineteenth century some of it was laid down to pasture. This account will begin at the highest point of the garden, to the west, and follow the flow of the waters as they make their way through the park.

The most obvious feature is the small lake (Pond B) just 50 m north of the former castle (Plate 18). The lake, which is aligned roughly north-west to south-east is around 100 m long by 80 m wide and bounded along its south-east side by a large earth dam up to 6.4 m high (Fig. 30). The lake is fed from a spring on the village High Street, and the water is brought under the road and into the park to fill a small pond known locally as the Horse Pond (Pond A). From there it is piped into the northern corner of the lake. Excavations in January and March 2015 (HANH) revealed that the side of the lake nearest to the castle had been bordered by a well-constructed stone wall; there was no evidence of

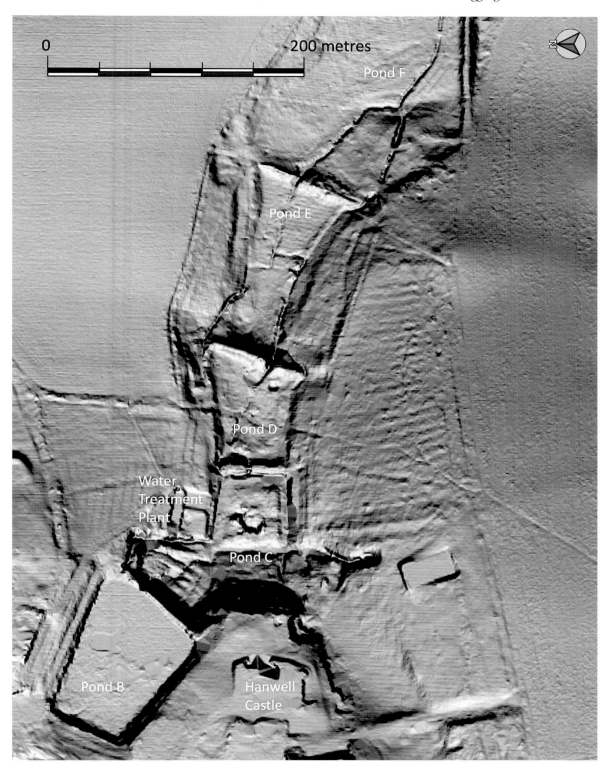

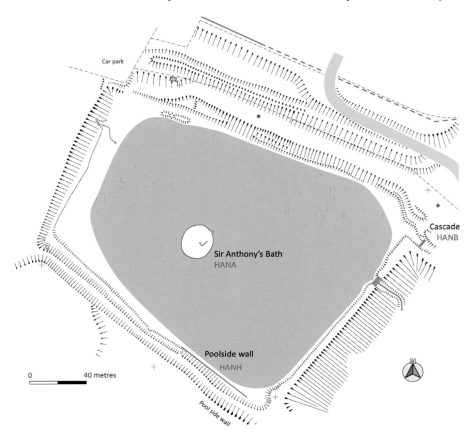

Car park

Cascade
HANB

Sir Anthony's Bath
HANA

Poolside wall
HANH

0   40 metres

Pool side wall

FIGURE 30. Hanwell, plan
of the lake (Pond B) and
associated earthworks.

such a feature around the rest of the perimeter (Plate 19). There was little silting built up above the puddled clay bottom of the lake, but what silts there were contained significant finds from the seventeenth century, including the neck of a Bartman bottle and a wine seal with a rose emblem and the initials IM or TM, presumably from a hostelry called the Rose Tavern. A large stone ball was also recovered from the lakebed silts closer to the southern corner, and this may have been part of an ornamental balustrade. Along the north-east side of the lake are two well-marked terraces, the lower being around 6 m wide, certainly adequate to accommodate Bacon's advice that walkways should be 'enough for four to walk abreast'. Just to the west of the centre point of the lake is a circular island rising around 1.2 m above the lakebed and measuring some 12.5 m in diameter. The perimeter had been severely undercut, and excavations in 2015 established that the original island was nearly 17 m across. The island is home to the remains of a structure known locally as Sir Anthony's Bath. Even today the view across the lake towards the castle is rather striking, and it is interesting to note that while the prospect towards the lake, of the building rising above the retaining wall, would have been of a quite formal built landscape, the opposite view, looking out from the castle towards the terraced walkway, would have had something of the 'wilderness' about it.

Water exited the lake by an overflow channel at the eastern corner. There would probably have been a sluice at this point, but the insertion of a stone cascade in the second half of the seventeenth century destroyed the remaining traces of this mechanism. Earthwork evidence indicates that the channel would have continued in an easterly direction, following the contour along the valley side for around 150 m before feeding into a lower pond. The exact route has been masked by the construction of a sewage treatment plant. The area below the main dam to the lake contains a complex series of earthworks, including to the north the original outflow channel (a) from the lake (Fig. 31). This is cut by a later channel associated with a modern, large-diameter pipe which takes some water from the spring in the High Street and empties it into a deep, little, rock-cut ravine (b) which defines the eastern edge of the area. There is no dating evidence for this feature, but it may be quite recent, possibly late-nineteenth or early twentieth century. A slope to the south of the overflow channel (c) appears to be make-up from silts, presumably dredged from the lake, and these partly obscure the three finger-like depressions to the south, which have been interpreted as medieval fishponds (d). An L-shaped ditch to the south and east (e) may be part of this complex, which has been cut through by a later overflow

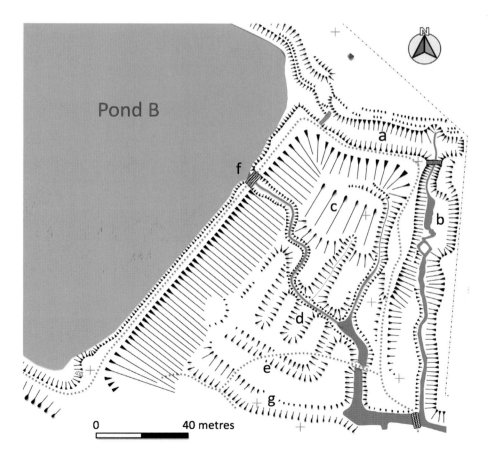

FIGURE 31. Hanwell, plan of earthworks east of the lake (Pond B).

Pond B

0   40 metres

channel (f) reputedly dug into the top of the dam in an attempt to search for treasure within the lake in the nineteenth century. A shallow, curving ditch to the south of the fishponds (g) could mark the line of the original stream that drained the valley.

The south side of the valley bends around to create the bluff on which the castle stands. The natural bank here is cut by a hollow that is worn into the face of the slope and may be the remains of an early hollow way associated with the medieval settlement and with the fishponds in the valley below. Further round, the slope had been terraced, and excavations in 2014 established the presence of walls, walkways and stairs. A long section (HANF) towards the northern end of the terraces had a fall of around 12 m. Work on it uncovered the remains of a very well-built stone wall that would have supported an upper-level walkway and possibly a balustrade. Below this was a bank, which sloped down to another walkway above a further retaining wall. A final slope ended at a stone-built drain. An additional small-area excavation towards the southern end of the terrace (HANG) picked up the end of the upper terrace wall, which terminated just before the slope turned towards the west. There was evidence of a partial rebuild here with the use of angled blocks, which may have been reused. If this was the case, it indicates a repair late in the seventeenth century. A secondary wall on unusually deep foundations ran down the slope from the face of the upper wall and was probably a seating for a stairway (Fig. 32). No specific dating

FIGURE 32. Hanwell, HANG14, terrace walling and base of stair looking west.

was recovered for any of the features on the eastern terrace, but the lack of brick and the high quality of the masonry in the context of large-scale groundworks suggests development during the early years of the seventeenth century. The levelled area between the top of the terracing and the east range of the castle may have been home to a conventional knot garden or parterre or, perhaps more likely, a bowling green.

Immediately to the west of the south end of the east terrace is an area known as the Sunken Garden (HANI). This consists of a roughly rectangular area, around 10 m by 15 m and cut into the north side of a shallow valley, to a depth of approximately 4 m. The north face of that cut drops down in two terraces. The lowest is faced by a stone wall, much of which has been recently rebuilt. Above that is a narrow walkway edged by an upward slope revetted with rubble after the fashion of a rockery. A curious steep little stair containing some reused stone rises in the north-west corner, and this may be one of the post-Civil War additions to the garden (Plate 20). Excavations in 2015 (HANI [E]) uncovered the lower courses of a dressed-stone wall defining the eastern limits of the site, while a trench dug down the full length of the western side (HANI [W]) revealed twentieth-century landscaping and debris from quarrying. Initial thoughts at the outset of digging here were that the sunken area may have been the location of a grotto or an elaborate sunken garden, similar to such examples as the one at the Villa Gamberaia, overlooking Florence. No traces of decorative materials, such as shell, were found, so the question of what the area was used for during the early life of the garden remains an open one. Foundations dug for the rebuilding of a stone wall along the southern margin of the Sunken Garden led to excavations in 2017 (HANI [S]) that uncovered a brick-lined drain and other remnants of walling, indicating further structures to the south. Further down the valley, in an area excavated opposite the south-east corner of the water parterre (HANL), there are indications, from the layout and depth of foundations, that a large, even monumental, gateway was positioned here. The complex area of walling at this point includes at least five different phases of development and is currently the subject of further exploration and study.

The complex, which occupies the valley bottom at the point where the lesser valleys to the north and south of the castle coincide, was first identified by earthwork survey in 2014 (Fig. 33). In places, the surviving earthworks were less than 30 cm high, and not until the LiDAR coverage for the area was accessed did the exact layout of the feature become evident. The form as expressed on the ground and in the LiDAR image was of a moated enclosure, about 45 m square, within which was a low, circular mound 15 m across, surrounded by a shallow ditch. This was linked to the outer moat by depressions to the north and south. The western arm of the moat still holds water and is known locally as the Lady Pool (Pond C). Other parts of the site have been drained by channels cut in the base of the moat and by a breach made in the retaining dam to the east, probably in the nineteenth century. Water currently flows into the Lady Pool via a later channel from the lake to the north-west. Another source of water

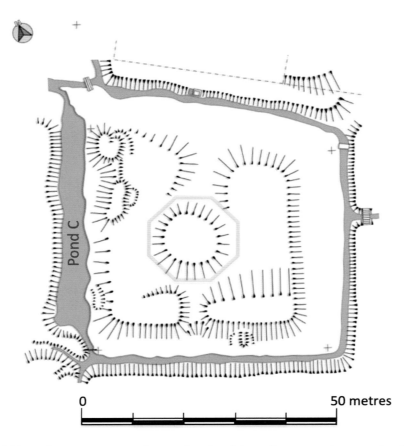

FIGURE 33. Hanwell, plan of earthworks on site of water parterre (Pond C); approximate line of octagonal island as later excavated shown in pale grey.

would have been a spring in the south side of the valley some 65 m south of the south-west corner. We came to describe this area as the water parterre on the basis of similar features seen at such locations as Raglan and Chipping Campden.

Excavations from 2017 onwards (HANK) demonstrated that the site began as a square pool, into which the island was inserted. As already noted, the valley side to the north is taken up by a modern sewage treatment plan. To the south of the parterre is a well-marked terraced walkway originally flanked by a stone wall taken down in the 1960s. The slopes above show evidence of additional terracing. A bypass channel exists at the north-east corner of the water parterre. An excavation was mounted here in 2015 (HAND) to examine traces of walling, in the expectation that it would be part of the remains of a sluice. In fact the wall represented a blocking of that channel which, from pottery evidence, can be dated to late in the seventeenth century.

The next pool (Pond D) down the valley was held in place by a huge dam, up to 8 m high at its centre point, which had created a body of water roughly 60 m east to west by 50 m north to south. The dam is rather longer, at 75 m, extending to the north to accommodate the natural fall of the northern side of the valley. There is no evidence of any features within this pool. An earthen ramp that drops down at its south-west corner may be a later addition to facilitate access for cultivation. The dam that retained the water for the following pool (Pond E) lies around 140 m farther east and, even allowing for damage by badgers, was not on the scale of the dams preceding and succeeding it. Standing at little more than 2 m high, it could only ever have formed a comparatively shallow pool. Terraces to the north and south gave a waisted effect to the pool's former outline. The upper section of the side of the valley to the north is marked by a ditch with bank which separates the valley from the flat land to the north and functioned to differentiate the water garden from the surrounding deer park. Running around 12 m below this is a terrace that may be the line of a previous pathway. Finally, below this, but aligned parallel to it, is a further broad terrace some 60 m long and 10 m wide that is exceptionally marshy and is defined in places along its southern edge by a low bank. This coincides with the spring line around the 120 m contour and may be the result of a land slip or, possibly, the location of a high-level rectangular pool, possibly for the mill.

The south side of the valley has a further series of earthworks running parallel to its east–west axis. Immediately above the terrace marking the south side of the pool is a shallow ditch, and above that is a small terrace which may be a pathway. Beyond that, and marking the limit of the woodland, is a second recent field boundary that has two large, timber gate posts set in it. Above the break of slope is an area of rough pasture bearing traces of the former open fields in the form of ridge and furrow. Other small, square earthworks over the ridge and furrow may be the remains of rabbit warrens referred to in a dispute of 1653 (TNA, C 4/58/66, Sir Anthony Cope, baronet, infant, v. [blank]). The boundary to this part of the garden, noted above and clearly cutting across the earlier field system, is a broad but shallow, flat-topped bank flanked on either side by ditches. This is very similar to perimeter earthworks seen around the small, seventeenth-century parks at Wormleighton and Farnborough, both in Warwickshire, and may represent a drive or bridleway for perambulating the inner part of the gardens.

The final pool (Pond F) in the sequence was maintained by a lengthy dam of nearly 150 m running east to west as the stream bends to flow south towards the River Cherwell (Plate 21). It is difficult to reconstruct the original footprint of the pool as there has been a considerable amount of modern dumping of builder's waste. To the south of the east end of the dam is an area of some disturbance formerly home to pens for pheasant rearing. Further earthworks have recently been recorded here, defining a rectangular area next to the stream. This may give a clue as to an alternate location for Sir Anthony's mill. The wider deer park stretches to the south and was bounded by a well-made, dressed-stone wall, still surviving to a couple of courses as part of a low, rubble-strewn bank. It is less clear where the northern boundary was, but remains of early walling can also be seen north of the lake as the presumed park wall approaches the village. All of these features are assigned to the suggested phase of garden development from the opening decades of the seventeenth century.

Two other Cope family properties exist in Oxfordshire, both of which retain evidence of early gardens. Bruern Abbey, located approximately 30 km south-west of Hanwell, in the Forest of Wychwood, was purchased by the Cope family in 1610. The former Cistercian Abbey had been dissolved in 1536, and the current house was constructed around 1720. There is no evidence about the accommodation prior to purchase by the Copes, but there must have been a house on the site as the family spent a considerable amount of time there. The main feature of interest is the remains of an elaborate, and previously unrecognised, water garden that, no doubt, was founded on monastic waterways and ponds. It has a distinctive period character, involving a main pond with island surrounded by walkways and subsidiary pools and channels (Fig. 34). Given the similarities with aspects of the works undertaken at Kensington and other contemporary water gardens it is possible that this was constructed by the Copes shortly after they took over the property.

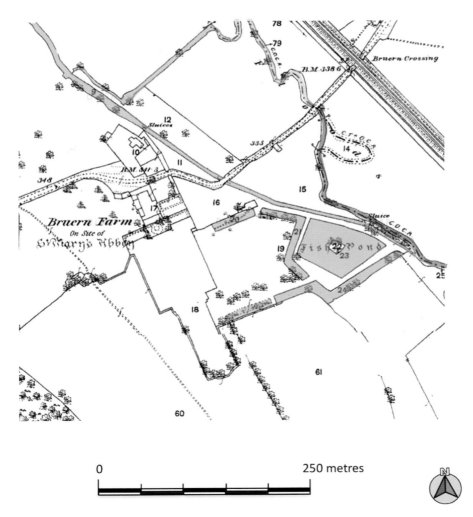

0   250 metres

FIGURE 34. Bruern, plan of water gardens from 1920 OS 6 inch map. © Crown Copyright and Landmark Information Group Limited (2021). All rights reserved.

Another local site in the hands of the Copes was Tangley Hall. This is around 4.5 km south-west of Bruern and was originally a grange of Bruern Abbey. A conveyance exists for the sale of the grange, dated 2 May 1551, between Edward Cope and Thomas Briggs of Cornbury (Hants. CRO, 43M48/12). Of all the Cope properties, it may be the most intact. The listing compiled by English Heritage in 1987 notes:

> Farmhouse, now disused. Late C16 or early C17 with later additions and alterations. Roughly coursed limestone rubble; artificial stone slate roof with stepped coped verges to south gable end of north-south range. Basic L-plan comprising hall range aligned east-west with roughly equal-length cross-wing projecting to north on west. 2 storeys and attic. (English Heritage 1987)

An early seventeenth-century well house roughly 20 m south-east of the hall is of particular interest. Earthworks to the east, generally ascribed to the medieval grange, look far more likely to be the remains of a formal post-dissolution moated garden, with viewing terraces and flanking walkways.

In considering questions of the overall design of Cope's early garden at Hanwell, one should perhaps enquire why it lacked the rather more elaborate compositions as identified at Kensington, Gorhambury and Bruern. The answer partly lies in the terrain defined by the valley the garden occupies. Here pools can be easily created by throwing a dam across the valley. There is no need to dig out ponds, and so the opportunity to create complex shapes is largely absent. In this context it is worth examining two other local parks, at Farnborough and Wormleighton, that share a similar approach to landscaping. At Farnborough, 5.5 km to the north and just over the county boundary into Warwickshire, is a small park to the east of the present hall. Early in the sixteenth century, the old, moated medieval manor at the bottom of the valley was abandoned and a new house built, with much better prospects, by the Raleighs. At the same time a small park was formed centred on a chain of fishponds, probably medieval in origin, occupying the valley bottom. The perimeter of the park was defined by a stone and brick wall and an earthwork consisting of, in places, a set of terraces and, along the crest of the hill to the south, a low, broad bank flanked by ditches (Wass 2016, 59). Wormleighton, a further 5 km north, was held by the Copes until they sold it to the Spencers, in 1506. A series of pools were inserted into the centre of the deserted medieval village. Again the boundaries of the small park were defined by an earthwork which could have doubled as a driveway. All three of these local examples suggest a shared practice of creating comparatively small-scale parks around pools and enclosing them with boundary banks and walks that concentrated the eye on these central bodies of water while turning one's back on the wider landscape.

Returning to the question of the dating of the primary works at Hanwell, we know that these demanded earth moving on a huge scale and the construction of considerable lengths of walling, but the dating evidence remains circumstantial. It seems unlikely, given the difficulties in getting the main residence completed, that much was done with the surroundings in the opening decades of the sixteenth century. Once the castle was complete, options would have existed for the Copes to develop the grounds. Anthony I (d. 1551) may well have picked up ideas in his continental travels on the design of gardens. While Sir Anthony II (d. 1614), with his puritan credentials, may seem an unlikely candidate for anything as frivolous as an elaborate garden, there were plenty of clerics prepared to argue in favour of such earthly paradises as models of order and good conduct. Indeed there is not necessarily an opposition between puritanism and expensive and fashionable consumption in this period. In establishing 'links between the activity of gardening and the social concerns and trends of the time', Jill Francis (2008, 26) stresses how garden publications of the period emphasised hierarchies, ordering and ranking while at the same time celebrating the puritan virtues of the commonwealth. Alternatively, taking an approach founded on the family's self-interest, given the clear desire to curry favour with King James I, we have a perfect context for investing in a fashionable garden as part of the preparations for a royal visit. Finally we have Sir Anthony's debt, which was passed on to his son William: £20,000 would have been more than adequate to undertake work on the almost heroic scale we see at Hanwell. All this argues for work to be underway possibly from the late 1590s, when Queen Elizabeth could reasonably have been expected as a visitor, through to the opening decade of the next century. Sir Anthony's brother Walter had, as discussed above, a well-documented interest, and indeed expertise, in garden making and may have been the driving intelligence behind work at Hanwell, with Sir Anthony footing the bill. Whatever the precise dating, and future archaeological work may clarify this, it seems likely that these works provided the setting and infrastructure for Anthony III (d. 1675), the 4th baronet, to develop his garden of wonders and marvels later in the century.

The Archaeology of the Gardens 1660–1675

As noted above, it is likely that most of the large-scale civil engineering tasks to create the garden were carried out in the opening decades of the seventeenth century. However, archaeological investigations have pieced together, in some cases with very secure dating evidence, the additions made to the garden by Sir Anthony Cope from the early 1660s onwards as an expression of his enthusiasm for all things scientific. It should be stressed that what follows is a summary of the main archaeological findings, and that a detailed account of the evidence is to be presented in the final excavation report for the site, which remains several years in the future.

The island in the lake (Pond B) was subject to excavation (HANA) between 2013 and 2015 on the mistaken assumption that this was the location of Plot's House of Diversion. The logistics for this task were quite demanding, as it was necessary to construct a ferry operated on a continuous loop to transfer staff and equipment over to the island. The most obvious feature, which was excavated, was a stone-lined sunken area known as Sir Anthony's Bath. The only deposits within this were of recent date, and it was obvious that it had been dug out at some time in the not-too-distant past. Once cleared, this revealed itself to be a rectangular, cellar-like structure 2 m long by 1.2 m wide and 1.4 m deep (Plate 22). At the base was a very well-laid, paved floor, which did not quite align with the rather less solidly constructed side walls, which contained some reused masonry. At the north end were a series of stepped-back, narrow courses of stonework dubbed by the excavators the 'fairy steps'.

Two trenches were cut to the north and east of this sunken feature to explore the possibilities of other structures on the island and in particular to look for evidence of features relating to the possible presence of pipework on this potential site for the House of Diversion. No such discoveries were made. One observation that is perhaps significant was the one made in 2015, when the level of the lake was so low that an additional trench was cut out across the lakebed on the south side of the island. This revealed that there had been considerable erosion around the island's edge and that it may have been lined by a stone wall nearly 2 m out from the current perimeter.

Islands were frequently incorporated into large pools to act as a refuge for nesting wild fowl. On a more elevated level, Maddalena Bellavitis (2017, 321) celebrates the social potential of an island in the Renaissance garden, writing, 'The island, the *isola felix*, has always been a very important *topos* for the concept of the *locus amoenus*, […] a magical land enclosed and separated from the outside where the court could retire, party and shine.' Other suggestions made for Hanwell's 'bath' have included a tank for breeding fish, a secure storage space for either valuables or reactive compounds, or a conduit house from which fresh water could be extracted. Perhaps the key observation is that water within the feature rises and falls according to the level of water within the lake. In all probability a bathing function is the most likely, although a cold bath on an island in a lake does not seem like an immediately enticing prospect. A parallel, although not a particularly close one, exists at Packwood House, Warwickshire, where a well-built and rather elegant outdoor cold bath is generally dated to the 1680s (Wass 2021, 231). It was certainly in place by 1723, which makes it quite an early example of the type of garden feature which became increasingly popular through into the eighteenth century. Outdoor pools of a similar type are uncommon for the seventeenth century. A couple of much larger pools purportedly for swimming existed at Emmanuel and Christ Colleges, Cambridge (Whittle 2017, 21). In some ways the closest structural parallels may be found in the baptistery pools that were becoming a feature of some chapels at the time, as for example recorded by English Heritage in the Old Chapel in Tewkesbury.

The element of reused stonework recorded associates this structure with the cascade at the outlet of the lake, which is dated to the second half of the seventeenth century. If this were Sir Anthony's bath, it could perhaps be another factor that steered Plot's thinking in the direction of *The New Atlantis,* as Bacon's House of Salomon was well provided with baths of various types. Whatever the case, there is no evidence to link this island to Plot's House of Diversion. Such was the lure of having a real island at Hanwell to explore that it was not until the project was in its third year that we noted that Plot's reference puts the House of Diversion to the east of the house, while the island lies to the north.

The outflow from the upper lake was managed through a bypass channel just past the northern end of the dam. The original sluice mechanism was almost certainly lost when a new construction was inserted. This initially seemed to consist of two stone piers that had later been blocked by a series of stone slabs with sloping faces. Once the vegetation had been cleared, several courses of this structure could be seen, and subsequent excavations in 2013 (HANB) explored this down to its lowest levels. An initial interpretation had viewed this as a two-phase structure, but it became clear that it was all built as a piece. Pottery and particularly clay pipes from the fill of the foundation cut dated this to the second half of the seventeenth century, and it appeared to have been built as a simple cascade to maintain levels of water in the lake yet permit outflow and at the same time create an attractive water feature. Many of the stones were obviously reused, the central blocks looking like large coping stones or possibly windowsills (Plate 23). Given the considerable destruction wrought in the area during the Civil War, there must have been something of a surplus of dressed stone available for reuse locally. Indeed Stephen Porter (1994, 96) records that 'Banbury Corporation petitioned for the demolition of the castle there and this was duly approved with, "the Materials bestowed upon the town of Banbury, to assist them in the Repair of the Ruins made in the late War".' He makes it clear that this process went on into the 1650s and even 1660s, and so it is not impossible that Banbury Castle could have been the source of Sir Anthony's stones. In a final attempt to validate the idea that the existing island in the lake could have been home to the fountains described by Plot, the possibility that a water wheel with attached pump could have been located here was explored with an additional area excavation on a terrace to the north. Nothing was found to support this suggestion.

Below the east terrace, an area adjacent to a small, rectangular pond known as the Lady Pool (Pond C) and described as a water parterre was subject to extensive excavations between 2017 and 2021 (HANK). Surface indications backed up by detailed survey work and most especially the LiDAR image suggested a possible ground plan. Excavations initially concentrated on the northern and western parts of the central island, but by 2021 the entire perimeter had been examined. The island proved to be octagonal and revetted with a stone wall. Evidence indicated that construction began with the draining of the pre-existing pool. A shallow, circular trench was cut into the gravelly silts across the pool's base, presumably after they had been allowed to dry out. This trench may have been dug to facilitate setting out the octagon; however, the finished result was far from being satisfactory (Fig. 35). The irregularity of the octagon may reflect instability in the silts on which it was founded, although there may be an element of simple incompetence here. Once the setting out had been completed, a foundation course was laid of quite large, up to 80 cm long, roughly shaped stone blocks. A further two courses of large, irregular blocks were laid on top

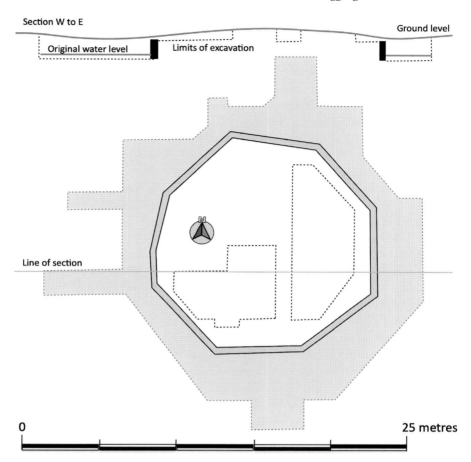

FIGURE 35. Hanwell, HANK21, plan of the perimeter wall to the central octagon.

of this at the same time as the middle of the island was built up with a series of dumps of clayey silt. The next two surviving courses consisted of well-shaped and fitted ashlar blocks, all of the local ironstone. None of the blocks recorded *in situ* appeared to have been reused. The lower of the two courses had suffered considerable frost damage as it had been set at water level and so subject to a cycle of wetting and freezing during the lifetime of the structure (Plate 24). At no point did the perimeter wall survive above five courses, and so its original height remains unknown; however, judging by the quantity of rubble and faced stone used to fill in the surrounding moat at the time of its destruction, it probably stood at least 1 m above water level and may well have been higher. The wall was capped with a set of extremely well-finished coping stones, with flat tops, 25 cm wide, and chamfered edges. A series of nearly sixty terracotta garden pots and urns were excavated from the moat at the foot of this wall, suggesting that they had originally been positioned along the length of this parapet. Some were plain and some fluted, interspersed with more decorative, handled urns. Amongst this extraordinary collection, one of the ornamental urns had the date 1664 inscribed into its base.

The only evidence available at present to date the construction of the island is a couple of large, unabraded base sherds of post-medieval Midlands Blackware sealed at least 1 m below its make-up. While there are no obviously reused stones in the standing remains that elsewhere have been used as an indicator for Sir Anthony's work from the 1660s, the question whether he was responsible for constructing the island or simply built his House of Diversion on top of an existing feature remains unresolved. However, it is likely, given the limited amount of silt that built up post-construction, that the island, and any associated structures, did not have a lengthy period of use. Unfortunately there were no traces from the interior of the island of any features, despite the huge amount of building debris filling the moat. The material in the moat is strongly indicative of a timber-framed building with tiled roof and plastered walls with glazed windows, and if this had been founded on sleeper beams, there would be comparatively slight traces of foundations on the ground. The material excavated from the deposits within the moat indicates a range of ac-tivities taking place on and around the island, specifically smoking, drinking and eating. Putting this in the context of what we know about the usage of ancillary garden buildings such as this one, we should perhaps compare the House of Diversion with contemporary banqueting houses.

We are still some way from being able to reconstruct with confidence the garden in its entirety for this period, and the identification and examination of the site of the elaborate water mill as described by Plot remains a high priority. What the archaeology does indicate is that a number of additions to the garden were made in the 1660s and 1670s, characterised by the reuse of materials and a slightly shoddy approach to construction, in marked contrast to the well-built walls probably from the opening decades of the century. This fits well with the idea of Sir Anthony as a young man full of enthusiasm for his passion for all things technological and in a hurry to incorporate such features into his garden. However, this remains speculation outside the strict limits of what the archaeology is telling us.

Reconstructing the House of Diversion

A key question must be how confident one can be that the site excavated is in fact the location of the House of Diversion as described by Plot. To recap Plot's description:

> There are some other *Water-works* at the same Sir *Anthony Cope's, in* a House of *Diversion* built in a small *Island* on one of the *Fish-ponds*, Eastward of his House, where a *Ball* is tost by a *Column* of *Water* and artificial *Showers* descend at pleasure; within which they can yet so place a *Candle,* that though one would think it must needs be overwhelmed with *Water,* it shall not be extinguish'd &c (Plot 1705, 74)

We are certainly on an island in the right location relative to the house, and, as it is described as 'built', we must assume a structure with walls and a roof inside which are the waterworks. Putting fountains and other water-powered special effects indoors is not particularly unusual, as has been noted at Enstone and Wilton, although in these instances the structures were elaborately decorated grottoes. Perhaps a relatively plain setting for the Hanwell waterworks underlines a more studied approach to the engineering involved and the science that this implies.

The evidence as to the precise conformation of the building is all rather circumstantial and based entirely on the destruction debris recovered from the moat. The presence of a high proportion of tapered ridge tiles suggests a pyramidical roof arising from a square or, more likely, octagonal floor plan. The survival of large quantities of wall plaster that had been pressed against timber laths indicates a timber-framed building with evidence of a 'pebble-dashed' or roughcast effect on some panels, possibly on the exterior, as well as combed decoration, sometimes known as pargetting or pinking. This is a technique to create a waterproof finish that, according to Ronald Brunskill (1978, 66), 'was most popular in the second half of the 17C.' John Steane and James Ayres (2013, 18) note examples from southern Oxfordshire at Markham and Denchworth and an example of roughcast, possibly medieval in date, from Abingdon. Although it was not a common technique in the region, there are examples of pargetting in Banbury: numbers 85–87, High Street, dated 1650, and number 12, Market Place, also of the seventeenth century.

There is ample evidence for glazing, with fine sheets of cylinder glass set within lead cames. The shaping of the surviving fragments of glass point towards a simple design of upright, rectangular panels with at least one of them being marked with a large, engraved star (Fig. 36). This star seems to be a unique find and hints at decorative elements that match quite well with an interest in natural phenomena, and that, indeed, may even have constituted an invitation to contemplate the heavens through the windows of the House of Diversion. Any flooring was removed as part of the programme of levelling the island and filling in the moat, but a number of thin, carefully finished stone slabs were recovered. A further series of slabs with rather roughly chased grooves may have been inserted into the floor to drain occasional splashes from the waterworks. It is assumed that the fountain, capable of suspending a ball in the air and creating descending showers, was placed centrally within the building. Evidence for this includes fragments of a large-diameter, up to 2.5 m, steep-sided bowl with external arcading, and a portion of a fluted stone bowl with a diameter of 2 m and pierced at three points for incoming pipework (Fig. 37). In addition, a small copper alloy quill, a thin-bore pipe used to create fine jets of water, was found, as well as a lead cone that may have been an element designed to create an umbrella-shaped spray. A number of faced blocks with a radius of just over 1 m could have formed the base for a fountain in the candelabrum style, as noted at Gaillon. Several finely shaped fragments of ironstone moulding were also excavated, none of which would fit with any conventional architectural element of such domestic features as door or window surrounds. The fact that the fountain also had to provide descending showers points to the fact that there may have been some kind of superstructure, a simplified version, perhaps, of the kind of canopies over

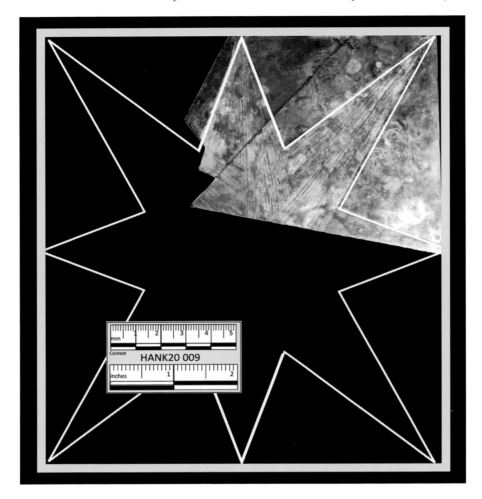

FIGURE 36. Hanwell, fragment of engraved window glass with restored outline.

the Carfax Conduit from Oxford or the early seventeenth-century fountain at Trinity College, Cambridge. Equally fanciful mouldings, in what has been termed the 'mannerist' style, featured in gardens from the late sixteenth and early seventeenth centuries, the extravagant arches above the garden walls at Montacute House, Somerset, being a case in point.

Given the setting and the likely presence of a central fountain on a circular base, an octagon is probably the most aesthetically satisfying arrangement for the ground plan of the building. In this context one's thoughts immediately turn to the octagonal Tower of the Winds in Athens, designed by the architect Andronicus of Cyrrhus between 100 and 50 BCE, and its Oxford incarnation on top of the Radcliffe Observatory building, completed by James Wyatt in 1794. However, a more useful parallel is the small, octagonal banqueting house within an octagonal moat at Hunstanton Hall, Norfolk, dated to around 1640. The earlier Tudor period saw many octagonal banqueting houses, for example at Hales Place, Kent, and Long Melford Hall, Suffolk, while timber versions were

erected at Hampton Court and at Windsor. Other architectural forms which
may establish a context for the construction of the House of Diversion include
small lodges, such as the Dutch Cottage, Rayleigh, Essex, which is dated 1621.
The building is octagonal, timber framed and plastered, over a brick plinth.
Polygonal dovecotes of the period also suggest contemporary forms, such as
the brick example dated 1641 at Hellens, Much Markle, Herefordshire (Hansell
1998, 131). The seventeenth-century examples at Wichenford and Hawford,
both in Worcestershire, while square in plan, are turriform, timber framed with
rendered wattle-and-daub infill and set on a coursed sandstone rubble plinth
under a tiled roof.

The overall dimensions of the House of Diversion remain a similarly speculative matter, although given that the diameter of the central fountain would have
been around 2.5 m (8 feet) and allowing room for circulation while avoiding
occasional splashing, then a minimum diameter of 6 m (20 feet) seems about
right. If the fountain was to perform such tricks as tossing a ball on a column
of water, given the possibility of a fairly elaborate superstructure in at least three
tiers, then we should perhaps consider a minimum height of 4 m (12 feet) for the
display to show at its best. Allowing for clearance above this, we must envisage
a structure equivalent to a building of two storeys, albeit probably open to the
roof on the inside. There is also the question of how much space there may
have been between the central structure and the perimeter wall to the island.
Despite it having been largely robbed out, the wall's line was clear, and the
recovery of several well-shaped coping stones enabled the setting for pots to be
recreated. The presence of the planted pots shows that access space around the

perimeter would be needed both to attend to the plants and, perhaps, to allow a walkway outside the building for further promenading. No evidence was found for a bridge to the island. This might have been confidently expected along the side facing the castle, with access being down the walkways and stairs of the east terrace. There were no traces either of springing in the perimeter wall for a stone arch or of timber posts in the moat or on the island for a timber bridge. It is possible that access was by boat only, but the most likely explanation is simply that the bridge was at a higher level and all traces were removed during demolition. All of this has enabled an initial attempt at reconstruction to be undertaken to create an image of a tall, octagonal, timber-framed tower with a rendered exterior and a pyramidical tile roof set centrally on its octagonal island and surrounded by the perimeter wall garnished with planted terracotta pots and urns. No doubt future work on the finds will enable us to refine this image, but it forms a valuable starting point for further discussion of the materiality of Sir Anthony's House of Diversion (Plate 25).

The Hanwell Pots and Other Finds

Unusually, for an exercise in garden archaeology, the excavation on the site of the House of Diversion resulted in many finds; indeed, one of the most remarkable discoveries of the entire programme at Hanwell was the assemblage of seventeenth-century terracotta garden urns. While there are both written and visual sources for the use of garden pots during the period, contemporary survivals are rare. As already noted, the pots were excavated from around the perimeter of the octagonal island identified as the probable location of the House of Diversion. The archaeology made it clear that they had been destroyed in a single act by being pushed or thrown from the perimeter wall and then having rubble from the demolition that followed dumped on top of them (Plates 26 and 27). It is likely that in total there were between 60 and 70 pots, which works out to 8 or 9 pots per side on average. This suggests quite close spacing, at around 70 cm, just under three feet (1 m). Although it is possible that not all pots were placed on the perimeter wall, this is the most likely arrangement.

Preliminary analysis has identified four main forms from the assemblage (Plate 28). All are in a well-fired, fine-grained, red fabric with few inclusions and appear to exist in roughly equal proportions. The first group (Type 1) consists of what one might term conventional flowerpots, large (typically 30 cm diameter, standing 35 cm tall), wheel-thrown pots with straight sides sloping slightly outwards but, unlike most modern pots, having the lip turned out in a broad flange to facilitate handling. Some had a band of reeding just below the rim. In all cases there were four or five small drainage holes around the perimeter of the base. The second form (Type 2) is a shallow pan with strongly everted sides, around 25 cm deep but flaring out to a diameter of 30 cm (Figure 60). Wheel-thrown with a single, large, central drainage hole, these pots were decorated with vertical finger-impressed fluting. Today such shallow, flared pans are frequently used for bulbs, which calls to mind the Dutch 'tulip mania' of the 1630s. The next two forms (Types 3 and 4) are closely related and are large-handled urns without bottoms. The smaller (Type 3) stands around 45 cm high and has a diameter of 25 cm at the rim and two lines of fluted finger-impressed decoration separated by a raised band. The larger (Type 4) is more than 60 cm tall and 45 cm in diameter and has a similar layout, except that the band of decoration has large, anti-clockwise spirals pressed into the clay.

Both types were hand built, almost certainly on a turntable, with the handles and their acanthus leaf plaques being taken from moulds. Similarly they are both, in effect, hollow tubes lacking a bottom. While some examples of these latter two types seem to have been presented in their natural finish, most were given a colour coating, either in cream or brown, in order to mimic the appearance of much more expensive stone vessels. None of the pots are glazed, although there are occasional smears of glaze indicating that they were fired alongside other types of pottery that was glazed. Remarkably one example of a type 4 pot has an inscribed date of 1664 on its foot, while another of type 2 has the initials RP incised on the base in an elegant cursive script, presumably the initials of the potter rather than Robert Plot.

There are still many questions that need to be answered through further scientific examination, perhaps most importantly, where the pots were made. Analysis of the clay should show whether they were imported or made at an established local pottery or, even, whether they were the product of an itinerant band of potters setting up in the park. Nor do we have any information about how they were planted. Extensive sampling was undertaken of deposits of silt from within the pots (even though the evidence indicates they were emptied of their planting before being discarded), as well as from the surrounding silts within the moat. Paleo-botanical analysis of these deposits should inform us at least as to what was growing in the vicinity.

Pots certainly figured in medieval gardens, sometimes as one-off pieces with a small tree, often depicted as being cut into a fanciful shape. As an architectural component of garden design, large terracotta pots were frequently associated with the cultivation of citrus fruits on a seasonal basis, especially in Italian gardens of the Renaissance. This practice in some places continues to this day, notably at the Boboli Gardens, Florence, and at the Villa Medici at Castelli (Fig. 38). Otherwise the use of potted plants as evidenced by contemporary images seems rather restrained, although they could, as rather ephemeral components of a garden's design, be simply underrepresented by the image makers. It is unlikely that there could have been much of an export trade in such bulky yet fragile items, although writing in 1706, Henry Wise (1706, 148) recommends that 'pots must be either of plain earth or Dutch ware, the latter being much larger'. Clearly complete decorative terracotta garden pots from the seventeenth century, either as antiques or archaeological finds, are extremely rare. The risks of accidental damage, to say nothing of the destructive effects of frost, are formidable. To give some idea of the rate of attrition, I note that Noël Ivor Hume (1974, 42) reported on the governor's palace in Williamsburg, Virginia, as follows: 'In 1768 the executors of the then deceased Governor Farquier sold

FIGURE 38. Current use of garden pots at the Villa Medici, Castelli, Italy.

to his successor, Lord Botetourt, 322 flowerpots at a cost of two pounds fifteen shillings and four pence, or twopence each. Three years later only 252 remained to be included in the governor's inventory', a loss of 22%. While some early urns survive in stone or lead, the Hanwell collection of ceramic decorative urns and flowerpots is unique. Of decorative urns, Currie notes, in reporting on a late eighteenth-century example, that

> Such horticultural urns were frequently shown in contemporary illustrations of 17th- and early 18th-century formal gardens, but have been considered by garden historians to have been made only in stone and lead. Since ceramic urns would have been susceptible to frost damage, it was thought unlikely that they were made in this material. (Currie 2005, 325)

The finds at Hanwell tend to contradict this view.

Where garden wares of the period have been excavated and recorded, they have usually been of the plain flower pot variety. Currie (1993, 227) published a general study on the archaeology of the flowerpot and came to the conclusion that 'functional non-ornamental flowerpots were not made in large numbers before the early eighteenth century', but he did not examine ornamental vessels. A small number of flowerpots were recovered in the excavations at Nonsuch Palace, Surrey. These were dated post-1667 and bore traces of 'purple red, orange–red and white-wash' on exterior surfaces (Biddle 2005, 198). The collection published by Brian Dix (1995, 291) for Kirby Hall, in Northamptonshire, consisted of six examples of three main forms of largely conventional flowerpot shape. One had lugs, and the larger examples had slightly everted rims. Holes were pierced both at the centre of the base and, in some cases, in the lower parts of the side walls. The pots all came from the western terrace of the 'Great Garden' and were dated to the seventeenth century.

The Kirby pots are similar to those recorded in the huge excavation of the Privy Garden at Hampton Court Palace, some of which date from the 1690s (Dix and Parry 1995, 110). Both sets also resemble those from contexts excavated at Colonial Williamsburg, in the United States. Apart from the rather eccentric crenellated urn from the moat of the Jewel Tower at Westminster, the only other major collection of decorated pots comes from the excavations at Basing House, in Hampshire, that had begun around 1875 (Moorhouse 1970, 31). Because of the early date of the excavations, the artefacts recovered were classified as unstratified, although a date range was ascribed to them as being after 1531, when work on the house was begun, and before 1645, when it was demolished after the Civil War siege. The horticultural wares are unusual, and, indeed, debate continues as to whether all the pieces identified were for planting. Certainly three urn-shaped flowerpots were made for the resident family specifically, as two of them bear the Paulet crest of a falcon and accompanying motto, *Ames Loyaulte*. A further four 'cylindrical pots' bear little resemblance to any known forms. Like some of the Hanwell pots, they have no base, but drainage holes are present and the existence of broad flanges on the bases of two of the pots and traces of mortar suggest they may have been permanently fixed to the top of a wall. Part of an urn of presumed seventeenth-century date was recovered by Currie (1995, 107) from Ham House, Surrey. The catalogue entry reads:

> Horticultural urn in a pinkish-beige, slightly sandy fabric with rare haematite inclusions to 6 mm. Zoomorphic ornamentation in relief, showing a goat's head with a leafy background. External surface treated with pinky-orange slip with traces of white paint overlaid. Deeply incised vertical combing internally. Rim diameter 190 mm. 14% of rim surviving. Unknown context, stored in Beer Cellar. (Currie 1995, 107)

Replicas of this urn were subsequently modelled by Whichford Pottery, in Oxfordshire, to provide a series of contemporary planters for use in the garden (Fig. 39). Part of a similar vessel was recovered at Gosport and was painted white in imitation of stone. Although there was no dating evidence from the archaeological context, Currie ascribed it to the seventeenth or early eighteenth century. One particularly interesting local find comes from a latrine pit in the grounds of Corpus Christi College, Oxford, whose fill was dated to between 1720 and 1740. It is described as

> [...] a complete profile of a remarkably elaborate red earthenware 'urn' shaped like a large chalice with a hollow pedestal base and with applied classical-style cherub masks and foliage (? acanthus) around the upper body. This highly unusual vessel is

FIGURE 39. Ham House, replica garden urn. Photo by Gary Marshall.

probably best interpreted as a flowerpot holder. Profiles of several other large conical flowerpots in a similar red fabric also came from the fills. (Bashford *et al.* 2014, 191)

The most comprehensive account of early flowerpots comes from Colonial Williamsburg, and while dealing primarily with material from the eighteenth century, there are some useful parallels. Apart from the example above, there is little published evidence of excavated examples of painted pots from England, but Hume reported on a later example from Colonial Williamsburg with fragments that were 'urn-shaped and bearing on the side a shield of arms cast in relief [...] The pots had initially been painted grey, perhaps as an undercoat, and thereafter a vivid pink, the arms picked out in deep yellow and the supporters in black' (Noël Hume 1974, 46).

A particularly unusual find was a large piece of a tin-glazed hanging flowerpot from a contractor's trench on the site of the Elizabethan garden at Beddington, Surrey (Phillips and Burnett 2005, 177). On the continent an important collection of large, decorated terracotta garden urns was excavated from a cess-pit in Haarlem, the Netherlands, and published in 1993 (Lindijer and Van Vlijmen 1993). Although they were discarded as wasters, they were finely made and with figurative, floral and heraldic decorations, making the Hanwell pots seem, by comparison, rather restrained.

As well as excavated examples, there are several contemporary references and illustrations of pots in use. John Evelyn in his unpublished *Elysium Brittannicum*, compiled over nearly forty years during the second half of the seventeenth century, provides a detailed account of contemporary garden practice. Throughout the work he offers advice as to the most appropriate pots for raising seeds, planting bulbs and managing grafts. It is in Chapter XI, *Of statues {Payntings}. Columns, Dyals, Perspectives, Pots, {Urns} Jarrs, Vas's and other Ornaments* that he gives his most comprehensive account of garden pots (Fig. 40).

FIGURE 40. Flowerpots illustrated in John Evelyn's *Elysium Britannicum.*

[Conventions used by Ingram in transcribing mss:

~~text lined through~~	Text lined through by Evelyn
{text in wavy brackets}	Interlineations by Evelyn
[text in square brackets]	Editorial comments

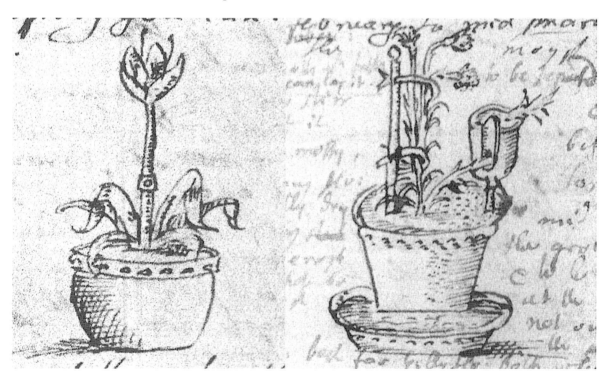

(text in parenthesis)   Evelyn's use of parenthesis
text in italic   Text underlined by Evelyn]

Finaly, amongst *Statues, Perspectives,* & other Ornaments, ~~suiting~~ exceedingly usefull; ~~in Gardens~~ {our ~~Elysium~~} *Pots, Vasas,* & the Urns, Jarrs or } Great *Amphoras* may be ranged: for they likewise stood in Gardens; And the Excussores & Figuilae, who carved repair'd, & formed these Vessels, were formerly reckned amongst the *Statuaries.* The first of these may be employed for the {Sowing}, Setting in & preserving of the choycest Flowers; especially the *Carnation, Auriculas, Amaramths, Anemones* etc; & for some shrubs, & plants of the rarest ~~sort~~ {kinds}: & therefore to be made of various sizes, depths, & diameters; frequently and commodiously enough ~~made~~ moulded ~~by our the potter~~ of common potters Earth; but always pierced at the bottom, for the passage of superfluous showers; which would other wise, overwash ~~& sta~~ {rott} & sterve the rootes they contained:

[Marginal note: but the best course to preserve your choyce Flo: potts is to place an ordinary flower pot filled with earth & wherein your flo: grow within the greater one, so as it be even at the orifice] (Evelyn 2001, 220)

Evelyn goes on to describe in detail rather elaborate arrangements for opening doors in pots to replenish the soil and pots manufactured for multiple plantings after the fashion of some present-day pots for herbs or strawberries. He then returns to questions of the form and materials to be used for planters.

We speake nothing here of the particular former of these potts; men are to please their phantsies ~~but the mos~~ though we should affect the most antique: & scubas we have described in Iconisme ~~And these brit Vessells may be~~

[Inserted on a separate piece of paper] Yet for a moderat proportion ~~let th~~ & generall Luke, they ought to be as broad at the Orifice as they are in height, two inches less at bottome (I speake for ordering ~~of~~ Carnation potts, etc) so as inverting ~~it~~ the whole masse of earth may come out intire upon occasion, and let there be holes at the bottom sufficient widenesse that the water may have convenient passage for which reason pibbles are better to strew & keeps the mould from clodding, thus tyle shards or oyster shells with which Gardners usually cover them. but in filling these potts with mould, be sure to let it exceede the brimms thereof by an inch, in regard of it sinking etc:]

But these materials are so fragile, that to have them cast in *Lead,* with their *frutiges, relievos,* {*Escutchions, Cyphers*} & other ornaments, were infinitely preferable to those of Earth; and after those such as are ~~made~~ {carved out} of hewen stone; But these for being commonely {bigger &} of lesse moderne shape, may be reckned amongst the *Vasas*; which were frequently ~~hew~~ cutt out of Porphyrie {Oriental Alabaster} ~~it~~ ~~selfe~~, & other rich {& lasting} materialls, with exquisite workmaneship, ~~and~~ for the adornement as well of Gardens, as the ~~most~~ famous of their Houses: For of these we have oftentimes beheld ~~pro Lavors~~ *Vasas, Urnes, Lavors,* & *Amphoras* of Prodigious capacity, & admirable arte, placed, as the rest, on *Pedistalls,* & Antique supporters about the~~ir~~ Roman Gardens, & in their ~~Porticos,~~ {Atrias} & Cimely{i}ums: And what a noble & grand effect, those goodly *Amphoras,* or *Jarrs* (Though but of simple ~~Earth~~ {clay}), cause, in that {spacious} area before the Villa of Pr: *Ludovisio,*

~~Every~~ {The} Traviler may observe: we have some in our ~~famous~~ {richer} Oyle shopps, much resembling them {in shape} & not much inferiour

[Marginal note: blacke lead dos very well being layd in oyle upon them, or but rubbed: cf]

And all these {fictilia} ~~airie vessells~~ may be painted & layd in oyle, of stone, ~~Colour~~, lead, bronz'd, or any other colour; some bestow the cost to gild them; but we, for our parts, do not affect it, unlesse it be universall, & all over the pott, which were an excessive charge: (Evelyn 2001, 222)

After a consideration of pots placed indoors for floral arrangements, Evelyn concludes:

Lastly, The proper places for these ornaments of Potts, {~~Vasas~~ etc:} ~~is~~ {are} at the sides of Alles & Gardens; Springling some about the *parterr* { & Trayle worke} as the designe invites: Also But for the larger *Vasas*; upon *Pedistalls*, of stone, ~~& the~~ betweene the ~~ranks~~ {files} of the *Statues*, Upon Balustrades, & the Ascent of stepps, & {generally on all elevated places} wherever we find them Gracefull: (Evelyn 2001, 223)

One author who managed to cover some of the same ground in print was John Worlidge, who, in his *Systema horti-culturæ,* published in 1677, said all he had to say about garden pots in these terms:

Other ancient Ornaments of a garden are Flower-pots, which painted white and placed on Pedestals, either on the ground in a straight line on the edges of your Walks, or at the corners of your squares, are exceeding pleasant.

They are usually made of Potters Clay and burnt, which when full of Earth and frozen in the Winter are apt to break unless you place another ordinary pot in Earth in the inside of it wherein to plant your Flowers, you design to propagate in them. But to prevent the casualty of breaking, some are made of Lead which are much to be preferred. (Worlidge 1677, 66)

There are several points of interest that relate quite closely to the Hanwell pots in these accounts. Evelyn suggests the placing of plainer pots within the choicest pots to preserve them, and he is backed up by Worlidge in this respect. This practice also supports a flexible planting regime as noted by the famous diarist, Samuel Pepys, who, in discussion with Hugh May at Whitehall on 22 July 1666, remarked on how appropriate it was that one had 'a little mixture of statues or pots, which may be handsome and so filled with another pot of such and such a flower or green, as the season of the year will bear'. Both remarks give a context for the fact that the Hanwell urns have no bottoms. There have been no instances of a basic pot remaining inside the more elaborate urns at Hanwell, and it is possible that, as noted above, planting here took place in sacks or baskets. Despite both Evelyn's recommendation and current gardening practices, it is perhaps surprising that in the more conventional flowerpots there have been no traces of deposits of pebbles, crushed tile or shell lining the base of any of the vessels.

Evelyn clearly was very conscious of the fragile nature of 'earth' pots manufactured from fired clay and would have much preferred to see them cast in lead or hewn from stone; however, there was obviously a cost issue here, although it is difficult to quantify. Evelyn goes on to praise the effect of painted terracotta

'*Amphoras*, or *Jarrs*' at the 'the Villa of Pr: *Ludovisio*'. This was probably the Villa Ludovisi, next to the Pincian Gate in Rome, now absorbed into the American embassy. While emphasising the variety of finishes available, Evelyn is less than enthusiastic about gilding, on the grounds of cost.

Contemporary illustrations include a large number of still life paintings, mainly Dutch in origin, where the flower-filled urns are generally of plain terracotta. The Spanish painter Tomas Hiepes (1610–74) painted similar compositions where there are instances of elaborate two-colour finishes which may have an element of the fantastical about them or, if realised in actuality, may have been for indoor use. More restrained finishes mimicking lead or stone are on show in the painting of the gardens at Pierrepont House, Nottingham, from 1705, although here the swags on the pots are portrayed as being picked out in gold or blue (Plate 29). Celia Fiennes, describing the gardens at Durdans, in Surrey, noted that there were flowerpots painted blue and red on raked gravel (quoted in Keeling 1990, 24). The well-known picture of the presentation of the first pineapple grown in England to Charles II shows a range of terracotta pots, indicating that plain pots were acceptable in the highest circles.

On a sheet of paper inserted into his manuscript, Evelyn illustrates a variety of forms of garden urn. Few of these seem suited for planting, and some draw heavily on classical forms; however, a pair of rather squat, handled urns are shown, both planted with flowers, possibly lilies. Similar pots holding small trees are depicted in *Aerarium philosophiae mathematicae,* by Bettini, to illustrate certain optical principles. Evelyn discusses the most appropriate settings for the display of garden pots and urns and includes 'Upon Balustrades', which perhaps comes closest to the Hanwell location around the perimeter of the octagonal island. The Pierrepont painting shows the pots spaced, judging by the scale of the human figures, quite widely, at something like 2 m apart. Here the rather severe regularity of the arrangement may reflect a desired ideal rather than the actual conditions, where pots are moved around and occasionally broken and replaced. The spacing of the pots along the top of the terrace walls in the 1662 painting of the gardens at Llanerch, Denbighshire, is broadly similar, while typically the pots shown in the 1639 portrait of the Capel family in the National Gallery are positioned on the piers of an open-work balustrade. By comparison with all these settings, the Hanwell pots were quite closely spaced. Finally, an extraordinarily elaborate array of colourful pots is portrayed on a large piece of embroidery dated from between 1710 and 1720 from Stoke Edith, Herefordshire, in the V & A Museum, London (Plate 30). It is not obvious if this is a depiction of an actual garden or an imagined landscape, but it clearly shows the great potential for variation in any given assemblage of pots, a situation demonstrated daily in any number of modern gardens.

Currently we have no information about planting at Hanwell, but list of plants growing in the gardens at Beaufort House, Chelsea, prepared for Mary, 1st duchess of Beaufort, in July 1691, gives an idea of the scale and range of planting attendant on a great house.

In the fore Court are 22 potts of Spruce ffirrs. In the West Walk next the Kitchin Garden is

01 potts of Lavender Cotton

15 potts of Campanulus Pyramidalis latescens

16 Potts of Scarlett Lychness

10 potts of ffraxinellas

10 potts of White Lillys

20 potts of Flos Cardinalis

26 potts of Ceders

02 potts of Heleborus verus Alb

02 potts of ordinary Honeysuckles

01 pott of Virginia Honeysuckles

12 potts of severall sorts of [left blank] 02 potts of Laurestina

01 Persian Jasmine

06 potts of Nasturtium arborescens

04 potts of Strip't Phillerea

04 potts of Juniper

10 potts of Abrotanum

02 potts of yellow Stoechas

12 potts of double Stock-gillyflowers 06 potts of Southernwood

01 of Myrtle

03 potts of Marum Syraicum

03 potts of double Sweet Williams 04 potts of Gentianellas

03 potts of Stript Thyme

01 of Jucos

100 Auriculas

100 potts of Julyflowers (Duthie 1990, 90)

Ruth Duthie (1990, 98) who transcribed the list remarks that 'It is clear that much use was made of pots of plants in the gardens of this period. Not only tubs and pots of large plants requiring winter protection but also pots of evergreens and ones containing flowering plants which could be removed and be replaced with fresh plants to keep a pleasing show.' Curiously, there are no citrus fruits in this list, unlike the situation at Ham House, where an inventory of 1682 lists '8 large orange trees and lemon trees, 22 smaller orange and lemon trees in tubs, 32 orange and lemon trees in potts, 11 great tubs with myrtles and several pots with greens' (https://www.nationaltrust.org.uk/features/potted-history-of-houseplants-in-our-houses-and-collections, accessed 9 October 2020).

Many of the questions about the Hanwell pots and their contents wait on the results of future scientific analysis; however, some preliminary suggestions can be made about their significance. The decorated pots are clearly all from the same manufacturer and can safely be dated as a group to 1664. The few conventionally shaped flowerpots have a finer fabric and are probably from a different source, although it is possible that they were brought together as part of a single decorative scheme, possibly following closely on the construction of the House of Diversion. The variety of forms suggests a corresponding variety in planting, although until further specialist reports are received, we cannot be specific about this, nor about whether the planting scheme was purely decorative or had an element of collection about it, or whether it focused on a particular category of plant – ornamental shrubs or medicinal herbs for example. It was hoped that the distribution of the four types of pots would give some indication as to their layout when displayed. However, there was no discernible pattern, and while the distribution was reasonably even, there was certainly a greater concentration along the south-east side, suggesting some additional pots were gathered at this location. Evidence for pots placed elsewhere in the garden is slender, although one might have expected to see them set out on the great eastern terrace. No horticultural wares were recorded from the excavations undertaken in 2014 in the immediate vicinity of the castle, nor were any sherds recovered from the lake-side excavation (HANH) or the Sunken Garden (HANI). It is likely therefore that the pots and planting around the House of Diversion made a striking and purposeful contribution to the scene that was not repeated in other parts of the garden.

Important though the pots are, their discovery within the moat surrounding the House of Diversion is just one element in a collection of other artefacts that provide clues to activities around, and the chronology of, this part of the garden. Apart from construction debris, the main finds of significance were glass drinking vessels, glass wine bottles and clay pipes. These alone, independent of any references from Plot, make clear that the site is a social one where drinking and smoking were regular occurrences. In addition, a small number of finds in lead and copper alloy hint at the functioning of the water works that were described by Plot.

Glass

As well as numerous fragments, five significant examples of fine-quality vessel glass were recovered, although they had all clearly been broken elsewhere and the pieces dispersed within the silts of the surrounding moat. One important example consists of the foot, stem and part of the bowl of a small glass, probably for drinking sack (Fig. 41). The stem is of the simple baluster form and bears a seal that, while indistinct, is almost certainly that of a raven's head, signifying its manufacture by George Ravenscroft (1632–83). Its most significant feature is the fact that the glass is crizzled (Truman 1984, 9). Ravenscroft probably learnt aspects of his trade abroad. He built his first glass house at the Savoy, in London, in 1673, and opened a second works with his brother Francis at Henley-on-Thames, in 1674. In 1676 permission for the use of the seal was granted by the Glass Sellers Company (Charleston 1984, 139). On 3 June of that

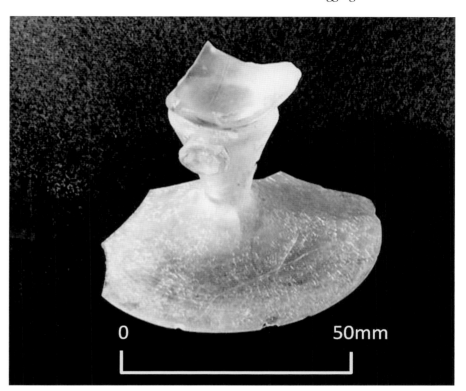

FIGURE 41. Hanwell, HANK19/009/G4, foot and stem of wine glass with crizzeling.

year the Company issued a certificate to the king and followed this up with announcements in the *London Gazette*, repeated several more times in 1677, to

> certify and attest that the defect of the flint glasses (which were formerly observed to crizzel and decay) hath been redressed severall months agoe and all the glasses since made have all proved durable and lasting as any glass whatsoever. (Plot 1705, 258)

It is possible that this is an example of 'experimental' glass that found its way into Sir Anthony's hands prior to his death in 1675, especially given the connection with Robert Plot, who was being consulted about the chemical basis of the process. Other glass specimens were of finer quality and finish, in particular a heavy, solid baluster or knop pattern stem and a foot, stem and part of the bowl with milled thread-work to the base of the bowl and a hollow knop that may be Venetian work from about 1670 (Charleston 2005, 246). Also found were the partial base and bowl of a pedestal bowl, generally used for serving sweetmeats, and a small flask in good-quality green glass of a type described by Paul Courteney (2004, 344) as an apothecary's bottle. Large quantities of glass from broken wine bottles were excavated, as well as two intact examples. Analysis of the fragments suggests that a minimum of 23 separate bottles were discarded into the moat. The 'onion' shape of the bottles accords well with production from the second half of the seventeenth century, although assigning more specific dates is problematic and the forms, as generally recognised, seem to belong more to the 1680s than the 1670s (Banks 1997).

Clay Pipes and Domestic Pottery

Around 2.8 kg of clay pipe remains were excavated, including 89 pipe bowls. They are all reasonably consistent in size and form and corresponded closely with Oxford type B, dated to the period 1650 to 1690 (Oswald 1984). A single example bears the initials E and G, although makers' marks on the foot or spur of the pipe were unusual prior to the eighteenth century (Oswald 1975). It has not proved possible to identify who this maker was from published sources. Comparatively little pottery of a domestic nature was excavated. The single most striking find, whose fragments were recovered over the course of two seasons, 2018 and 2019, was a complete tin-glazed earthenware plate with cobalt blue under-painting, generally known as Delftware (Fig. 42). The composition consists of an arrangement of fruit, probably pears and grapes, set on what may be a shelf or a tabletop, with a drape bearing a snake-like motif. The plain rim and simple, free style of painting, with a slightly abstract feel, argues for an early date, perhaps around the middle of the seventeenth century. The question whether it is of English or Dutch provenance is not easily resolved, as Dutch potters and materials were present in English manufactories throughout the seventeenth century (Ray 2000, 4). The closest parallel, bearing strikingly similar iconography, has been identified as Dutch and dates from well into the following century; it may represent an elaboration on a well-established pattern that has perhaps evolved over decades (Mellors and Kirk 2021). Further fragments of a large, tin-glazed earthenware container banded in blue and pink, probably the base of an apothecary's jar, were recovered, together with small quantities of salt-glazed stoneware.

FIGURE 42. Hanwell, tin-glazed earthenware plate (HANK19/009), left; Dutch polychrome Delftware dish, c. 1770, right, Mellors and Kirk, by kind permission Mellors and Kirk, Auctioneers, Nottingham

Coins

Coins in general were few and far between in the garden, but a particularly significant example was recovered from the moat. This was a seventeenth-century copper alloy tradesman's token. On the obverse it was marked RICHARD. SHORT. IN. WARDENTON, with the arms of the Grocers Company, and on the reverse IN. YE. COVNTY. OF. OXON. MERCER, with, in the centre, HIS HALF PENY. Coincidentally, Alfred Beesley had an example in his collection. The British Museum also has a specimen, which they date from between 1648 and 1672. An authority for the Portable Antiquity Scheme explained the context.

> To deal with a lack of small denominations in the regal coinage civic institutions and individual business people issued copper-alloy tokens between 1648 and 1672 (1679 in Ireland); the end date resulting from the reintroduction of farthings in copper alloy by Charles II. (Portable Antiquities Scheme, https://finds.org.uk/counties/findsrecordingguides/tokens/#17th-century_trade_tokens, accessed 6 July 2021.)

Short was born in 1638, and his wife, whose name was unrecorded, gave birth to a daughter, Anne, in 1674. It seems likely, therefore, that the token dates from the late 1660s or early 1670s. His headstone in Warmington churchyard reads, 'Here lyeth the body of Richard Short who departed this life April 1st 1715.'

Metalwork

Although such items were not specifically referred to by Plot, one might have expected to see a variety of other devices or curiosities displayed within the House of Diversion. Presumably some of the 'instruments' removed by John Cope after Anthony's death may have been shelved here. There is limited evidence for this, although a turned copper alloy finial discovered in 2019 almost certainly came from a lantern clock after the pattern of one by George Harris, the maker of the Hanwell church clock, sold by Bonhams in 2006. A curiously twisted fragment of lead was initially thought to have been a folded section of window came, but closer examination revealed it to be a section of cast lead made to mimic a fine, twisted cord or perhaps braided hair and so is almost certainly an element from a fine figurative lead sculpture. Surviving examples of lead sculpture of the period are quite rare, largely because of the ease with which the metal can be melted down and reused, and a convincing parallel has yet to be found.

Although there are several more years of analysis and research to be done, the assemblage of finds from the moat surrounding the site of the House of Diversion begins to tell of a very specific pattern of activities within a defined time frame. The fine-quality drinking vessels, numerous wine bottles and frequent clay pipes, together with comparatively little in way of other forms of domestic debris – pots for cooking and animal bone for example – all suggest gatherings that are primarily social and, unsurprisingly, probably male focused. While clearly the garden pots were deposited as part of the process of demolition, there is no recognisable separate phase of occupation, although the domestic debris tended to be sealed by the destruction rubble and much of the glass had sunken into the underlying silts. Quantities of finds recovered argue for a fairly short period of occupation and presumably quite intermittent, as visitors came and went. The demolition is dated based on the concept of *terminus post quem;* it cannot have taken place prior to 1664, the date on one of the pots. Indeed it is hard to imagine a context prior to Sir Anthony's death, in 1675, where such destruction could have been countenanced. Evidence from the glass demonstrates activity on site in the 1670s, although from a stylistic point of view both the wine bottles and clay pipes hint at the possibility of occupation continuing into the 1680s. These are important dates when considering the activities of Sir Anthony's brother John in the later decades of the century.

Bibliography

Bacon, F., *The New Atlantis* (originally published London, 1626), in Bruce, S. (ed.) *Three Early Modern Utopias: Utopia, New Atlantis and The Island of Pines* (Oxford, 2008)

Banks, F., *Wine Drinking in Oxford 1640–1850* (Oxford, 1997)

Bashford, R., Dodd, A. and Poore, D., 'Medieval and Post-medieval Remains from Excavations on the Site of the New Auditorium, Corpus Christi College, Oxford', *Oxoniensia* 79 (2014)

Bellavitis, M., 'The Dukes of Este and the Garden as Scenery and Representation of the Magnificence of a Dynasty', *Studies in the History of Gardens and Designed Landscapes* 37(4) (2017)

Biddle, M., *Nonsuch Palace: The Material Culture of a Noble Restoration Household* (Oxford, 2005)

Brunskill, R.W., *Illustrated Handbook of Vernacular Architecture* (London, 1978)

Charleston, R., *English Glass and the Glass Used in England c. 400–1940* (London, 1984)

Charleston, R., 'Fine Vessel Glass', in Martin Biddle, *Nonsuch Palace: The Material Culture of a Noble Restoration Household* (Oxford, 2005)

Courteney, P., 'Vessel Glass', in Rodwell, K. and Bell, R., *Acton Court: The Evolution of an Early Tudor Courtier's House* (London, 2004)

Currie, C.K., 'The Archaeology of the Flowerpot in England and Wales, circa 1650–1950', *Garden History* 21(2) (1993)

Currie, C.K., 'Horticultural Wares from Ham House, Surrey', *Post-medieval Archaeology* 29(1) (1995)

Currie, C.K., 'A Zoomorphic Horticultural Urn from Gosport, Hampshire', *Post-medieval Archaeology* 39(2) (2005)

Dix, B. and Parry, S., 'The Excavation of the Privy Garden', in S. Thurley (ed.) *The Privy Garden, Hampton Court Palace* (London, 1995)

Dix, B., Soden, I. and Hylton, T., 'Kirby Hall and Its Gardens: Excavations in 1987–1994', *Archaeological Journal* 152(1) (1995)

Duthie, R., 'The Planting Plans of Some Seventeenth-Century Flower Gardens', *Garden History* 18(2) (1990)

Francis, J., 'Order and Disorder in the Early Modern Garden, 1558–c.1630', *Garden History* 36(1) (2008)

Hansell, P. and Hansell, J., *Doves and Dovecotes* (Bath, 1998)

Hants. CRO, Conveyance (Counterpart Bargain and Sale) of Teyngle or Tyngle [Tangley] Grange, Oxon, 43M48/121

Keeling, J., *The Terracotta Gardener* (London, 1990)

Lindijer, T. and Van Vlijmen, S., *Om de Tuinpot Geleid: 17e Eeuwse Tuitten uit Haarlem* (Haarlem, 1993)

Mellors and Kirk, 'A Dutch Polychrome Delftware Dish, c1770', sale catalogue (Nottingham, 2021)

Moorhouse, S., 'Finds from Basing House, Hampshire (c. 1540–1645): Part One', *Post-medieval Archaeology* 4(1) (1970)

Noël Hume, A., *Archaeology and the Colonial Gardener*, Colonial Williamsburg Archaeological Series 7 (@@@, 1974)

Oswald, A., *Clay Pipes for the Archaeologist* (Oxford, 1975)

Oswald, A., 'Clay Pipes', in Hassell T. *et al.* (eds.) 'Excavations in St. Ebbes, Oxford, 1967–1976', *Oxoniensia* 49 (1984)

Phillips, J. and Burnett, N., 'The Chronology and Layout of Francis Carew's Garden at Beddington, Surrey', *Garden History* 33(2) (2005)

Plot, R., *The Natural History of Oxfordshire* (London, 1705)

Porter, S., *Destruction in the English Civil War* (Stroud, 1994)

Ray, A*., English Delftware* (Oxford, 2000)

Steane, L.J. and Ayres, J., *Traditional Buildings in the Oxford Region c. 1300–1840* (Oxford, 2013)

TNA, C 4/58/66, Sir Anthony Cope, baronet, infant, v. [blank]: 1638 to 1653. https://discovery.nationalarchives.gov.uk/details/r/C9129536, accessed 14 September 2020

Truman, C., *English Glassware to 1900* (London, 1984)

Wass, S., 'A Way with Water – Water Resources and the Life of an 18th-Century Park', *Industrial Archaeology Review* 38(1) (2016)

Wass, S., 'Waterworks at Packwood House, Warwickshire', *Garden History* 49(2) (2021)

Whittle, E., 'Ornamental and Utilitarian Water Features and Their Water Supply in Cambridge at the Beginning of the Seventeenth Century', *Garden History* 45(1) (2017)

Wise, H., *The Retir'd Gardener: In Six Parts, the First Two Being Dialogues Between a Gentleman and a Gardener* (London, 1706)

Worlidge, J., *Systema horti-culturae, or, The Art of Gardening: In Three Books: The I. Treateth of the Excellency, Scituation [sic] of Gardens...: the II. Treateth of All Sorts of Trees... the III. Treateth of the Kitchin Garden* (London, 1677)

CHAPTER SIX

The End of It All

The Aftermath, the Family and the Estate After 1675

In June 1675, following Sir Anthony's death, there was the potential for the family to be disrupted by an acrimonious dispute resulting from the marriage of his brother and heir, John, to a lodging house keeper from Dunkirk. Beesley gives a succinct account of events which had their roots back in the late 1650s, when Richard Allestree was engaged in facilitating correspondence between the exiled Prince Charles and royalist supporters at home.

> One of the organs of communication was a Mistress Ann Booth, an English woman resident at Dunkirk, who seems to have been a lodging-house keeper. Sir Anthony's brother John Cope was in command of a troop at Dunkirk at the time of the Restoration: he married a Mistress Ann Booth, who appears to have been a person of low origin, since in the pedigrees of the Cope family she is described as being the daughter of *Mr*. Philip Booth. (Beesley 1841, 473)

It seems that offering loyal and possibly dangerous service to the king in waiting was insufficient to raise her status in the eyes of the 4th baronet. Sir Anthony's will, dated 22 January 1674, begins with a significant bequest. 'Unto the Poore inhabiting in Hanwell and the neighbouring Country and Roundabouts the summe of fortie pounds to be appointed amongst them' (TNA, Will of Sir Anthony Cope, PROB 11/350/249). He goes on to list his manors of Hanwell, Hardwick, Drayton, Bruern, Tangley and Shelswell, in Oxfordshire, as well as a variety of other properties, including quays, wharves and warehouses in the City of London, and then writes of measures 'for the providing […] for Mary my dearly beloved wife and for the better securing of the payment of my debts […] and the settling my said Mannors and Lands to continue in my Name and Family so long as it shall please God'. As trustees he appoints 'my worthy and good Friends Sir Francis Fane the Elder, Knight of the Bath, Sir Thomas Chambourlaine Baronet, Sir Edmund Bray knight, William Thursby Esq, Dr. Richard Allestree Provost of Eaton Colledge, William Garnacke esq, John Draper the elder gent'. The situation they were charged with managing may have been a challenging one. His brother John was left use of the properties for the term of his natural life, apart from the manor of Drayton, which went to Mary; however, it was made clear that sons of Sir John would only inherit providing they were 'other than from that issue of said Anne Booth'. Beesley ascribes this hostility to the fact that Booth was of 'low origin', but there could have been other factors, unknown to us, at play here. Indeed Sir Anthony may have met

Anne during his short time of service with the army, when he may also have been posted to Dunkirk. Plot records that John had some continuing involvement in his brother's interests, and Sir Anthony's will does leave to 'Brother John Cope my Studie of Books'. Presumably these formed the core of what was later catalogued in 1898 as the library at Bramshill (Hants. CRO, 43M48/2017–2018). Beyond that he also made bequests to 'Richard Allestree fifty pounds, Dr. Say Provist of Oriele Colledge, formerly my Tutor fifty pounds, in remembrance of my love to them'. It may be significant that Robert Plot is not listed either as trustee or legatee, but of those others mentioned in the will, the playwright Sir Francis Fane (d. 1691), Sir Anthony's first cousin once removed, had been involved in a drainage scheme in the fens and was elected a member of the Royal Society in 1663 (*ODNB*). Beesley takes up the story.

> It appears that Hanwell continued to be the residence of the Hon. Lady Cope, the widow of Sir Anthony, until her death in 1714. Grief for the loss of her husband and children seems to have deprived this lady of her reason; and, from an expression in the Register of Hanwell, it would appear that the Hon. W. Spencer, her brother-in-law, was appointed to her committee under a commission of lunacy– *Information from the Rev. W. H. Cope*. (Beesley 1841, 508)

It is clear that there was a measure of both dispute and cooperation between Mary Cope and her brother-in-law, Sir John, after Sir Anthony's death. On the 20 November 1675 an agreement was sealed to submit to arbitration outstanding disagreements regarding her late husband's personal estate (Hants. CRO, 43M48/389). Subsequently a further agreement between them, dated 3 December 1675, ironed out a variety of issues relating to the settlement of debts and the disposal of Sir Anthony's personal estate. Perhaps most tellingly, Mary surrendered her claim to her late husband's 'instruments' in exchange for fifty guineas while retaining at Hanwell 'all armour and standards', to be surrendered at her death (Hants. CRO, 43M48/391). This not only demonstrates Sir John's interest in his brother's scientific pursuits, but may also be the source of the instruments he was to leave to his son in his will of 1713. It also helps explain Plot's favourable comments about him despite the difficulties of inheritance.

We cannot be sure what Mary's state of mind was at this juncture, although a draft of a letter she wrote, presumably late in 1675, exists concerning financial matters, including the stopping of a legacy to John Draper, one of her husband's trustees, pending a conversation with Sir John (Hants. CRO, 43M48/387). According to an anonymous writer who transcribed it, the note was poorly drafted. 'The whole letter is very blotted and corrected' (A/TC, Anonymous, Century Note Book). This, along with the slightly rambling contents of the text, may be evidence of an unsettled mind or simply someone under pressure or in a hurry. However, there also survives a note written by her prior to Sir Anthony's death regarding a 'demand that persons withholding any writings belonging to her, or writings falsely made concerning her estates, will forfeit lands to which they had real right' and endorsed with the contemporary anonymous comment: 'a very extravagant silly nonsensical paper written by Lady

Cope in Feb 1674' (Hants. CRO, 43M48/386). There appears to be something of an air of distraction in both of these missives, which may have been retained as evidence of Mary's deteriorating mental health. Whatever the case, a set of court papers regarding her committal as a lunatic exists from 30 January 1677 (TNA, C142/734/65). Beyond that, from 1678 onwards, there is a series of receipts from Henry Guy, from 1678–81; William Spencer, from 1681–88; Elizabeth Spencer, from 1688; and Thomas Wharton, from 1689, relating to their role on the 'committee of the body of Dame Mary Cope' (Hants. CRO, 43M48/413–437). Henry Guy (1631–1710) was a lawyer and groom of the bed-chamber to Charles II and may have been a court appointment pending a final settlement. Elizabeth Spencer was half-sister to Mary and married to William Spencer, son of the 2nd baron Spencer of Wormleighton. Those charged with her care were probably not resident in the parish, although a memorandum in the church register for 4 April 1686 records the loan of a large silver chalice and paten,together with payment for setting up communion rails by 'The Honble. Will. Spencer Junr. Esqr. Committee of the Body and Estate of the Lady Mary Cope' (Oxfordshire History Centre, PAR122). Something of a crisis erupted in February 1689, when there are recorded

> Proceedings upon the petition of Sir John Cope. Stating that Lady Cope, the widow of his late brother, Sir Anthony Cope, is a lunatic, and that upon the lands in her jointure great waste has been done, these being upon part of the petitioner's estate in Oxfordshire. Prays that she and the estate may be committed to the custody of Thomas Wharton comptroller of the household. Granted. (Proceedings upon the petition of Sir John Cope (February 1689), http://www.british-history.ac.uk/cal-state-papers/domestic/will-mary/1689-90/pp1-11, accessed 11 January 2021.)

This suggests that all was not well with the management of the estate in Sir John's absence, although it could equally have been a ploy to increase his influence over the property. Even so, it may give some context for the destruction of the House of Diversion and associated features.

Following the Poor Law Act of 1601, justices of the peace and parish officers were normally responsible for ensuring that the nearest lineal kin undertook appropriate care, sometimes with financial support of the parish. In the case of the wealthy, it was usual for the Court of Chancery to be given responsibility for the estates of lunatics. After the Restoration, according to Michael MacDonald (1981, 5), 'the court usually appointed relatives or friends of mad landowners to see that they were cared for and their property preserved. King James had instructed the courts to ensure that "lunatics be freely committed to their best and nearest friends, that can receive no benefit from their death".' Certainly Mary's guardians' efforts in this respect were exemplary, as she survived in her confinement for 37 years. We have no detailed information about the care Mary received. In terms of a diagnosis, this amounted to little more than a label. The words used, according to A. Fessler (1956, 902), were 'mad, melancholic, lunatic, frantic, raving, furious, frensic, crazed, hunted, *non compos mentis*; or it is stated that they are distracted in their mind, in their senses or in their wits; or that they are suffering from a trouble in the brain. Of the various medical terms which appear in the petitions, the term "melancholy" is most often used, very likely because this diagnosis was one of the favourite diagnoses of the period.' If the advice penned by Thomas Willis (1695, 476), Sedleian Professor of Natural Philosophy from 1660 to 1675 and an individual known to Richard Allestree and also presumably to the Copes, was being followed, that 'the affectations of the mind are either to be appeased or subdued by others opposite' and that use should be made of 'Advices, Deceptions, Flatteries, Entreaties and Punishments', her lot would not have been a happy one. However, Willis also recommends 'being, compos'd to a Cheerfulness and Delight: Let a merry or *jocose Discourse, Singing, Musick, Painting, Dancing, Hunting, Fishing* and other pleasant Exercises be brought in use', and so one imagines her treatment would have been very much down to the temperament and expertise of her carers.

As well as residing at Bruern, Sir John Cope had a property in Chelsea, from where he was able to maintain links with the scientific community in London. In November of 1688 Robert Hooke records in his diary meeting him at Jeremy's Coffee House in the company of Sir Christopher Wren and others (quoted in Gunther 1920, vol. 10, 75). Plot (1705 Tab II) evidently hoped that the 'learned and curious artist' John would follow in his brother's footsteps as a patron of scientific enquiry. Given this, the likely abandonment of the garden at Hanwell and its devices seems particularly unfortunate. The whole episode of his marriage and inheritance clearly troubled Sir John deeply, and in his will, of 1713, he made the following statement:

> And now before I proceed towards the disposal of my temporal estate […] I think it fit to declare something of my past and present circumstances to the world […] after having spent many years of my youth in travel beyond the seas in France, Italy, Germany, Flanders and Holland, I returned home with a great desire and a firm resolution to marry, but with consent and approbation of my friends and relations and in order there unto proposed several matches to my elder brother Sir Anthony Cope then living but he not complying with any of them nor consenting to make any settlement upon me in marriage whereby I may better my fortunes (tho his own children were all dead) I did there upon contract myself to Mss. Anne Booth a neighbouring gentlewoman and took her to wife but very privately lest my brother should come to know it he might have been so far displeased as to have given his estate wholly from me. (TNA, Will of John Cope, PROB 11/609/21)

This clearly places the onus for the family dispute on Sir Anthony's refusal to consent to earlier proposals, but the fact that Anne Booth is described as a 'neighbouring gentlewoman' is perhaps being economical with the truth. He goes on to say,

> I understood by his will how unkind he had been in making me only tennant for life and disinheriting my children I then had or should have by my said wife I cast about how to make the best of a Bad Market and finding that he left me his Estate only for my Life yet I had a power of committing wast and of making a joynture to my said wife or any other wife I should after marry, of the whole estate or any part of it by which means I thought I might bring the person on whom the estate was settled after me to a Composition (as accordingly I did) upon his marriage with Sir Thomas Fowles daughter. (TNA, Will of John Cope, PROB 11/609/21)

The heir he is referring to is his cousin Jonathan Cope (1664–94), who went up to Christ Church in 1681 and married Susannah Fowle, daughter of a London goldsmith, in 1688. As Sir John stated, he was trying to 'make the best of a bad market' by being accommodating to the other branches of the family; however, this was within the context of him having 'the power to commit wast'. William Blackstone (2007, 1762), in his *Commentary on the Laws of England*, first published in 1765, gives as instances of committing waste, 'pulling down their houses, extirpating their gardens, ploughing their meadows and cutting down their woods' or more generally, 'Whatever does a lasting damage to the freehold or inheritance is waste' (Blackstone reprinted 2007, 1762). Further legal clarification comes in the 1808 case of Williams v. Williams, where Lord Chancellor Eldon cites Edward Coke, who earlier in the seventeenth century stated that the 'power of committing waste [...] proves that a tenant for life without impeachment of waste has as great a power to do waste, and to convert the property at his own pleasure, as tenant in tail had' (Vesey 1822, 428). This is clearly important in considering the fate of the garden in the latter part of the seventeenth century. We have no specific documentation relating to Hanwell, but a series of valuations and related papers concerning timber and coppice wood on the Bruern and Tangley estates survive indicating there was a determined exploitation of this particular resource (Hants. CRO, 43M48/469–479).

Sir John continued his will by noting that he had, 'with my said wife lived faithfully ever after (being above forty yeares) producing a single daughter, who died, and seven sons, of who four are living'. He then proceeded to consider the portion he could pass on to his children. His oldest son, John, received most of his assets, but his second son, Anthony, in addition to five thousand pounds, is given 'one thousand pounds I formerly sent him to Constantinople'. There follows a lengthy list of items, primarily silver ware, that he distributed amongst his family, including an exotic 'letter case formerly sent me from Constantinople with my Arms embroidered on it in Gold'. There are further mentions of items that may have been part of his brother's collection but must also have reflected Sir John's own continuing interests:

> Item I further give to my said oldest son Sir John Cope the immediate possession after my death of all my books mathematical instruments Optik glasses Marking Tools and other such like things in my Study Lumber Rooms Forge House and elsewhere about the house by me commonly called lumber or Gimcracks and I do advise him to appropriate a Room or two upon the first floor of his house for a Repository (or as I used to call it a Repository) to keep them in for a Diversion sometimes (as they were to me in my younger days) to keep him from idleness or being many times worse employed as some of my predecessors have often been while I have diverted myself with these or such like Trifles and much more to the satisfaction and health both of Body and mind and the increase of my estate. (TNA, Will of John Cope, PROB 11/609/21)

This is the kind of statement that one might have expected to have read in Sir Anthony's will had he had a son to whom he could have passed on his instruments and interests. The fact that it is made by Sir John is a strong indication that Plot's description of him as the 'equally Ingenious Brother Sir *John Cope,* the Heir of his Virtues as well as Estate' is an apt one and may also provide a context for his 1675 London sighting in the company of Robert Hooke and John Ray mentioned earlier. His son John, who was the recipient of the collection of scientific 'lumber or gimcracks', matriculated at his uncle's old college, Oriel, in 1689 and purchased Bramshill House with a loan from his father in 1699. Pevsner remarks that Bramshill 'is one of the largest Jacobean Houses. What Bramshill has in common with the other grandest Jacobean Houses – Hatfield, Audley End, Holland House Charlton House Greenwich – is the concentration on a really spectacular piece of display with few decorative embellishments otherwise' (Pevsner and Lloyd 1985, 138). No doubt there would have been ample spaces for a 'repository' for his 'gimcracks'. The old castle at Hanwell must have seemed rather cramped and old-fashioned, to say nothing of the unfortunate detention of his aunt there. However, Plot, writing in 1692 to Edward Lloyd, 'Keeper of the Museum in Oxon', says, of the fossil illustrated in his *Natural History,* that 'I hope it still remains at the Lady Cope's at Hanwell'. It is possible that elements of Sir Anthony's collection were retained there until a fire and consequent partial demolition of the castle late in the eighteenth century. Books from the library from Hanwell were transferred to Bramshill, where they remained until their sale at Sothebys on 4 March 1913 (Sotheby, Wilkinson and Hodge 1913).

Mary, Sir Anthony's widow, remained confined at Hanwell accompanied by her relations and guardians from the Spencer family until her death, in 1714. Hanwell passed, under the terms of Sir Anthony's will, to Jonathan Cope of Bruern who had been elected M.P. for Banbury for the parliament of 1713 (*HOP*). The *VCH* account notes that

> there is little evidence of early inclosure and Hanwell probably remained largely an open-field parish until the 18th century. In *c.* 1768 Sir Charles Cope, lord of the manor, who probably already owned most of the land, bought out the common rights of copyholders, life- and lease-holders, and other proprietors than the rector, and inclosed the parish. (*VCH:* 122)

They go on to suggest that the remains of the castle were converted into a farm on the death of Sir Charles Cope in 1781 and sum up the later history of the landholdings that

> were divided between his sisters Catherine Ann and Arabella Diana. Catherine, relict of the elder Sir Charles, married Charles Jenkinson, later created Earl of Liverpool, who held Hanwell in trust for his step-daughter Arabella until her marriage in 1790 to John Frederick Sackville, Duke of Dorset. After the duke's death in 1799 Arabella married Charles, Earl Whitworth, with whom she held Hanwell until her death in 1825. Hanwell then passed to her younger daughter Elizabeth, wife of George John West, later Sackville-West, Earl de la Warr (d. 1869). In 1946 Herbrand, Earl de la Warr, made over the estate to his son William, Lord Buckhurst, by a marriage settlement. (*VCH:* 122)

George Berkeley, a later resident, states that in 1782, 'the house came to grief owing to a fire. In that fire part of it was consumed and some of the remainder had to be pulled down as being unsafe' (A/TC, George Berkeley, Notes for book on Hanwell (Undated), 2). He gives no source for this information. The French family became tenants and worked the site as a farm for the next hundred years or so. At the start of the twentieth century, George Fitz-Hardinge Berkeley (1870–1955) took on the lease of the property for 70 years, at a rent of £55 a year. He recorded his impressions of Hanwell as he first saw it in 1902.

> I found myself caught, so to speak, by the charms of an old tower standing rather solitarily in a large rough grass field. It is true that with the tower there was a block or two of red-brick buildings, with a charming Oriel window but it was the glimpse of the tower, looming through the mist that caught me. […] On the north side was a rough grass field and a pond; upon the south and westward two farmyards of brown clay, with bits of old iron and carts and all the litter of a farm. (Ibid., 1)

The Berkeley's plan was to refurbish and to a certain extent rebuild the castle, an enterprise that would 'include the planting of gardens and lawns, shrubs and fruit trees by the hundred; until one day the old tower would seem to be standing in a sea of blossom' (Ibid., 3). His wife, Caroline, had been brought up at Eynsham Hall, Oxfordshire, at a time when her father, James Mason, had been actively engaged in a huge campaign of planting and garden making there. Berkeley's account of effects achieved by the conversion of the brown clay farmyards with lawns, herbaceous borders, a rockery and pool captures some of the flavour of early twentieth-century gardening.

> From end to end of the great barn was a wide herbaceous border where in late summer phlox grew particularly well and made a beautiful mass of colour. A second herbaceous border ran from the loggia (newly built in 1908) on the line of old cow sheds down to a little arbour shade by a medlar tree of which Car[oline] was particularly fond. On the right the border was backed by a low wall crowned with old coping from part of the boundary wall which had been demolished at some time or other. The wall ceased half way down the border which here opened onto Cynthia's garden, a pleasant expanse of mown grass under fruit trees sloping down to the rockery and pool which had been contrived from the farmyard drinking place. This was one of the prettiest parts of the garden. Car had kept the old drinking trough which was fed by a strong spring on the far side of the pool and she had cleverly concealed the prosaic iron pipe which conducted the water across with an arrangement of stones covered with ferns and musk. The overflow from the trough flowed into a little runnel which was dug down the slope and disappeared into an old stone drain to emerge finally into another little pool in the sheepfold. (Ibid., 6)

It is fascinating to see water engineering carried on, albeit on a small scale, in the twentieth-century garden. Drinking water was a priority, as earlier wells within the farmyard had been condemned, so a new well was dug across the other side of the small valley to the south, and an engine installed there to pump water also powered a generator for electricity. Work was done to create an appropriate boundary; Berkeley says with some pride that 'the iron railing which we put up was an extremely good and expensive one' (Ibid., 9). The provision of the present, curving driveway that approaches from the west, replacing the original entry next to the church, proved to be challenging. 'After a good deal of debating we hired a professional landscape gardener from Messers Dickson at Chester. The man came down and lodged here at the public house and got out his suggested plan. We liked his design. It was for virtually the little drive as it remains today' (Ibid., 10). Work to the north of the house focused on planting fruit trees and horse chestnuts, but it was the lake that was 'a great joy to Car […] We bought a punt and a double paddle and used to take friends to see Sir Anthony Cope's bath.' Such joy was not unalloyed, and Berkeley records that 'because poor Car with her illness was rather morbidly sensitive about people looking at her during her last years there were walks that were covered by hedges' (Ibid., 16). Caroline died in 1933 and George remarried, before his own death, in 1955, after which his widow, Joan, auctioned her effects and moved out. The freehold of the property that had been held by the Berkeleys was sold (A/TC, Midland Marts sale catalogue, 1956). In 1957, the castle was opened as an 'educational centre for the training of 27 students from 11 different nations in examinations to gain admission into university' (A/TC, Cutting, *The Oxford Mail*, 1957). Known as the Woodnewton Tutorial Establishment, under the direction of the Reverend Charles Brown, as well as offering preparation for the General Certificate of Education, the school also boasted boating on the lake and 'ample supplies of fresh milk and vegetables from our own gardens' (A/TC, undated school brochure). The claim that the 'establishment has well equipped laboratories' may be a slight exaggeration. The school closed early in the 1960s and the freehold was sold in 1977, at which point the property was divided up into several lots. The surrounding agricultural land remained in the hands of the Sackvilles, earls De La Warre. Since their purchase of the coach house and the greater part of the gardens in 1984, Rowena E. Archer and Christopher Taylor have carried out extensive additional planting and have opened the gardens annually for an event known as 'Stars and Snowdrops', which also showcases the work of the Hanwell Community Observatory, founded in 1999, and enables visitors to admire the huge colony of wild snowdrops on the eastern terrace.

The Archaeology of the Gardens from 1675 to the Present Day

The extent to which Sir John capitalised on his 'power to commit wast' is unclear, as is the time frame. Given that arrangements for Sir Anthony's widow, Mary, were in place by 1677, it suggests that Sir John may have had some control of the estate fairly soon after Sir Anthony's death. Even so, it seems likely that there may have been a period during which care and maintenance of the gardens were neglected, possibly to the point where locals felt that they could move in and help themselves to materials with impunity. The fact that the collection of decorative garden pots was still in position indicates a comparatively short time span between Sir John's takeover and the demolition of the House of Diversion, although the archaeological evidence certainly leaves room for this not to have taken place until the 1680s. What is certain is that these elaborate gardens could fall into disuse and become overgrown and prey to the depredations of vandals remarkably quickly. Even the prestigious gardens at the Villa d'Este were not immune to such attacks. According to Philip Jacks, 'In the two decades following Cardinal Luigi's death in 1586, the Fontana dell'Organo, like much of the gardens, fell into serious neglect. Already four years earlier, the copper pipes and ducts of Venard's apparatus had been vandalised' (Jacks 2019, 271). Closer to home, neglect to the gardens at Beddington, the seat of the Carews, is recorded in John Evelyn's diary for 20 September 1700.

> In decay as well as the Grotts & other curiosities, cabinets and fountaines in the house and abroade, thro the debauchery & negligence of the Heires, it being now fallen to a child under age, and onely kept by a servant or two from utter delapidation. The Estate & Parke about it also in decay: the negligence of a few years, ruining the elegances of many.' (Evelyn 1955, 354)

However, the archaeological evidence at Hanwell argues for a process of careful and controlled demolition, at least of some features, and the reuse or sale of materials. At the House of Diversion, the process of demolition was clear to see. Initially the perimeter pots had been pushed or thrown off the parapet into the moat. Most were close to the foot of the wall, although a few had been thrown or kicked and lay at a distance of up to 3 m in some cases. Although these pots appear, at first glance, to be ideal candidates for reuse or resale, examination of some the best-preserved examples shows a degree of damage, especially spalling caused by frosts, to the extent that they were probably not worth saving, however, the plants seem to have been removed.

The coping stones to the perimeter wall were taken down and, along part of the north-west side of the octagon, three were laid on the bed of the moat, presumably to give a secure footing for the demolition work. Curiously, the body of a medium-sized dog, perhaps a spaniel, was laid on the northern-most slab, before being buried in rubble pulled down from the wall. The angled coping stone from the corner at the west end of the north side had simply been levered off and had fallen into the moat end on, where it remained until excavated. Many of the facing stones must have been removed for reuse, although a surprising number of well-dressed stones were abandoned, together with large quantities of rubble. Mixed in with the upper strata of this spread of rubble were several kilograms of roof tiles, the vast majority ceramic, but with a significant number of stone examples. In addition, many fragments of wall plaster, which had been attached to timber laths, were recovered, some with combed decoration. The fact that a large dump of broken roof tile was found on the north side of the island with architectural fragments gathered on the south side and that most pieces of window glass and lead cames were excavated along the south-west side argues for materials being gathered together and sorted into piles on site before removal. Spills of molten lead recovered suggest that this material was melted down and probably cast into ingots before being taken away. Given the almost total lack of plaster or tile from the island itself and the absence of features, such as foundation trenches or post holes, there is a strong possibility that as part of a levelling process, its upper layers were removed to fill the surrounding moat, with a view perhaps to making the ground more cultivable. A curious set of narrow ridges running north to south that survive to the south-east of the octagon may be the remains of a later asparagus bed. The valley is now drained by a series of open channels cut through the remaining dams, a measure probably from the nineteenth century intended to improve drainage and the productivity of the land. The base of the former fourth pool is dissected by a variety of drainage channels, and in 2017 a stone sluice was excavated (HANJ) on the south side of one of these water courses. It appears to have been part of a sluice similar to those used to flood and empty traditional water meadows and so may have been connected with some form of cultivation of the valley bottom instituted after the draining of the pool. A number of shallow ditches mark later divisions of the land to form small fields, a pattern reflected in an estate map of 1799 and First Edition Ordnance Survey map of 1882. Material remains from the Berkeley tenancy and subsequent ownership from the first half of the twentieth century include elements of the levelled iron rail fencing and a shallow, concrete-lined pool within the Sunken Garden that was probably built for paddling or yachting with model boats (Fig. 43).

FIGURE 43. Hanwell, HANI, twentieth-century paddling pool, looking southwest.

Recent planting and other works have been well documented by the current owners, and present-day phenomena, such as the site of an outdoor gathering for an illegal party, have also been recorded. It is a curious coincidence that in the twentieth-first century the garden is home to scientific endeavour, through the presence of the Hanwell Community Observatory, in much the same way that it was in the seventeenth century, and it is to an appraisal of the claim that Hanwell had a part to play in the birth of modern science that we finally turn.

Bibliography

A/TC, Anonymous, Century Note Book entitled *Transcript from Some of the Cope Papers in the Bodleian at Oxford*

A/TC, Berkeley, G., Notes for Book on Hanwell (undated)

A/TC, Midland Marts sale catalogue (22 September 1956)

A/TC, cutting, *The Oxford Mail* (22 October 1957)

A/TC, school brochure (undated)

Blackstone, W., *Commentaries on the Laws of England in Four Books* (New Jersey, reprint 2007)

Cope, J., Proceedings upon the Petition of Sir John Cope (February 1689), http://www.british-history.ac.uk/cal-state-papers/domestic/will-mary/1689-90/pp1-11, accessed 11 January 2021

Fessler, A., 'The Management of Lunacy in Seventeenth Century England: An Investigation of Quarter-Sessions Records', *Proceedings of the Royal Society of Medicine* 49 (1956)

Hants. CRO, Two Volume Catalogue for Bramshill Library, July 1898, 43M48/2017-2018

Hants. CRO, Agreement between Mary Cope and Sir John Cope, 20 November 1675, 43M48/389

Hants. CRO, Agreement between Mary Cope and Sir John Cope, 3 December 1675, 43M48/391

Hants. CRO, Part of Letter from Dame Mary Cope, 43M48/387

Hants. CRO, Letter and Disclaimer by Lady Mary Cope, February 1675, 43M48/386

Hants. CRO, Valuations and Related Papers Concerning Timber and Coppice Wood on Bruern and Tangley Estates, 43M48/469–479

Hants. CRO, Receipts from Henry Guy and His Successors, 1678–1689, 43M48/413–437

Hooke, R., *Diary*, quoted in Gunther, R., *Early Science in Oxford*, vol. 10 (Oxford, 1920)

HOP, Matthews, S., 'Cope, Sir Jonathan (?1691–1765)'

Jacks, P., 'Pirro Ligorio and the Design of the Fontana del Diluvio at the Villa d'Este', *Studies in the History of Gardens and Designed Landscapes* 39(4) (2019)

MacDonald, M., *Mystical Bedlam, Madness, Anxiety and Healing in Seventeenth-Century England* (Cambridge, 1981)

ODNB, Vander Motten, J.P., 'Fane, Sir Francis (d. 1691)'

Oxfordshire History Centre, Parish of Hanwell, Church Registers Vol. 1 (1586–1753), PAR122

Pevsner, N. and Lloyd, D. *The Buildings of England: Hampshire and the Isle of Wight* (London, 1985)

Plot, R., letter to Edward Lloyd (1692) quoted in Gunther, R., *Early Science in Oxford*, vol. 12 (London, 1939)

Plot, R., *The Natural History of Oxfordshire* (London, 1705)

Sotheby, Wilkinson and Hodge, *Catalogue of Valuable Books and Manuscripts, Recently the Property of Sir Anthony Cope, Bt. Selected from the Library at Bramshill Park, Winchfield, Hants Which Will Be Sold at Auction... on Tuesday, the 4th of March, 1913* (London, 1913)

TNA, Will of Sir Anthony Cope, PROB 11/350/249

TNA, Chancery Inquisition, Cope, Mary (lunatic), C142/734/65

TNA, Will of John Cope, PROB 11/609/21

Vesey, F., *Reports of Cases Argued and Determined in the High Court of Chancery 1808–1809* (Philadelphia, 1822)

Willis, T. *The London Practice of Physick* (London, 1695)

CHAPTER SEVEN

Oxford, Science and Gardening

Oxford, Hanwell and Early Scientific Thinking

The transformation of thinking and, as a result, teaching relating to natural philosophy at Oxford was brought about by a combination of historical events, a certain social milieu and, of course, the individual talents of a number of profound thinkers and experimentalists. The condition of Oxford studies at the start of the seventeenth century was summed up, perhaps with unnecessary bleakness, by the philosopher Thomas Hobbes as being 'based on incomprehensible logic and sterile physics' (quoted in Feingold 1997, 359). The course of events that supported change, particularly in the 1650s, and that contributed to the founding of the Royal Society in the early1660s, was partially played out in the colleges, coffee shops and gardens of Oxford, where there was an 'essentially liberal environment prevailing which in turn facilitated the swift and largely unchecked dissemination of the new modes of thought among teachers and students alike' (Ibid., 361). A precursor to the eventual development of a school of scientific thought at Oxford was the arrival of physician William Harvey (1578–1657). As the king's physician, Harvey came to Oxford in 1642 and became warden of Merton College. This enabled him to gather a circle of acquaintances, particularly anatomist Nathaniel Highmore (1613–85) and George Bathurst (1610–44), of Trinity College. George was older brother to Ralph Bathurst (1619–1704), another physician, who was at Trinity from 1637 and went on to be an influential member of the Oxford experimental group and the Royal Society. The group was able to support Harvey in his work towards the publication of *Exercitationes de generatione animalium,* in 1651 (Cooke 1975, 186). Trinity also had its own tradition of an experimental interest in mathematics and mechanics going back to the time of the mathematician Thomas Allen (1542–1632). Harvey left Oxford in 1646, after the surrender of the city to Parliament.

Subsequent to the defeat of royalist forces, and following the second civil war, in 1648, attempts were made to tame the university through a series of purges. One of the parliamentary visitors appointed in 1647, and from 1648 president of Trinity College, was Robert Harris, who had been evicted from the living at Hanwell by royalist troops five years previously and who would, of course, have known the young Sir Anthony well (*ODNB*). The puritan reformers, appointed to undertake the visitations by Parliament, required from 1649 that an oath of engagement be sworn by members and employees of the university.

One of the consequences of the anti-Anglican sentiments embraced by the new parliamentarian rulers of Oxford was the setting up of a cavalier congregation at Beam Hall, in Merton Street, by cleric John Fell, who had been ejected from Christ Church. Beam Hall was the lodging place of his brother-in-law, physician Thomas Willis, who, as well as being at the centre of a like-minded group of fellow physicians, also became an active member of the experimental philosophy group. Fell was joined there by two other churchmen, John Dolben and Richard Allestree, the latter Sir Anthony Cope's future house guest. Through the early 1650s they 'kept up the forbidden offices of the Church of England' (Beddard 1997, 805). It is possible to over-emphasise the internal conflicts between differing political and religious factions within the university during the 1650s, and Worden (1997, 771) states that 'the partisan loyalties of puritans and royalists, deep and socially divisive as they often were, were time and again softened or sublimated by common enthusiasms, by scholarly collaboration, or by private kindness'. He cites the care administered to Robert Harris, the ailing head of Trinity College, by royalist physicians Ralph Bathurst and Thomas Willis. Perhaps Sir Anthony's transition from undergraduate to virtuoso was not quite such a fraught process as one might have imagined.

In the aftermath of the parliamentarian visitations there was a series of new appointments that marked the starting point for what was once termed 'the Scientific Revolution'. This began with the arrival of John Wilkins (1614–72) as master of Wadham College, in 1648, who was, as already mentioned, Aubrey's 'principal reviver of experimental philosophy at Oxford'. That same year physician and experimenter William Petty (1623–87) was given a fellowship of Brasenose College and incidentally, as noted earlier, Sir Anthony Cope matriculated at Oriel College. These events were followed closely by the appointments of John Wallis (1616–1703), mathematician and cryptographer, as Savilian professor of geometry and Seth Ward (1617–89) as Savilian professor of astronomy, in 1649. Ward collaborated with Wilkins when, shortly after his arrival, he fitted out a room as an observatory in the tower above the gate at Wadham. Given that the average age at appointment of Wilkins, Petty, Wallace and Ward was 31, it is perhaps possible to attribute some of what followed to the 'activity of youth'. Christopher Wren (1632–1723) went up to Wadham in the summer of 1650, the beginning of a long association with Oxford, which saw him graduate in 1651 and receive his M.A. in 1653. Subsequently he was elected a fellow of All Souls College. Robert Hooke (1635–1703) secured the post of chorister at Christ Church in 1653 or 1654. His future employer Robert Boyle (1627–91) moved to Oxford in 1655 or 1656. While all these individuals would have been well versed in the writings of Francis Bacon, the influence of the French philosophers René Descartes (1596–1650) and Pierre Gassendi (1592–1655), representing, respectively, dualist and materialist perspectives, was also becoming current. Indeed Aubrey credits Robert Hooke as inducting Robert Boyle into Cartesian philosophy. Unified by a common interest in experimentation, many of these individuals came together under the aegis of

Wilkins to form the 'experimental philosophy club'. We have no evidence as to Sir Anthony's direct involvement in this group; indeed the club's statutes of the 1680s purposefully excluded undergraduates. As Sprat (1734, 323) expressed it, 'the *Art* of *Experiments* is not thrust into the hands of Boys'. However, it is possible that during the early stages of the association, before the adoption of a formal constitution in October 1651, rules may have not been quite so prescriptive. Other experimental groups included

> the small chemistry group that used Thomas Willis's rooms at Christ Church and Ralph Bathurst's at Trinity during 1648–49, the group that held regular meetings at William Petty's lodgings in 107 High Street (Buckley Hall) between 1649 and 1651, the much larger group that met weekly at John Wilkins's lodgings in Wadham College between 1651 and 1659 and, on a somewhat smaller scale, the group that met sporadically at Robert Boyle's lodgings at 88 High Street (Deep Hall) between about 1657 and 1668. (Gouk 1996, 265)

Obviously there were plenty of other opportunities for social contact that could have advanced the young Sir Anthony's acquaintance with those whom Henry Oldenburg, first secretary to the Royal Society, dubbed 'the *Oxonian* Sparkles' and Gouk termed, more prosaically, 'scholars and practitioners'. Gouk emphasised the fact that 'One of the most distinctive features of Oxford "scientific life" […] was the habit of small groups of like-minded individuals to meet informally on a regular basis […] to perform experiments and discuss their findings' (Ibid., 262). She argued the case for the close association between 'cultural and intellectual production' and documented the particular contribution made by music. Gatherings to enjoy performances by musicians, such as Thomas Baltzar, drew together many of those with an interest in natural philosophy, with which music was seen to be inextricably linked. These social and, by inference, intellectual exchanges continued in the taverns and coffee shops of Oxford. The garden at Wadham College was used to demonstrate a number of devices, as well as functioning as a social space and a space for reflection. We assume that Sir Anthony would have had access to these grounds both as an undergraduate and presumably later, when, as Baltzar's patron, he maintained links with Wadham. The first historian of the Royal Society, Thomas Spratt, writing in 1667, summarised the coming together of, as Margery Purver expressed it, 'the man and the moment', in these terms:

> It was therefore, some space after the end of the Civil Wars at *Oxford* in *Dr. Wilkins* his lodgings, in *Wadham College*, which was then the place of Resort for Virtuous, and Learned Men, that the first meetings were made, which laid the foundation of all this that follow'd. The *University* had, at that time, many Members of its own. who had begun in a *free way* of reasoning; and was also frequented by some gentlemen of Philosophical minds. (Purver 1967, 102)

No doubt Sir Anthony could have been counted amongst this body of 'gentlemen', given an *entrée* into matters scientific on the basis of what Frank (1973, 209) calls abundant 'ties of kinship and college'. The 'Learned Society of

Virtuosi, that, during the late Usurpation lived obscurely at *Tangley*', referred to by Plot, is presumably a further extension of these ties.

Following the restoration of Charles II, in 1660, many of the key participants moved away, some to London, and though far from becoming a backwater, Oxford was perhaps no longer at the leading edge of scientific thought and practice. Wilkins had been moved, at the behest of the fellowship there, to become the master of Trinity College, Cambridge, in 1659, a post from which he was dismissed in 1660, after which he moved to London. At a meeting chaired by Wilkins in the capital in November of that same year, 'something was offered about a design of founding a College for the promoting Physico-Mathematicall, Experimental Learning', according to Purver (1967, 110) 'an occasion generally regarded as the birth of the Royal Society'. In 1662 the society was incorporated with a royal charter, a measure that Purver (Ibid., 129) notes would 'enormously strengthen their position: prestige and legal standing'. In its early years the Society made much use of the premises of Gresham College in Bishopsgate, London, a small, private foundation whose curriculum was adapted to 'the understanding and practical outlook of a non-academic audience' (Ibid., 187). Debate continues as to the precise make-up and indeed significance of the Royal Society. As Michael Hunter (1976, 209) remarked, 'though it is generally accepted that the Society comprised some sort of elite of Restoration science, the precise relationship that it bore to the contemporary English scientific community is far from clear'. What a number of commentators have noted from analysis of membership lists is that the Society was predominantly made up of royalist, Anglican, university-educated gentlemen and that, not surprisingly, fewer members were drawn from the class of artisans and tradesmen. Lotte Mulligan characterises the membership this way:

> On the whole, then, the royalists were academically well-qualified men of affairs, out in the world, holding Court and government positions, interested in science as well as in history; many of them were trained at the law or in the church, and some were London businessmen. The parliamentarians were proportionately less formally educated. Their graduates were either practical medical men or less worldly academics. (Mulligan 1973, 107)

This may perhaps be an oversimplification of a complex situation, but it does seem to contrast with the more ecumenical approach enjoyed by the earlier Oxford experimentalists.

After Wilkins's departure, Boyle continued to host meetings of the experimental philosophy club in Oxford, but by the early 1660s there remained few of the personnel with the ability, or the inclination, to continue the pursuit of natural and experimental philosophy. In 1664, the year Sir Anthony was commissioning his garden urns, John Evelyn reported coming across Christopher Wren, Robert Boyle and John Wallis in the Schools Tower at the Bodleian 'with an inverted tube or telescope observing the discus of the sunn for the passing of Mercury that day before the Sunn', evidently still actively engaged in their researches. However, a serious decline had set in. Feingold (1997, 441) records that 'less than a quarter of the hundred scientists and virtuosi who participated in the work of the various Oxford groups in the 1640s and 1650s were still in residence when Robert Boyle left for London in 1668'. What these days might be termed a 'brain drain' had led to a significant diminution in scientific interest and output that not even the combined enthusiasm of Aubrey, Evelyn and Plot could entirely reverse. It appears that during the decade that Sir Anthony would have had the opportunity to expand his involvement in experimental philosophy, interest in Oxford was waning. The founding of the Ashmolean Museum, in 1677, and the construction of its first premises, in Broad Street, with its basement laboratory, together with the appointment of Plot as its first keeper and professor of 'chymistry' six years later, all came too late for Sir Anthony (Martinón-Torres 2012, 25).

Gardens and Science

As noted previously, a key component of the House of Salomon in *The New Atlantis* was the garden, which provided not only the setting for a variety of science-focused buildings, but also outdoor spaces for further observation and investigation (Fig. 44). In her account of musical performances in Oxford in the late 1650s, including those by Thomas Baltzar, Gouk (1996, 257) stresses that 'where the making of scientific knowledge is generally understood as arising out of a set of collective practices, the spatial dimensions of this process have come to the fore'. In examining the locations of colleges, coffee shops, lodging houses, and gardens and the routes between them, she defined an environment within which 'traditional boundaries can be temporarily overlooked and conventional behaviour suspended in favour of an atmosphere more conducive to the exchange of skills and ideas'. She concludes that, in considering the twin domains of music and natural philosophy, 'activities now judged as innovative in each sphere initially emerged in informal and highly unstable contexts where practitioners from very different backgrounds were unexpectedly brought together in a new way' (Ibid. 287). This is part of a wider understanding of 'spaces of discursive exchange', whereby 'ideas are produced in, and shaped by, settings' that, of course, included gardens (Livingstone 2003, 7).

A consideration of the gardens at Hanwell, in the light of archaeological investigations and Plot's account of them, with his *New Atlantis* claim, suggests a variety of ways in which they may have both embodied and promoted certain modes of scientific thinking. Remmert (2016, 12) remarks that, 'If designed accordingly, the fashionable gardens of the rich and powerful would demonstrate the sophistication and hence the prestige of their owners; but at the same time, they would be promoting the mathematical sciences among the most influential members of society.' This reflects comments by Hubertus Fisher *et al.* (Ibid., 2) that 'With their many facets, the mathematical sciences and botany point to the increasingly "scientific" approach that was being adopted in garden art and garden culture in the early modern period.' Michael Lee and Kenneth Helphand (2014, 1) go further. In their assessment of Leo Marx's book, *The Machine in*

NEW ATLANTIS

a. *Wildfires burning in water*
b. *Engine houses to study motion*
c. *Ability to fly in air*
d. *Instruments for seeing distant objects in the heavens*
e. *Light intensified and thrown great distances*
f. *Glasses to see small bodies perfectly*
g. *Perspective houses to study light and color*
h. *Pools to strain fresh water out of salt*

i. *Gardens bearing more speedily than their nature*
j. *Animals bred both greater and smaller than their kind*
k. *Fruit much larger than its nature*
l. *Aids to improve hearing*
m. *Sound houses for studying sound*
n. *Sound conveyed in tubes over distances*
o. *Deep caves for refrigeration*
p. *Ships sailing under water*

FIGURE 44. The gardens of *The New Atlantis*, illustration by Lowell. Hess, 1970.

the Garden, they note that 'he posited that modernity came into being when the "machine" – a symbol and artefact of technology – entered the pastoral "garden" of the preindustrial world'. Whether consciously or unconsciously Sir Anthony was certainly embracing this modernity when he introduced features, such as his multi-faceted mill, into the gardens at Hanwell. Indeed gardens themselves have always been available for many different purposes, inter-leaved and inter-layered in a way which creates both tensions and opportunities. The contrasts between gardens as active spaces full of movement and restful places of tranquillity parallels the social versus the contemplative role they have enjoyed. John Evelyn experienced something of these tensions as he

> wanted [Sayes Court] and his other gardens, to become the locus of philosophical discussion among the learned gentlemen he styled *paradisi cultores* or 'hortulan saints', but fretted that, by inviting friends to visit and admire it, even if under the rubric of what he called a 'deipnosophisse', a re-enactment of Athenaeus' philosophical supper, he was violating the spirit of Epicurean withdrawal. (Barbour and Preston 2015, 477)

In thinking about the significance of Sir Anthony's additions to the gardens at Hanwell in the 1660s and early 1670s it is worth considering the role gardens played in the development of scientific thinking. Stephen Shapin (1988, 377) explains that 'the performance and the consideration of experimental work in mid to late seventeenth-century England took place in a variety of venues. These sites ranged from the apothecary's and instrument maker's shops, to the coffee house, the royal palace, the rooms of college fellows, and associated collegiate and university structures. But by far the most significant venues were the private residences of gentlemen.' These residences would, of course, have generally had gardens attached that would have been to hand for a variety of purposes. Mathematical sciences were clearly important in the creation of gardens as can be seen by referring back to Bettini's *hortus mathematicus*, in his *Apiaria universae philosophiae mathematicae* of 1642 where he 'made expert use of the notion that everything to create a garden of amusement and edification – geometry, architecture, perspective, optics, music etc. – could be derived from the mathematical sciences' (Remmert 2016, 12). It appears that Sir Anthony's interests were less mathematical and more earthy with his enthusiasm for rocks, minerals and fossils but, whatever the case, the gardens at Hanwell afforded many opportunities for study and reflection. In general terms there were a number of routes by which gardens could be exploited for advancing scientific thought.

The Garden as the Artisan Test Bed

As fundamentally practical engineered spaces gardens could act as showcases for the activities of a variety of craft workers whose knowledge and skills were often used to inform more structured scientific thinking. So it is that we see engineers such as Salomon de Caus and mathematicians such as Bettini publishing garden designs as exercises in geometry and perspective. There was a symbiotic relationship between garden design and layout and the development of new and improved methods of surveying, especially those relying on optical instrumentation came about as 'a bottom-up contribution of landscape architecture to optical technologies' (Farhat 2014, 26). As John Henry (2001, 36), pointed out, 'The mathematical sciences were always concerned with practical useful knowledge and the practitioners were generally empiricist in their orientation.' By seventeenth-century standards the gardens at Hanwell were not excessively formal although the geometries of knot work could have been explored on the upper terrace next to the house. Careful surveying would have been required for the management of the water supply to the mill. However, the layout of the octagonal island is so poorly executed that it speaks of ignorance or incompetence rather than expertise, a perplexing situation far removed from that in an illustration from 1648 by Benjamin Bramer (1588–1652) depicting the setting out of a polygonal pond which then, through a wooden sluice, feeds a water mill (Fig. 45). This is clearly a situation that echoes some elements of the arrangements at Hanwell.

The installation of such features as fountains and related pumping mechanisms enabled savants such as Bacon and later Evelyn to document and indeed celebrate the practical skills of the artisans they employed. Jim Bennett (1986, 1) noted that there was an intimate connection between the scholar and the craftsman as exhibited in many gardens. In commenting on the 'contribution of the mechanical arts to the rise of empirical and experimental methodologies within the new sciences of the seventeenth century' Pamela Long (2001, 2) also registered the primacy of the practical. Katherine Rinne's (2014, 111) comments on the Italian experience are instructive in this respect: 'Hydraulics, the scientific study of the dynamic and static behaviours of liquids, including water, was an area of intense theoretical and practical concern between the fifteenth and eighteenth centuries.' There is an intermingling of craft skills with more conceptual endeavours, as shown by practical and theoretical studies by

FIGURE 45. Surveyors at work, from Braemer, 1648.

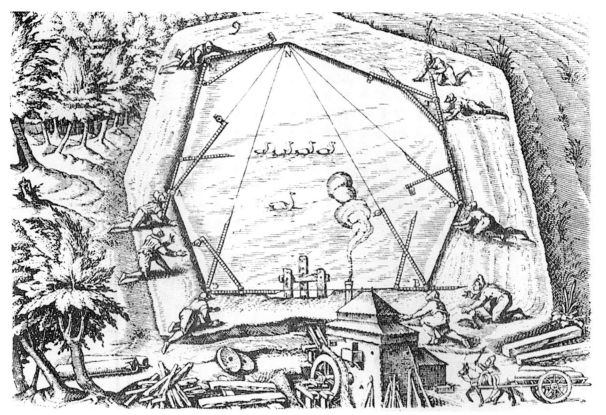

Geralamo Cardarmo (1501–76), Jacques Besson (1540–73) and Benedetto Castelli (1578–1643). In the case of Hanwell, both the plumbing at the House of Diversion and the grinding, cutting and boring mill would have been venues where Sir Anthony could have observed, and to a certain extent taken ownership of, a range of skills that demonstrated mastery of a variety of natural processes and in particular the application of De Caus's *'forces mouvantes'*.

The Garden as Laboratory

An important element in Bacon's *New Atlantis* was 'laboratories for every kind of research as well as orchards, gardens, parks and lakes where experiments in every field of nature could be carried out'. This was a consciously constructed artificial environment. 'The gardeners were not concerned with beauty. They were concerned with which soils best suit which plants. They artificially accelerated growth, artificially obtained fruit of greater sweetness in a variety of colours, tastes, and shapes, and created new kinds of plants' (Jaroszyński 2007, 150). There is nothing in Plot, apart from the appellation 'virtuoso', to suggest that Sir Anthony was actively involved in such experimentation. Clearly opportunities existed. In St James's park in London, 'After the Restoration, a 40-foot-long telescope was mounted in the middle of the park which, with its plants and exotic animals was a kind of outdoor laboratory for the horticulturalists, botanists zoologists and astronomers' (McDayter 1995, 136) Experiments, such as those on human flight, were carried out in the Warden's Garden at Wadham (Garnett and Davies 2014, 19). Of course physical evidence of such activities is hard to come by, but it is not impossible that at some point excavated material may emerge at Hanwell akin to the remains of crucibles and retorts dug up in the back garden of the original Ashmolean Museum (Martinón-Torres 2012).

The Garden as Collection

The concept of a botanic garden as an ordered collection of plants, 'a living encyclopaedia', is an important one. It has its origins in the Middle Ages when 'the *Hortus Medius*, where plants were cultivated above all for their pharmacological properties, evolved into the *Hortus Botanicus*, whose scope was the disinterested pursuit of knowledge' (Tomasi 2005, 102). This transition was first expressed in the botanical gardens founded in Italy at Pisa (1543) and Padua (1545). The Botanic gardens at Oxford originated as the Oxford Physic Garden in 1621 at the behest of Henry Danvers, earl of Danby. Its status as a place of learning was spelt out from the outset as a facility 'whereby learning, especially the faculty of medicine might be improved' (quoted in Batey 1982, 31). A 'conservatory for evergreenes' accommodated, at the time of a survey in 1648, a variety of tender plants, including orange, myrtle and pomegranate, all heated when a 'grated iron wagon filled with burning charcoals was hauled around the pathways' (Woudstra 2014, 84). Sir Anthony would no doubt have had access to the physic garden but despite Plot's account of the distinctive variety of small-leaved elm at Hanwell and the current presence of the rare herb, Saracen's Woundwort, there is no evidence that Sir Anthony had any specific or unusual interest in plants. As well as accommodating collections of plants subject to study, many botanic gardens, for example at Leiden, Montpellier and Pisa, as well as the occasional aristocratic garden, were also home to 'cabinets of curiosities'. John Dixon Hunt (2001, 267) reminds us that 'in sixteenth-century English the word "cabinet" had a sense of summerhouse or bower in a garden and it continued to be so used at least until Miller's Gardeners dictionary of 1712'. Such collections of what today we might view as the weird and wonderful often facilitated 'Bacon's brand of supposedly "theory-free" fact gathering' (Henry 2001, 40). Bacon in his *Gesta Grayorum* elevates the business of collecting to the creation of a microcosm, being 'a model of the universal nature made private'. There is nothing to say that Sir Anthony was aware of his great-great-uncle Walter's well-known collection nor whether Sir Anthony had his select items on show in a dedicated space either inside the house or in a structure located in the garden, possibly within the House of Diversion itself. What is clear is that he did have a special interest in rocks and fossils and particularly in stones that could be cut in his mill and polished to create attractive handles for his cutlery. An inventory of Hanwell, drawn up in 1658 in connection with a valuation associated with the family's debt to Milton (French 1939, 349), demonstrates that there was no shortage of rooms in which a collection could be housed but nothing in the list of contents indicates anything that reflects on Sir Anthony's collecting interests or status as a virtuoso.

The Garden as Social Space

There was little place for the solitary researcher in the world of natural philosophy in the seventeenth century, rather there was a clear understanding of the importance of social contact and collaboration. A typical expression of this can be read in a letter from John Dury (1596–1680), a member of Hartlib's circle of learned correspondents, that listed the requirements for a proposed house of investigation and experiment to be set up at Vauxhall. This suggested that it be 'a place of resort where unto Artists and Ingeneers from abroad and at home may repair to meet with one another to confer together and improve in many ways their abilities and hold forth profitable Inventions for the use of the Comon-wealth' (quoted in MacGregor 1989, 208). This was another Utopian scheme that came to nothing although the gardens were eventually opened to the public in 1661 for purposes far from scientific (Corfield 2012, 7). Boyle's conversation with Carneades and Eleutherius in the *Sceptical Chymist* of 1677 is set in a garden below 'one of the arbours to enjoy under its cool shades a delightful protection from the yet troublesome heat of the sun', a clear contrast with their 'Dark and Smokie Laboratories'. This is not only symbolic of the 'property and private wealth' of these gentlemen practitioners but also must reflect on the day-to-day reality of social interactions (Preston 2015, 127). Given that a community of like-minded individuals is a key requisite for a *New Atlantis* the expectation might be that Sir Anthony maintained a household where such groupings came together regularly. Again one calls to mind the 'Society of Learned *Virtuosi*' at his property at Tangley. Certainly the opportunities were there, thinking of the collegiate appearance and layout of the castle itself, the broad terraced walkways along the north side of the upper pool and the venue termed the House of Diversion with its associated debris of clay pipes and broken wine bottles conjuring up these social spaces. However, apart from the late 1650s when we have Allestree and Baltzar in temporary residence, there are no records of anyone, either resident or local or transient making use of the gardens for scientific or philosophical conversations.

The Garden as Thinking Space

It seems absurdly reductionist to suggest that the straight paths and enclosed spaces of the formal garden promote logical thinking while the meandering paths of a woodland garden inspire all that is poetic, yet such assumptions colour both interpretations of historic gardens and support a range of modern texts, both popular and academic, on engineering spaces to promote creativity. There is no doubt that thinkers of all persuasions have sought out gardens as places where a measure of solitude coupled with gentle stimulation can be used in support of serious thought as well as idle speculation. Undoubtedly the most famous instance of a garden based scientific discovery is the tale associated with Newton's apple. Despite this event frequently being relegated to the status of fable an account by William Stukeley, Newton's biographer, seems quite unequivocal.

> On 15 April 1726 I paid a visit to Sir Isaac at his lodgings in Orbels buildings in Kensington, dined with him and spent the whole day with him alone.... After dinner, the weather being warm, we went into the garden and drank tea, under the shade of some apple trees, only he and myself. Amidst other discourse, he told me, he was just in the same situation, as when formerly, the notion of gravitation came into his mind. It was occasion'd by the fall of an apple, as he sat in a contemplative mood. (quoted in Hastings White 1936, 19)

An earlier instance was documented by Julian Jaynes who described Descartes's reaction to the automata housed in the grottoes below the terraces at St Germain-en-Laye.

> Descartes tells us himself how he made them move without knowing it; how, on entering, he trod on hidden plates that, for example, when he approached a bathing Diana, caused her to hide her bronze allurements in bronze rose bushes, and when he tried to follow her, caused a stern Neptune to clank and hiss forward to intercept him, creaking his dripping trident puritanically over the delighted philosopher's head.

> These images, [...] with their paradigms of behavioural control, perhaps stayed at the very depth of Descartes' thinking. (Jaynes 1970, 224)

A particular example of observation and experience informing a scientific conclusion is the contention that Harvey's discovery of the circulation of the blood was part inspired by the examination of sluices and other garden water features in Italy and elsewhere (Boyle 2008, 1). In terms of a more general structural and indeed symbolic approach to creating a thinking space the gardens surrounding Tycho Brahe's observatory at Uraniborg from late in the sixteenth century were severely symmetrical suggesting a focus on 'fundamental aspects of Pythagorean mysticism which were common property during the sixteenth century' (Parrot 2010, 68).

The 'Scientific' Garden at Hanwell

Apart from the gardens at Wadham college described earlier it is difficult to identify in this country any other outdoor spaces seriously dedicated to science. Perhaps the closest parallel is the garden of Henry Winstanley (1644–1703) with its remarkable 'House of Wonders' at Littlebury, in Essex. Winstanley was a 'printmaker, horologist, architect, engineer, inventor and businessman' (Taylor 2014, 39). His premises were operated as a commercial venture, Winstanley charging a shilling for admission at a turnstile. The attractions featured a variety of devices constructed 'allegedly to amuse his new wife whom he married in 1683'. The garden, probably laid out around 1677, included a moated mount with summerhouse and a windmill that according to Taylor was 'an exhibit […] used to fill garden ponds, to drive hydraulic curiosities and to show that Winstanley was familiar with the then "modern" technology.' However, Taylor also records that the attraction, together with his London based 'Water Theatre' was not opened until 1693 and apart from a tentative connection with Christopher Wren there is no evidence of a link back to Hanwell. Winstanley's garden was part of a money-making venture and sits well within the framework suggested by Pamela Long as she sets the scene for the early modern transformation of points of view on technology that Winstanley and Sir Anthony may have been swept up in and considers the relevant factors to be

> the development of commercial capitalism, the expansion of artisanal trades in general, the increasing cultural importance of objects and the development of conspicuous consumption on the part of elites. Construction and fabrication became connected not just to craft know-how and the making of things but to knowledge about the world itself. (Long 2001, 246)

All of these could have been factors in the development of Sir Anthony's 'garden of science' but without testimony from those who used the garden it is impossible to cite specific instances of particular thoughts being sparked by individual locations. We know that Plot examined and indeed collected specimens of the small-leaved elm within the park and searched, unsuccessfully, for freshwater oysters. He was clearly impressed by Sir Anthony's mill. We do not know if any of these encounters inspired any particular new insights, rather, it is safe to say that the experiences contributed to his developing understanding of a variety of natural histories. We can also reasonably conclude that the garden was an arena within which Plot (1705, 73) was able to establish and expand his acquaintance with Sir Anthony and develop the kind of dialogues that led him to identify his host as 'the most eminent *Artist* and *Naturalist* while he lived, if not of *England*, most certainly of this *County*'. Given the appellation *The New Atlantis* one can deduce that other learned and ingenious individuals exploited the gardens for scientific gain but they remain unidentified.

The varied terrain at Hanwell within such a large park would have meant that there were many opportunities for both solitary and social exploration of a range of stimulating environments. For the sake of completeness in examining the Hanwell environment a consideration of the castle building itself is useful. There were clear advantages to be had from arranging accommodation around a central courtyard, benefits shared by late-medieval colleges and hospitals. As well as conferring feelings of security and solidarity, there is also the expression of the concept of community. The courtyard plan has many practical advantages relating to the control of resources and the management of risk. Casual incursions are prevented, visitors are monitored and controlled and strangers easily identified within the community of the courtyard. Beyond that the courtyard is above all a social space within which casual interactions can take place. The more formal business of walking and talking in a small group matches well with the terraced walkways at Hanwell where there is ample room to exchange learned discourse or witty banter with the distant prospect of the castle encouraging a different sense of perspective on whatever issues were being debated. Walking literally in the footsteps of kings may have contributed to general feelings of approbation. The Sunken Garden could have offered opportunities for more intimate conversations while the descending terraces and stairways east of the castle no doubt provided an element of stimulation and excitement as the view of the lower part of the valley opened out on the approach to the House of Diversion. The strong west to east linear design of the garden is maintained by the positioning of the water parterre at the foot of the east terrace and demonstrates a powerful sense of order. Not only is there an alignment but also, whether consciously or by topographical circumstance, the areas occupied by the castle, possible bowling green, terraced walks and water parterre are broadly similar. The height of the eastern terrace overlooking the water parterre obviated the need for that distinctive presence in early modern gardens: the mount. The topography alone provided the view. There is evidence in a letter from Anthony Cope to the earl of Salisbury that the castle had an enclosed gallery, sub-divided in 1605 prior to his visit, that would have commanded a view of the valley. The geometric surrounds to the House of Diversion and its contents express both order and wonder. We know something of the contents of the House of Diversion with its balanced balls and descending showers that would doubtless have provoked reaction and discussion. We do not know if Sir Anthony kept any of his collectibles here and the finds from the surrounding moat speak primarily of the social activities of eating, drinking and smoking rather than of any experimental undertakings. Somewhere in the park the mill and its great engine indicate calculation and industry as well as offering opportunities for practical engagement or 'tinkering'. Longer walks would have made it possible to explore the lower reaches of the valley and new perspectives obtained from the deer park to the south with its views of the Cherwell valley and the distant town of Banbury. This is, of course, essentially an, in the imagination but it chimes well with other accounts of the benefits of gardens to intellectual undertakings. The many roles a garden could play are summed up in the thinking of Evelyn.

> Evelyn came to see the garden as a heterotopia, that is, as a space that exists as a physical reality and is part of the world. But at the same time, it was a place to retreat from that world where one could critically and systematically study the same, and was thus simultaneously positioned outside of it. The pleasure garden and the microcosm of learning, the kitchen garden and the laboratory, the real and the imaginary garden could no longer be separated. (Remmert 2016, 20)

Plot's multiple references to aspects of the grounds at Hanwell and the additional features revealed by archaeology all support the conclusion that this was indeed an environment rich in challenge and stimulation.

The Tangley Mystery and Hanwell as *The New Atlantis*

Both Plot's reference to the 'Society of *Virtuosi*' gathered at the Cope family property at Tangley as living 'obscurely' during the interregnum and his claim that the Hanwell household in some way was the real *New Atlantis* point to Sir Anthony Cope having an active role in promoting associations of like-minded individuals and providing them with some measure of resources to advance the cause of natural philosophy. There is no particular reason to doubt what Plot has to say and one must assume he had some grounds for making these assertions, presumably on the basis of information that was gathered from Sir Anthony himself and other interested parties with whom Plot met during the composition of his *Natural History*. Difficulties arise because of the lack of corroborative evidence from or about any other participants in these gatherings. The identities of the members of the Tangley society remain as obscure today as they were, presumably, in the 1650s and apart from what we know of Allestree and Baltzar we have nothing further from Hanwell for the fifteen years between the Restoration and Sir Anthony's death, a period when one might have expected the need for secrecy to have largely vanished. Indeed the issue of secrecy is one that must be confronted in any attempt to explain the vanishingly low profile of Sir Anthony's 'new Atlanteans'.

Many authors have commented on the way both scientific practice and thought were advanced in the early modern period by a move towards greater openness and collaboration. In writing of the change from alchemy to chemistry Clay Shirky remarks:

The problem with alchemists was not that they failed to turn lead into gold; the problem was that they failed uninformatively. Alchemists were obscurantists, recording their work by hand and rarely showing it to anyone but disciples. In contrast [the chemists] shared their work, describing and disputing their methods and conclusions so that they all might benefit from both successes and failures to build on one another's work. (Shirky 2011)

As progress was made from loose arrangements of friends and colleagues meeting in coffee houses and each other's homes to the more formal setting of colleges and lecture theatres this trend towards openness became codified. The quasi-legal 'importance of public witnessing of experimental results, emphasised by Boyle and other fellows of the Royal Society as a guarantee of the reliability of the Society's pronouncements' (Henry 2001, 102). Given this and the many avenues open for publication, or at the very least correspondence, it is hard to reconcile Plot's claim for Hanwell as *The New Atlantis* with the apparent lack of any communications from or to Sir Anthony or any other references to science based activities. It is true that despite the new openness there remained something of a tradition of secrecy with some experimentalists continuing to operate *sub rosa*. Mayling Stubbs (1982, 470), in writing about the 'philosophical gardener of Herefordshire', John Beale (1608–83), states that 'Beale's early astronomical studies coincided with his participation in a secret society (*sub rosa*) which included Wotton and his friend Sir Edmund Bacon'. Beale reported to Hartlib in 1659 the 'phansical discourse' on angelic cosmology that he had heard 'when wee were all undr the Rose'. One advantage of meeting secretly was that the participants frequently felt themselves to be freer to indulge in fancy and speculation. Plot himself was less than forthcoming about aspects of his chemical preparations although his 'secrecy had largely to do with the economic necessities of his position' (Roos 2014, 89). Nevertheless the tendency was towards 'collaboration and communication between practitioners, learned humanists, other university-educated men and ruling elites' (Long 2001, 246). One early aspect of this was the loose grouping of virtuosi around Robert Boyle in the 1640s known as 'the Invisible College'. As Charles Webster (1974, 19) noted, 'straightforward identification of the Invisible College is ruled out by the paucity of evidence'. However, the sense here is that this was a college that was free from material boundaries rather than one that was confidential, indeed communication was at the heart of their association. We can speculate on what may have caused Sir Anthony to go against this trend and be less than forthcoming about any of his potential science-related activities. The fact that Richard Allestree successfully maintained a veil of secrecy over the authorship of his 1657 publication, *The Whole Duty of Man* may have inspired Sir Anthony to operate in a similarly clandestine fashion. In this context he may have been sensitive to the opinions of his neighbours. In his preface to *The Natural Historie of Wiltshire* begun in 1656 John Aubrey described his own motivation. 'I was carried on with a secret [strong] impulse to undertake this Task; I know not why bundles for my own private pleasure; Credit there was none, for it gets the contempt [disrespect] of a man's neighbours. But I could not rest till I had obeyed this secret call.'

A further consideration that may have inspired a tendency to obscurity is that aspects of the deliberations of Sir Anthony and his friends may have embraced 'forbidden' topics related to the occult and especially the art of astrology that, as we have seen, was of particular interest to Richard Allestree. At its height in the sixteenth century 'it was less a separate discipline than an aspect of a generally accepted world picture' (Thomas 1991, 338), and thus part of everyday life, in much the same way as it is in present-day India. However, as the seventeenth century wore on two challenges began to assail it as a pursuit: a puritan distaste for things 'magical' and the growing appeal of a more rationalistic understanding of the universe. There was no doubt a considerable degree of equivocation on the part of the parliamentarian and puritan establishment towards astrology during and after the Civil War. Astrologers, such as William Lilly, were consulted by both sides during the conflict. Indeed Nicholas Nelson (1976, 352) argued that 'heretofore they had been kept at the periphery of respectable society however, the new Puritan government appeared to favour and even foster their new status'. This is evidenced by the authorisation and popularity, especially in London, of a range of astrological almanacs. However, there was also a distinct trend through the 1650s towards the condemnation of such 'ungodly' acts as divination. As far back as 1561 John Calvin (1509–64) had attacked astrology in his *An Admonicion against Astrology*. Whether they saw them as professional rivals or practitioners of the black arts many clergy were vociferous in their condemnation of astrologers (Thomas 1991, 425). While there was no great opposition to astrology at Oxford Sir Anthony may have been subject to scrutiny by ministers closer to home and hence not advertised his interests too widely. Beyond theological niceties there was also a growing sense that astrology had 'had its day'. Peter Wright (1975, 400) described the period from the sixteenth to the late seventeenth centuries as one 'in which England became a leading nation in scientific advance, and during which astrology largely lost its hold among the educated'. However, the mechanism whereby this transformation was effected is not immediately apparent. Wright comments how little publicly stated criticism there was of astrology by the scientific luminaries of the time, a notable exception being Seth Ward, who, in 1654, proclaimed it to be 'that ridiculous cheat made up of nonsense and contradictions' (Ward 1654, 30). In general there seems to have been a dwindling away in the face of new social realities and intellectual preoccupations. If astrology had been one of Sir Anthony's interests, he may have felt silence was the only response to growing indifference to, or worse, mockery, about the subject.

Of course, a more prosaic explanation could be that Sir Anthony simply preferred the quiet life and his perspective may well have been that outlined by David Beck (2014, 72), 'Common reactions among period intellectuals were an avoidance of (public) conflict, and a strong desire to preserve the world immediately around them, once the situation made it possible.' So it is that any measures to populate the communities at Tangley or Hanwell remain intensely speculative.

One might perhaps look towards the University of Oxford itself as a recruiting ground for Sir Anthony's first undertaking: the assembling of the Tangley set. A possible reason for a number of 'learned virtuosi' taking what sounds very much like internal exile is the series of visitations and resultant expulsions that took place at the university under parliamentarian control in 1647, 1652 and 1655, a process described by Major-General John Desborough (1608–80) as 'to purge loose and profane persons' (quoted in Worden 1997, 746). Given that several key members of the Oxford experimentalists decided to stay in the city it is difficult to imagine significant defections from there to Tangley nor do circumstances appear extreme enough to force scholars into hiding. Worden comments on the fact that 'The well-documented resolve of Wilkins and his fellow experimental philosophers to avoid the discussion of state affairs at their scientific meetings, and to elevate intellectual enquiry above the divisive passions of the times, should not be taken for political innocence or abstinence' (Ibid., 738). The internal exiles at Tangley may have been less accommodating. In his exhaustive account of seventeenth-century medical and other studies at Oxford Robert Frank (1980, 63) undertook a detailed analysis of the personnel involved in early scientific pursuits, 'from the eve of the Civil War to the mid-1670s'. In examining in detail Franks list and linking it to those individuals who were early members of the Royal Society, yet who maintained a low profile during the 1650s, it is possible to identify men who could have had a Tangley connection. Frank listed 104 'participants' putting them in three groups: 14 'major scientists', including Boyle, Harvey, Hooke, Petty, Wallis, Ward, Wilkins, Willis and Wren, 46 'minor scientists', of which Austen, Bathurst (Ralph) and Plot are numbered, and under the heading of 'Virtuosi' he names Allestree, Aubrey, Bathurst (George), Lydall and Sprat. Sir Anthony is not listed, nor is Sir Thomas Pennyston, who, as we saw, had his own home laboratory. Frank recorded college affiliations, revealing, surprisingly, that 13% of his sample had no formal association with any college but were a mixture of tradesmen, such as apothecaries, or interested foreigners residing in Oxford. Of those who were part of the university the largest grouping, not surprisingly, was linked to Wadham at 15%. Christ Church's 13% may simply reflect its status as Oxford's largest college at the time. The figures for Merton at 13% and Trinity with 8% are both probably a result of particular groupings around individual enthusiasts. Of those associated with Sir Anthony's old college, Oriel (3%), we have William Clark, a Somerset gentleman who was up from 1660 to 1666 and who went on to become a physician in Bath, Christopher Merrett from Winchcombe who left in1648 to become a physician in London and Richard Lydall who moved from Oriel in 1641 to Merton, where he eventually became warden in 1693 as well as acting as a physician in the town. It appears that Sir Anthony's college did not engender a great number of experimental philosophers. Frank also recorded subsequent occupations, again not surprisingly 52% were listed as physicians.

The next largest group was of clerics and divines which comprised 29% of his sample while 20% had largely academic careers. Only 4% were noted as aristocrats or gentlemen having no formal employment. Despite Sir Anthony's evident interests he came from a college with no great tradition of scientific endeavour and was not a member of one of the professions which formed the core of the Oxford alumni; he was something, perhaps, of an outsider and does not appear to be an obvious 'port in a storm' for researchers if the winds of censure were blowing particularly strongly.

While Oxford remained a comparatively benign environment for many royalist experimentalists another potential source of disaffected natural philosophers was the capital. A number of royalists were expelled from London and Philip Major (2008, 731) describes how 'more royalists were affected by internal exile than by external: whereas banishment abroad was restricted to specific individuals who had earned the opprobrium of Parliament, blanket exclusions from London were applied at various times to every "delinquent"'. One example of such a 'delinquent' was John Berkenhead who went up to Oriel College in 1632 and became editor of the royalist newsletter *Mercurius Aulicus* in Oxford between 1643 and 1645 (*ODNB*). Both a literary figure in his own right and a royalist agent, he later became a founding member of the Royal Society and was the type of person who may have found sanctuary with Sir Anthony. Marika Keblusek gives a more general context for this: 'Ejected from their livings and universities, the Anglican exiles in particular formed a close-knit community, collaborating on intellectual projects, assisting each other financially and logistically, travelling together, exchanging and sharing materials and books' (Keblusek 2010, 83). Many who chose exile on the continent, such as Charles Cavendish or Robert Moray, decided to immerse themselves in experimental studies abroad and P.H. Hardacre (1953, 366) noted that 'of the ninety-eight original Fellows of the Royal Society about a fifth were old royalists who had gone into exile during and after the Civil War'. Of course it was possible to follow a less dramatic course of action and simply live in obscurity. William Brounkner (1620–84), first president of the Royal Society, graduated in medicine from Oxford in 1646 and according to Caoimhghín Breathnach (2006, 224) 'shrewdly avoided the political uncertainties of those turbulent times by devoting himself to the cloistered study of mathematics […] in his country retreat'. He corresponded frequently through the 1650s on mathematical topics with his ideological opposite, John Wallis, and in 1660, 'surfaced as a loyal royalist' (*ODNB*). He was part of the same group as Sir Anthony Cope that worked through General Monck to bring about the Restoration but whether they had any closer acquaintance remains uncertain.

Thomas Henshaw (1618–1700) is another interesting case study, not only because of his potential connections with the Cope family but also because of his propensity for involvement with 'chemical clubs' and learned societies of various kinds. Henshaw matriculated at University College, Oxford in 1634 and went on to study mathematics with William Oughtred. After an abortive attempt to join royalist forces at the outbreak of the Civil War he toured Europe largely in the company of John Evelyn (*ODNB*). On returning to England early in 1649 he took up residence in Kensington. It was here that he assembled 'a research collegium of chemists known as the 'Christian Learned Society or the Chymical Club'. A handful of people lived or worked at his manor house in Kensington, called Pondhouse or Moathouse because close by were some large fish ponds '"intersected with grand walks" and the islands in the middle of the ponds were connected by wooden bridges' (Dickson 1997, 58). This was, of course, the former residence of Sir Walter Cope that he inhabited while build-ing Cope Castle and was attached to his elaborate water gardens. The property had passed by marriage to the Rich family, but the Cope connection must have been well known. As we have seen, Henshaw was recorded as participating in a discussion that featured stones from Sir Anthony's collection at a meeting of the Royal Society in 1681. Henshaw's circle included fellow alchemists Robert Child and Thomas and Rebecca Vaughan. Elias Ashmole made use of his library and Samuel Hartlibb was a regular correspondent. Once again there are plenty of potential points of contact but no evidence of any meetings with Sir Anthony let alone taking up part-time residence with him.

The question remains, were any of the Tangley virtuosi recruited from Oxford or London? Exile from Oxford seems at odds with climate there as described by Frank (1980, 43) as being a place where 'cooperative scientific activity was possible because Commonwealth Oxford provided institutional support, intel-lectual resources, and a congenial environment for a core of scientific leaders'. However, Tangley was only a journey of around 25 miles from Oxford, easily accomplished on horseback in a day and perhaps accessible as a temporary refuge. Coming from London would be a more challenging journey and any such visitors would have had to be at least semi-resident. One individual who was known to be present at Tangley in 1654 for the birth of Sir Anthony's third son was Henry Cary, Fourth Viscount Falkland (1634–63). He was the son of Lucius Cary who had been convener of the Great Tew circle that had assembled in his Oxfordshire manor house in the 1630s to debate matters religious and literary. As well as having something of a sense of the workings of a private 'society', Henry Cary was also a royalist supporter who was secretly commis-sioned as a colonel that same year and almost certainly moved in the same clandestine circles as Allestree. In 1655 he narrowly escaped arrest by protectorate forces. One cannot but help wonder if the Tangley group were royalist agents masquerading as virtuosi, and with this in mind recall that 'He [Falkland] and another of the presenters, Sir Anthony Cope, had worked together to promote the rising of 1659' (*ODNB*).

It is possible to identify a number of other early members of the Royal Society with royalist leanings who seem to have been keeping a low profile for at least some of the 1650s and may have been similarly working under cover and grateful for the respite that a stay at Tangley or Hanwell could offer. John Pettus (1613–90), a soldier during the Civil War with an interest in mining, corresponded with and sent cash to Prince Charles while John Talbot (1630–1714) of Lacock Abbey was arrested in 1659 for his involvement in the Cheshire Rising, the last of a series of local rebellions in which Henry Mordaunt, 2nd earl of Peterborough (1632–97), was complicit. Walter Pope (1627–1714) is certainly a candidate for being well known to Sir Anthony, if not a member of his immediate circle. Pope was grandson of the Puritan cleric John Dod, patronised by the Copes as the vicar of Hanwell from 1585 to 1607 and half-brother to John Wilkins from his mother's previous marriage. He gained his BA in 1649 from Wadham College where he was employed until the Restoration when he went on to become professor of Astronomy at Gresham College. He succeeded Christopher Wren and was an active member of the Royal Society (*ODNB*) His parliamentarian connections may have distanced him from Sir Anthony although his resistance to the puritan proposal to abolish caps and hoods at the university indicates his 'hostility to the Puritan republicans who had taken over the University in the 1650s' (Gibson 2010, 44). As part of his campaign he summoned, 'all the Antediluvian Cavaliers, I mean the fellows of colleges, who had good fortune to survive the flood of the [Puritan Parliamentary] visitation, and keep their places, and who had ever since that liv'd retir'd in their cells, never meddling with public affairs in the University, nor appearing in the Convocation, or Congregations' (Pope 1697, 42) This could be a description of those who were part of the Tangley group and Pope himself would certainly have been a contact worth maintaining in Commonwealth Oxford. A further family connection that may be significant is with Sir Anthony's uncle on his mother's side, Sir Francis Fane (1611–81), royalist governor of Doncaster, and later Lincoln Castle, Fane demonstrated his scientific interests by becoming a founding fellow of the Royal Society in 1663 although he seems not to have been a particularly active member. We have, as far as the membership of Tangley's 'learned society of virtuosi' is concerned, many candidates but no appointees. The situation regarding Hanwell is similarly difficult.

Plot's accounts of Hanwell together with the evidence from the archaeology strongly suggests that the opportunity was there for a simulacrum of the House of Salomon to exist in the physical sense given that the house is not a particular structure but rather an institution based on multiple locations. If one were to represent this landscape of wonders in any concrete form it would be within the setting of a garden. However, the more important element had to be the community of like-minded individuals of 'New Atlanteans' who could work together and capitalise on whatever facilities Sir Anthony was able to provide for them. It is unclear why Sir Anthony's hospitable inclinations shifted later in the 1650s from Tangley to Hanwell. It seems unlikely that Richard Allestree and Thomas Balzar were solely the ones Plot had in his mind as residents of *The New Atlantis* when he came to write about it over fifteen years later but with possible exception of the weather-wise shepherd, John Claridge, we have no other individuals who might have qualified as participants. It is probable that a variety of specialists could have stayed at the castle while assisting Sir Anthony with the construction of his wonders and marvels although we have no record of who they may have been apart from George Harris who would have been involved in installing the clock that Sir Anthony gave to the church in 1673.

Of course some of those members of the Tangley group may have continued both their association with Sir Anthony and their habit of secrecy through into the 1660s and the move to Hanwell. Equally other interested parties may have taken up with him and shared their enthusiasms. There are several individuals mentioned in Plot's *Natural History* who may have formed part of a Hanwell circle. A strong candidate and neighbour was fellow 'eminent virtuoso', Thomas Pennyston of Cornwell, a village just under 7 miles north of Tangley. Born in 1648 and so 18 years younger than Sir Anthony, he could not sensibly have participated in the Tangley group; however, he had clearly become a 'fellow traveller' by the 1670s when Plot (1705, 54) notes him for his attempted identification of a new source of fuller's earth. Plot (1705, 60) goes on to celebrate a quarry 'about An Hundred Yards from the Right Worshipful Sir *Thomas Pennyston's* House', that contained a white clay known as *Lac Lunae*. Work on other forms of 'earth' in Sir Thomas's laboratory has already been referred to and he was also busily examining his house coal as he discovered in it a fossil 'that seems to represent a *Carp* or *Barbel*' (Plot 1705, 99), However, he is probably best remembered for his discovery of a stone 'that has exactly the Figure of the lowermost part of the *Thigh-Bone* of a Man, or at least of some other *Animal*'. Plot (1705, 134) identifies this as a 'real *Bone*' possibly belonging to an elephant brought over by the Romans. This was actually 'the earliest discovery of a dinosaur bone on record', a bone that can now be identified as belonging to a Megalosaur (Delair and Sargeant 1975, 7). The eighth table of *Natural History* is dedicated to 'the learned and curious Artist Sir Thomas Penyston' and illustrated further geological specimens he had collected. Pennyston was acquainted with Anthony Wood who records an encounter with him at the Mitre Inn in July 1671 (Keissling 209, 126). He was in the company of the Woodstock lawyer Sir Littleton Osbaldeston (1631–91) who had been ejected from Magdalen by the parliamentary visitors back in 1648 (*HOP*). In May 1675 Wood travelled to London in a borrowed coach and took Sir Thomas with him. It is clear that Pennyston enjoyed a range of social interactions with a variety of individuals on the fringes of the scientific community, but we have no record of him even having met Sir Anthony Cope.

Other potential recruits for Sir Anthony's *New Atlantis* can be identified in the pages of Plot's *Natural History* amongst the ranks of those with special interest in earths and stones. George Pudsey Esq. (d. 1690) of Elsfield just outside Oxford was commended for his discovery of '*a light and hollow sort of Marl*'. (Plot 1705, 54) As an M.P. he was 'fervent Tory' and 'sycophant' whose speeches were 'permeated with High Anglicanism' (*HOP*). He does not appear to be a natural companion for Sir Anthony. Doctor Perrot (1594–1684) of North Leigh, Plot's 'worthy friend', produced a form of pyrites that 'gave the tast of *ink*' (Plot 1705, 71). This is probably Charles Perrot (1627–77) who was also a friend of Anthony Wood and a fellow of Oriel College (Toynbee 1946, 132). The 'Worshipful' Edward Sheldon Esq. (1624–76) of Steeple Barton collected fossils while one 'Mr. *Wildgose, Physician* at *Denton*, and an ingenious *Chymist*' was noted for his exciting '*effluviams*' (Plot 1705, 89). An intercepted letter from January 1655 in the state papers of John Thurloe (1616–68), head of intelligence for the Protectorate from 1653, mentions a Mr Wildgose as paying the sum of £10 possibly as a contribution to secret royalist funds (Anonymous, letter to George a Lion). Again while there are a number of individuals who shared in Sir Anthony's enthusiasm, none can be securely placed at Hanwell.

As, at least according to Plot, the county's leading naturalist one must ask why Sir Anthony did not become a member of the Royal Society during the last decade of his life. However, as Michael Hunter points out,

> For more minor provincial enthusiasts, membership of the Royal Society was a rarity and not all were even associated with it. The correspondence of the Secretary, Henry Oldenburg, with rural virtuosi like Samuel Colepresse in Devonshire, Nathaniel Fairfax in Suffolk or Peter Nelson in Durham, provides glimpses of a widely scattered interest in the new philosophy, but these isolated figures, though gratified by correspondence with the Society's Secretary, were hardly ever awarded the accolade of membership of the Society itself. (Hunter 1976, 11)

However, given that the statutes expressly permitted an exception, 'for any of his majesty's subjects [...] having the title and place of a baron', Sir Anthony may have been able to attend without actually being a fellow. If Sir Anthony's focus was on his Hanwell estate with perhaps occasional trips to Oxford but rarely to London, full membership would have brought few benefits.

An interesting possible parallel to Sir Anthony's Tangley group and subsequent 'New Atlanteans' potentially based at Hanwell is the Towneley Circle. Prior to the Civil War Christopher Towneley (1604–74) gathered around himself a group of young astronomers while his nephew Richard Towneley (1629–1707), after a continental education, was able to continue aspects of his uncle's work at the family seat of Towneley Hall near Burnley in Lancashire. As Webster puts it, 'when tranquillity returned during the Commonwealth, [he] again established Towneley Hall as a centre for the informal discussion of scientific problems' (Webster 1966, 66). Amongst the group were the 'mechanical philosopher' Henry Power (1623–68) and astronomer John Flamsteed (1646–1719). Key to the ongoing success of the group was access to both the Towneley library and the set of instruments the family owned; however, their Catholicism, reduced financial circumstances post–Civil War and distance from London all contributed to reducing their influence. Towneley did not join the Royal Society. He may have felt, and Sir Anthony could have shared this feeling, that, as the originator of his own society, the London based institution had little to offer him.

Despite all the intriguing biographical details of various potential contributors to Sir Anthony's community of 'New Atlanteans' Plot remains our only source for the existence of the group at Tangley and the attribution of the title of *The New Atlantis* to the Hanwell household. We come therefore to the question of Plot's veracity. His contemporary, H.S.J. in the 'Short Account of the AUTHOR', in the introduction to the 1705 edition of *Natural History* commended his 'great Integrity'. In general terms Plot was held in high regard as a collector and recorder of information that was to be trusted. Even if his interpretations sometimes appear suspect to modern understanding the data with which he worked was sound. Mendyk (1985, 165) is clear that 'Plot was able to separate fact from fancy, in most instances at least'. The flowery language that Plot uses in his histories to describe his friends, acquaintances and correspondents appears flattering, even sycophantic, but while examining other texts, it became clear to me that these forms of address were essentially the courtesies of the age. David Beck (2009), examined this issue and queried, 'how important was gentry status to Plot? Did he accept testimony given by a gentleman over and above that by a tradesman, or even his own eyes?' He concluded that Plot was an effective and comparatively impartial observer. Summing up Plot's approach to scholarship Turner (*ODNB*) says his strength lay in 'providing rational accounts of things which were described in detail'. On this basis we can safely dismiss the idea that Plot's references to Sir Anthony's societies were fabrications although, of course, there could have been a degree of elaboration or exaggeration. Plot was known for his sociability. As the curator of the Ashmolean he had a reputation for acquisitiveness but Gunther (1935, 320) is of the opinion that 'he was one who gave ten-fold more than he received, and he had many friends'. As someone who knew the Copes well there may be an element of flattery and given that Sir Anthony could have been unwell and in the throes of his final illness this may have inspired a degree of memorialising by Plot. It is also possible that Plot may have wanted to demonstrate Sir Anthony's achievements out of a sense that his own efforts to create a permanent college, as embodied in the revived Oxford experimentalists from the 1660s, had come to nothing. Mendyk (1985, 171) concluded 'That Plot's scholarship was held in high esteem is evident in the fact that a new post, that of "Mowbray Herald Extraordinary" was created specifically for him about one year before his death, at which time he was also appointed Register to the Court of Honour.' This appraisal was echoed by Turner who suggested that it was during his 'years of teaching and study that Plot must have laid the foundation of the formidable erudition that earned him the sobriquet "learned Dr Plot", learning which is evidenced on every page of his writings' (*ODNB*). We may perhaps allow a certain warmth of feeling to colour Plot's writings about Hanwell but there is no reason to doubt his assertions about the gathering at Tangley or the status of Hanwell. As we have seen, there is no shortage of candidates be considered as associates of Sir Anthony Cope and the balance of probability surely must be that, even in the absence of hard evidence, some of them were indeed part of a grouping, however loose, that he facilitated.

Conclusions

Our starting point was Plot's extraordinary assertions about Sir Anthony Cope and his household that provoked this investigation into him, his family and his estate. We have seen how the development of the park at Hanwell was characterised as something that arose out of an established tradition of garden making that began with medieval designed landscapes, both secular and monastic. Post reformation an existing body of expertise was drawn on that continued working with water to create landscapes that were both productive and decorative and that, in the hands of certain engineers and virtuosi, became a showcase for matters technological and thinking scientific. While there was a nodding acquaintance with continental practice, especially in the engineering of the more elaborate waterworks during the early years of the seventeenth century, much of what was undertaken was firmly grounded in local practices.

The Cope family having set themselves up at Hanwell early in the sixteenth century became associated through the agency primarily of Sir Walter Cope not only with the court but specifically with the Cecils and indulged themselves in the design and development of water gardens on a large scale, an interest shared with Sir Francis Bacon. The evidence suggests that the garden so created in the early decades of the seventeenth century became a kind of playground for the 4th baronet, Sir Anthony Cope, who, inspired by his time at Oxford and supported by like-minded individuals, turned his garden into something resembling a science based theme park. However, after the death of Sir Anthony and the consequent disputes within the family the gardens fell into disuse. The archaeology has been able to discover and document some of physical remnants of this story from traces of the medieval landscape through to the creation of the terraced and walled water garden of the early seventeenth century and the later setting up of the House of Diversion celebrated by Plot. Evidence on the construction and use of this feature informs our understanding of contemporary garden structures. The excavation and recording of the unique collection of terracotta garden urns from the 1660s have the potential of making a major contribution towards knowledge about this aspect of gardening practice for the period. In charting the course of the growth of a scientific mindset at Oxford around the middle of the seventeenth century, links have been made with the households at Tangley and Hanwell in an attempt to explain and justify Plot's references to a 'learned society' and 'the real *New Atlantis*' and to set the works at Hanwell in a broader context of the contributions gardens made to the development of scientific thinking.

Had Sir Anthony's house at Hanwell truly been *The New Atlantis*? In answering this question, given the appearance to an archaeologist's eye of the destroyed House of Diversion as something of a crime scene, it is perhaps appropriate to consider the question in terms of motive, means and opportunity. Sir Anthony seems to have been driven by a strong interest in aspects of natural philosophy thus supplying a motive. He certainly had the means at his disposal in terms of physical resources and he had the opportunity to create an environment conducive to scientific enquiry. Even so, the only evidence we have to convict him of virtuosity is the title given him by Plot, the physical fact of the garden's existence and a few hints about the company he kept at various stages in his life. However, like the evidence for the House of Diversion, this is all circumstantial. Extending the criminological metaphor, perhaps it is fair to say that the jury is still out, but where lies the balance of probability? The key to a just verdict may lie in penetrating the veil of secrecy in which Sir Anthony cloaked himself and his possible associates in and while we have plenty of suspects, we have little proof.

At the start of this study it was characterised as a single story but in actuality Hanwell is a place where many stories intersect: the rising fortunes and the ultimate decline of a gentry family, the almost ruinous spending by the litigious Copes and their attempts to achieve status, the comings and goings of the spy, the musician, the weather-wise shepherd and the clockmaker and the triumphs and tragedies of Sir Anthony Cope, a man in love with science and secrecy. If Plot chose to describe this locus as the 'real *New Atlantis*', who are we to disagree (Plate 31)?

Bibliography

Anonymous, letter to George a Lion (June 1655), http://www.british-history.ac.uk/thurloe-papers/vol3/pp587-599, accessed 21 January 2021

Aubrey, J., *Memoirs of Natural Remarques in the County of Wiltshire*, ed. Britton, J. (London, 1847)

Aubrey, J., *Brief Lives,* ed. Bennett, K. (Oxford, 2015)

Bacon, F., *The New Atlantis* (originally published London, 1626), in Bruce, S. (ed.) *Three Early Modern Utopias: Utopia, New Atlantis and The Island of Pines* (Oxford, 2008)

Bacon, F., *Gesta Grayorum,* ed. Greg, W. (Oxford, 1914)

Barbour, R. and Preston, C., 'Discursive and Speculative Writing', in Cheney, P. and Hardie, P. (eds) *The Oxford History of Classical Reception in English Literature*, vol. 2 (Oxford, 2015)

Batey, M., *Oxford Gardens: The University's Influence on Garden History* (Oxford, 1982)

Beck, D., 'Plot's Investigation of Nature'. Paper presented at The Making of Early Modern Scientific Knowledge: Objects, Spaces, Practices and Epistemologies conference, Warwick (2009)

Beck, D., 'County Natural History: Indigenous Science in England, from Civil War to Glorious Revolution', *Intellectual History Review* 24(1) (2014)

Beddard, R., 'Restoration Oxford', in Tyacke, N. (ed.) *The History of the University of Oxford, Vol. IV: Seventeenth-Century Oxford* (Oxford, 1997)

Bennett, J., 'The Mechanics' Philosophy and the Mechanical Philosophy', *History of Science* 24 (1) (1986)

Boyle, M.O., 'Harvey in the Sluice: From Hydraulic Engineering to Human Physiology', *History and Technology* 24 (1) (2008)

Boyle, R., *The Sceptical Chymist* (Oxford, 1677)

Bramer, B., *Bericht zu M. Jobsten Burgi sel. geometrischen Triangular Instruments. Mit schönen Kupfferstücken hierzu geschnitten* (Cassel, 1648)

Breathnach, C., 'William Brouncker MD Viscount Castlelyons (c 1620–84) First President of the Royal Society'. *Journal of Medical Biography* 14(4) (2006)

Calvin, J. (trans. Mary Potter), 'A Warning Against Judicial Astrology', *Calvin Theological Journal* 18 (1983)

Cooke, A.M., 'William Harvey at Oxford', *Journal of the Royal College of Physicians* 9(2) (1975)

Cope, A., letter to earl of Salisbury (August 1605), http://www.british-history.ac.uk/cal-cecil-papers/vol17/pp374-409, accessed 11 January 2021

Corfield, P., *Vauxhall, Sex and Entertainment* (London, 2012)

Delair, J. and Sarjeant, W., 'The Earliest Discoveries of Dinosaurs', *Isis* 66(1) (1975)

Dickson, D., 'Thomas Henshaw and Sir Robert Paston's Pursuit of the Red Elixir: An Early Collaboration Between Fellows of the Royal Society', *Notes and Records of the Royal Society* 54(1) (1997)

Farhat, G., 'Optical Instrumenta[liza]tion and Modernity at Versailles', in Lee, M.G. and Helphand, K.I. (eds) *Technology and the Garden* (Washington, 2014)

Feingold, M., 'The Mathematical Sciences and New Philosophies', in Tyacke, N. (ed.) *The History of the University of Oxford, Volume IV: Seventeenth-Century Oxford* (Oxford, 1997)

Frank, R.G., 'John Aubrey, F.R.S., John Lydall, and Science at Commonwealth Oxford', *Notes and Records of the Royal Society of London* 27(2) (1973)

Frank, R.G., *Harvey and the Oxford Physiologists* (Berkeley, 1980)

French, J.M., *Milton in Chancery: New Chapters in the Lives of the Poet and His Father* (New York, 1939)

Garnett J. and Davies, C., *The Invention of Modern Science* (Oxford, 2014)

Gibson, W., '"The Remembrance Whereof Is Pleasant": A Note on Walter Pope's Role in the Attempt to Abolish Academic Dress during the Commonwealth', *Transactions of the Burgon Society* 10 (2010)

Gouk, P., 'Performance Practice: Music, Medicine and Natural Philosophy in Interregnum Oxford', *British Journal for the History of Science* 29 (1996)

Hardacre, P., 'The Royalists in Exile during the Puritan Revolution, 1642–1660', *Huntington Library Quarterly* 16(4) (1953)

Henry, J., *The Scientific Revolution and the Origins of Modern Science* (Basingstoke, 2001)

HOP, Naylor L. and Jagger, G., 'Osbaldeston, Sir Littleton, 1st Bt. (c.1631–91)'

HOP, Naylor L. and Jagger, G., 'Pudsey, Sir George. (d. 1688)'

Hunt, J.D., 'Curiosities to Adorn Cabinets and Gardens', in Impey, O. and MacGregor, A. (eds) *The Origin of Museums* (Oxford, 2001)

Hunter, M., 'The Social Basis and Changing Fortunes of an Early Scientific Institution: An Analysis of the Membership of the Royal Society, 1660–1685', *Notes and Records of the Royal Society* 31 (1976)

Jaroszyński, P., 'Science and Utopia: From the House of Solomon to the Royal Society', *Science in Culture* 185 (2007)

Jaynes, J., 'The Problem of Animate Motion in the Seventeenth Century', *Journal of the History of Ideas* 31(2) (1970)

Keblusek, M., 'A Tortoise in the Shell: Royalist and Anglican Experience of Exile in the 1650s', in Major, P. (ed.) *Literatures of Exile in the English Revolution and Its Aftermath, 1640–1690* (Farnham, 2010)

Kiessling, N.K. (ed.) *The Life of Anthony Wood in His Own Words* (Oxford, 2009)

Livingstone, D., *Putting Science in Its Place: Geographies of Scientific Knowledge* (Chicago, 2003)

Long, P.O., *Openness, Secrecy, Authorship: Technical Arts and the Culture of Knowledge from Antiquity to the Renaissance* (Baltimore, 2001)

MacGregor, A., '"A Magazin of All Manner of Inventions", Museums in the Quest for "Salomon's House" in Seventeenth-Century England', *Journal of the History of Collections* 1(2) (1989)

Major, P., '"Twixt Hope and Fear": John Berkenhead, Henry Lawes, and Banishment from London during the English Revolution', *Review of English Studies,* New Series 59(239) (2008)

Martinón-Torres, M., 'Inside Solomon's House: An Archaeological Study of the Old Ashmolean Chymical Laboratory in Oxford', *Ambix* 59(1) (2012)

McDayter, M., 'Poetic Gardens and Political Myths: The Renewal of St James's Park in the Restoration', *Journal of Garden History* 15(3) (1995)

Mendyk, S., 'Robert Plot: Britain's "Genial Father of County Natural Histories"', *Notes and Records of the Royal Society of London* 39(2) (1985)

Mulligan, L., 'Civil War Politics, Religion and the Royal Society', *Past and Present* (59 (1973)

Nelson, N., 'Astrology, *Hudibras,* and the Puritans', *Journal of the History of Ideas* 37(3) (1976)

ODNB, Doyle, C., 'Birkenhead [Berkenhead], Sir John (1617–1679)'

ODNB, McIntyre, G.S., 'Brouncker, William, second Viscount Brouncker of Lyons (1620–1684)'

ODNB, Smith, D., 'Cary, Henry, fourth Viscount Falkland (bap. 1634, d. 1663)'

ODNB, Wright, S., 'Harris, Robert (1580/81–1658)'

ODNB, Speake, J., 'Henshaw, Thomas (1618–1700)'

ODNB, Turner, A., 'Plot, Robert (1640–1696)'

ODNB, Clerke, A.M. and McConnell, A., 'Pope, Walter (bap. 1628, d. 1714)'

Parrott, V., 'Celestial Expression or Worldly Magic? The Invisibly Integrated Design of Utaniborg: A Look at some Philosophical Aspects of the Ground Plan of Tycho Brahe's House and Garden, 1576–97', *Garden History* 38(1) (2010)

Plot, R., *The Natural History of Oxfordshire* (London, 1705)

Pope, W., *The Life of the Right Reverend Father in God Seth, Lord Bishop of Salisbury, and Chancellor of the Most Noble Order of the Garter. With a Brief Account of Bishop Wilkins, Mr Lawrence Rooke, Dr Isaac Barrow, Dr Turberville and Others, Written by Dr Walter Pope, Fellow of the Royal Society* (London, 1697)

Preston, C., *The Poetics of Scientific Investigation in Seventeenth-Century England* (Oxford, 2015)

Purver, M., *The Royal Society: Concept and Creation* (London, 1967)

Remmert, V., 'The Art of Garden and Landscape Design and the Mathematical Sciences in the Early Modern Period', in Fischer, H., *et al.* (eds) *Gardens, Knowledge and the Sciences in the Early Modern Period* (Basel, 2016)

Rinne, K., 'Garden Hydraulics in Pre-Sistine Rome', in Lee, M.G., and Helphand, K.I. (eds) *Technology and the Garden* (Washington, 2014)

Roos, A.M., 'The Chymistry of "The Learned Dr Plot" (1640–96)', *Osiris* 29(1) (2014)

Shapin, S., 'The House of Experiment in Seventeenth-Century England', *Isis* 79(3) (1988)

Shirky, C., *The Invisible College,* http://www.msuedtechsandbox.com/MAET/year3-2011/wp-content/uploads/shirky.bw_.pdf, accessed 12 January 2021

Sprat, T., *The History of the Royal Society of London: For the Improving of Natural Knowledge* (London, 1734)

Stubbs, M., 'John Beale, Philosophical Gardener of Herefordshire', *Annals of Science* 39(5) (1982)

Stukeley, W., quoted in *Memoirs of Sir Isaac Newton's life,* ed. Hastings White, A. (London, 1936)

Taylor, C., 'The House and Garden of Henry Winstanley, Littlebury, Essex', *Landscape History* 35(2) (2014)

Thomas, K., *Religion and the Decline of Magic* (London, 1991)

Tomasi, L. 'The Origins, Function and Role of the Botanical Garden in Sixteenth- and Seventeenth-Century Italy', *Studies in the History of Gardens and Designed Landscapes* 25(2) (2005)

Toynbee, M.R., 'Charles I and the Perrots of North Leigh', *Oxoniensia* 11 (1946)

Ward, S. (published under the anonymous authorship of 'H.D.'), *Vindicae Academiarum* (Oxford, 1654)

Webster, C., 'Richard Towneley, the Towneley Group and Seventeenth Century Science', *Transactions of the Historic Society of Lancashire and Cheshire* 118 (1966)

Webster, C., 'New Light on the Invisible College the Social Relations of English Science in the Mid-Seventeenth Century', *Transactions of the Royal Historical Society* 24 (1974)

Worden, B., 'Cromwellian Oxford', in Tyacke, N. (ed.) *The History of the University of Oxford, Volume IV: Seventeenth-Century Oxford* (Oxford, 1997)

Woudstra, J., 'Much Better Contrived and Built than Any Other in England: Stoves and Other Structures for the Cultivation of Exotic Plants Hampton Court Palace 1689–1702', in Lee, M.G. and Helphand, K.I. (eds) *Technology and the Garden* (Washington, 2014)

Wright, P., 'Astrology and Science in Seventeenth-Century England', *Social Studies of Science* 5 (1975)

Index

....